NEW YORK:
LIVERMORE & RUDD,
310 Broadway.

CINCINNATI:
MOORE, WILSTACH, KEYS & OVEREND,
25 West Fourth Street.

Stereotyped and Printed by
WILLIAM OVEREND & CO.
CINCINNATI.

PREFACE.

GREEN PEAS! an odd title for a book, is it not? Yet who can say it is inappropriate? Has not the press issued "The Daisy," and "The Violet," the "Opening Rose" and the "Withered Flower," and an hundred more as prettily titled volumes? If poets can clothe their dreams in the lovely language of Flora, and borrow titles for their volumes from her favorite flowers, why cannot Invisible descend into the more humble but not less popular vegetable kingdom, for a name for his first book? GREEN PEAS! Is there not music in that sound? Does it not smack of something palatable? Is it not new, pleasant, refreshing? In fact, is it not a good name?

What the book contains, the reader will ascertain by perusing it. Invisible has no hesitation, however, in making the prefatory assurance, that the pods are all full of peas. Some of the peas are large, and some are small, some are plump and savory, and some—if the truth must be told!—will require strong applications of seasoning to make them relishable.

Many of the sketches in this book have been written for recreation, while performing the labors of reporter to a daily newspaper. As a reporter in pursuit of "items,"

Invisible often met with characters which afforded him pleasure to describe, and events in the career of individuals which were all sufficient

"To point a moral or adorn a tale."

To sketch such characters and arrange such incidents in short stories has been to him the source of numerous pleasant hours. Many queer people indeed does this world contain—men, and women too, with odd manners, odd features, and such odd actions, that they are walking humorists, sure to excite merriment wherever they go. And how many people there are, too, whose hearts are rent by the most sorrowful afflictions, and who suffer without the sympathy of even one kindred spirit,

"In secret, in silence, and tears."

In this volume, Invisible has endeavored to array this kind of people — the queer, the sorrow-stricken, the eccentric and the suffering. He has attempted to combine the humorous with the serious, by the presentation of incidents as he has observed them, dressed in a style to please himself. He hopes that GREEN PEAS will gratify the much talked of reading community, and that those who purchase it will, to use a very common but proper expression for the day, "Get their money's worth."

CONTENTS.

POD I.

POD II.

PICKINGS FROM INVISIBLE'S CITY OBSERVATIONS.

POD III.

POLICE SKETCHES.

POD I.

GREEN PEAS,

PICKED FROM INVISIBLE'S PATCH.

UNCLE BARNEY:

OR, AN EARLY MORNING ADVENTURE OF AN ECCENTRIC OLD BACHELOR.

WERE you ever in the City of D——, which rests so prettily in the Valley of the Great Miami? It is a charming city, with its broad streets, its costly and handsome public buildings, and its spacious gardens, in the midst of which, in buildings of varied architectural beauty, the more fortunate portion of the community reside. It is a small city, but being in the centre of one of the prettiest and most productive valleys in the country, wealth flows easily into the coffers of its thriving inhabitants. A good portion of the population is made up of families whose "heads" were among the early settlers of the country, and who have become wealthy through the constant and rapid increase of property. Among these is "Uncle Barney," known to almost every resident of the place, and really a very eccentric character. It is said, he was a lively and vivacious youth, and as such was quite a favorite with the early settlers of the neighborhood. In early manhood, being an only child, he inherited all his father's estate, which, even in that early day, was a competency. Soon after this event Barney became sad and demure, and, refusing at all times to explain his altered conduct, kept aloof from all company.

Time rolled on, and Barney remained the same. His property had increased in value until he had become immensely rich; and yet he was the same demure, incommunicative Barney. After various conjectures as to the cause of his eccentricities, it was generally concluded, as is usual under such circumstances, though without any apparent foundation, that he had been crossed in love.

A year ago, though age had silvered his hair, and he had received the title of Uncle Barney, he still preserved his singularity. He never possessed more than two suits of clothes at one time, one being woolen and the other linen; and his changes from thick to thin, or from thin to thick, were more regular than the seasons. On the first of April, every year, no matter how cold, he would don his Summer suit, and keep it on, though Winter lingered long in the lap of Spring. On the first day of October, he would resume his Winter garb, and retain it, even if the mercury rose to boiling heat. From this habit, he had never varied within the memory of his oldest neighbors.

As singular was he in regard to his hours of rest. When he sported his linen, he retired promptly every evening at 9, and rose each morning as promptly at 4. While wearing the woolen, 8 o'clock of every evening beheld him in bed, and nine hours after, to the minute, was he up, on the morrow. And Summer or Winter, in rain or snow, mud or dust, he was no sooner dressed than he started upon a morning walk, traversing the same path every day, and returning to his lodgings, with the precision of a locomotive running "on time."

These were some of the eccentricities of Uncle Barney a year ago, which made him still an object of wonder to his neighbors, and of interest to the stranger. But about that time, another sudden change came "o'er the spirit of his dream," a change as astonishing as that of his earlier days, but more readily accounted for. It happened in this way.

One beautiful morning in June, as he was taking his usual walk, his course led him along the banks of the gentle Miami. As the early dawn broke upon the earth, Uncle Barney was impelled to stop and enjoy the advent of the "god of day;" for it was one of his chief pleasures to witness the earliest blushing of the skies.

A few light clouds were floating in the eastern sky, and the morning zephyrs wafted them gently onward, until they formed a gauzy veil o'er the hill tops, behind which the rising sun was ascending. These light clouds soon assumed a grayish hue, and were not unlike misty banners floating in the air. As the light from the rising god became stronger and more diffused, they assumed more brilliant hues, and soon the whole of the eastern sky was covered with a sheen of the richest and most varied dyes. A little longer, and the golden streaks from the Summer's sun burst o'er the hills, and pouring their welcome beams across the valleys destroyed the charming formations of the clouds. Instantly all nature was alive. The birds left their tiny Summer homes, shot forth into the pure air, and warbled their sweetest notes. The beasts of the field aroused themselves as if summoned by a voice, and prepared for their daily toil, and even the waters seemed to glide more happily along, proclaiming, as it were, a greeting to the sun.

It was such a scene as this, one of our glorious western sunrises, so beautiful, yet witnessed, alas! by so few,—which caused Uncle Barney to pause. From his youth he had loved the beautiful in nature; and it was only such scenes as these, witnessed by him when alone, that sent a thrill of pleasure to his heart. He was still standing in the same spot, now listening to the warbling of the birds, and the music of the dancing waters, and then watching the advance of the sun, when suddenly a heavy moan fell on his ear. He listened.—It was repeated, and quite near him. Looking into a recess in the bank of the river near him, he saw a female stretched upon the ground, her face and the earth about her covered with gore. Startled at the sight, he instantly hurried away. It had been many years since he had been brought in contact with a woman, dead or alive; or had, in person, administered relief to any one, though he had frequently sent large donations, anonymously, to the various benevolent societies of the city, in whose success he secretly felt a lively interest. His first impulse, therefore, was to withdraw from the vicinity where immediate help no doubt was needed.

He walked very fast for a few rods, when he suddenly paused.

"Hold on, Uncle Barney," he soliloquised, "this aint never a goin' to do, by gee-ko, (his favorite oath). Afore you git to a house the gal might die, and if you was to be the first to tell 'em where she is, and they was to find her dead they might think you killed her. By gee-ko, that wont do.

Better say nothin',Uncle Barney, by gee-ko. Strange world, and strange people, you know, Uncle Barney," and shaking his head, he slowly continued his walk.

He had not proceeded far before another and a strange thought appeared to strike him. He wheeled suddenly around, and hastily retraced his steps.

"By gee-ko, I may save the poor gal's life," he exclaimed, as he hastened onward. "Nobody may n't hear tell on it, and if they do, by gee-ko, I do n't care, for there's somethin' here, in my heart, tells me I ought to do it, and I will."

Arriving at the spot, he found the woman moaning most piteously. Not responding to his questions he lifted her in his arms, and carried her to the water's edge, where he gently bathed her face, putting aside the long tresses of hair, which, clotted with gore, hung over, and almost concealed her countenance.

He then recognized her as the mother of a family residing in a cabin not far distant, and being familiar with her condition, readily divined the cause of her terrible situation. — The water revived the woman, and she was soon able to speak.

"By gee-ko, gal," said Uncle Barney, as she opened her eyes, "I had almost gin you up for gone. What on airth brought you here so early?"

"Don't let him hit me again, oh! for God's sake, don't let him hit me again," faintly exclaimed the poor woman, looking wildly about her.

"By gee-ko, he shant," soothingly responded the Good Samaritan. "It's Uncle Barney that's holdin' you, and there wont be no hitten of any body now."

As the woman continued to revive she told the cause of the

night's disaster. She was the wife of a drunkard. The evening previous her husband had come home a raving maniac from the effects of liquor. She fled from his presence. He pursued her; felled her with a club; and that was all she recollected. Uncle Barney helped her home, where he also found the drunken husband stretched upon the floor, and in the agonies of death. His miserable career was about ending. Uncle Barney saw him breathe his last, and then hurried to the city for medical aid for the almost dying woman.

There was some excitement in the city that morning.—Uncle Barney had not returned from his morning walk, and was not at his breakfast. Such a thing was unknown before, even to the oldest inhabitant, and fears were entertained for his safety. Persons were about starting in search of him, when he appeared, walking out of his usual gait, down the main street. He said nothing, and was asked no questions. He hastened to his rooms, dressed himself, and hurried away again. That day he buried the husband, and watching over the unfortunate woman, day and night, until she recovered, he then — married her!

He is no longer an old bachelor, spurning society, but a comparatively happy husband. He takes no more long morning walks, though he holds to his queer notions of dress, which he still insists are correct, "accordin' to natur'," and he is still studiously silent as to the cause or causes of his long years of stupidity and silence. Was he not an eccentric old bachelor?

A PRACTICAL ILLUSTRATION:

OR, HOSS HEAD AND THE FOPS.

HOTELS have now become so numerous in cities, and the fare so reasonable, that they are the resort, at times, of nearly all classes of society. The man who can afford to travel from home, can afford to stop at a hotel; and as landlords are smart enough to regard the wants of the million as well as those of the millionaire, we find the rich and the poor, the high and the humble, side by side at hotel tables. Homespun there sports a silver fork with as much gusto as Mr. Broadcloth, and the humble 'Sally' is as much entitled to, and enjoys as fully, the good things of life at the richly loaded table of the hotel, as the accomplished Miss Josephine Martha Washington Victoria Maria. Consequently the hotel is a good place to study human nature, for there we see men, and women too, from all the walks of life, and of all classes of character. Often 'extremes meet,' and when such is the case, amusing circumstances are sure to transpire.

Sitting one evening in the office of the O——House of Cincinnati, my attention was attracted toward two genuine, and unadulterated fops, who occupied seats near me. A description of them would be uninteresting, for there is no community in this broad land of ours without its fops, and a fop is a fop and nothing else, the world over. They admit of but one distinction—city fop and country fop; and they differ only

2

in the extent of their dress, or exterior display, it being conceded I believe, that all fops possess merely sufficient brains to make an animal a human. The individuals referred to were city fops, diminutive specimens of humanity, in every regard.

One of them had received a letter from a lady, which he read to his companion, to whom he declared the writer was "chawmingly beauchiful," but, as she was without a pwospect (for a fortune,)he could not consent to return her love. He vowed that the *billet doux* annoyed him exceedingly, as he disliked to "bweak the dwear cweature's heart."

While they were thus engaged in conversation, a tall strapping Hoosier entered the hotel. He had a 'Buena Vista' on his head, and a red flannel 'wamus' on his shoulders, while his lower extremities were encased in brown linsy pants, and the stoutest kind of hog-skin boots. His hair was long and scraggy, his face unshaved, at least for a week, while his whole form was covered with dust, which indicated that he had just arrived by railroad, In one hand he carried a bundle, which was evidently clothing, tied up in a 'span new' yellow and red cotton handkerchief, and in the other he held a stout but rude walking stick, not long since from its mother hickory. He had that awkwardness of gait, peculiar to countrymen whose days are spent almost entirely upon their farms, and whose minds are devoted to the one thing most sought after, but not the most desirable, the accumulation of wealth.

He paused a moment at the door, glancing at the crowd within, and at once attracted the attention of the fops, who immediately gave a sort of consumptive laugh or snickering sneer, at the homely appearance of the stranger.

"Is this yere place a tavern?" he inquired of the fops.

"A twavern? howwible!" exclaimed one of the fops holding up both his hands.

"A twavern, indeed!" said the other, "he must be from the woods, Chawlee," and both renewed their laughter.

The Hoosier gave them an indignant look, and was about to reply, when the clerk, who had observed him, approached, and informed him he was at a hotel, and inquired if he wished to stop.

"Stop! sartin I do," was his response, "you don't reckon a feller to cum to such a smart tavern as this yere, without stoppin', do you Kurnell?"

"Hardly, sir—allow me to take your baggage, and furnish you with a room."

"Just as you're a mind—I'm not partic'lar so I get six feet o' bed, and a hull plate at the table.—Golly! but aint this a scrouging town?"

"Quite a place, sir. Walk this way, if you please, and I will attend to you, instantly," said the clerk, as he took the Hoosier's bundle.

"Wall, now, you're uncommon polite, stranger, but I reckon you make a feller pay for it all in the course of sarcumstances. But as you're sort o' human—set right up to a feller what's in a strange country, I'm the chap to squar your bill for fodder to a figure, when you fotch it up. That's my way o' doing business, Kurnell."

"I have no doubt of it, sir," said the clerk, smiling, and handing him the book for that purpose, asked him to register his name.

"Do what?" inquired the stranger, somewhat astonished.

"Register your name and residence in this book, sir."

"Write it down thar?"

"Yes, sir."

"Cum, now, Kurnell, none o' your tricks," said the Hoosier, with a sly smile on his countenance, and after a moment's pause.

"O, sir, it's no trick I assure you. We require this of all visitors, as much for their own as our benefit."

"You don't tell?"

"Yes, sir, that is a fact."

"Want to know whether they kin write, I reckon. Wall, that's on the squar. When a feller goes away from hum, he ought to show his edication. I not only larned to write when I was a shaver, but got up purty high in the figures. I'll give you a specimen of my chickography, as old Squire Smith calls writin, in darned short order;" and the traveler took the pen, turned the book in an oblique direction, and squaring himself to suit, leaned over the book to write. His oddity attracted the attention of all in the office, including the two fops, who, amused at his remarks, gathered about him at the clerk's desk. The pen in his hand had touched the book, when he paused, and, after reflecting a moment, raised his head, and addressing the clerk, said:

"Kurnell, do you want all of a feller's name?"

"We would like to have your full name."

"Full name! Wall, that's a puzzler. You see my family name is Hempfield, then my Christian name is John Isaiah, that thar's John Isaiah Hempfield, aint it?"

"Yes, sir."

"Wall, then, the boys down our way, considerin' me a right smart chap, kind a gin me a second christenin'—they call me Hoss Head."

This information, so innocently given, caused a loud burst of laughter from the crowd. Hoss Head participated in it, for he loved a laugh, and could be as merry as the next one.

"A rale smart name, aint it boys?" he asked, after the laughter had ceased. "Would you put it down in the books?"

"Certainly, certainly," cried all.

In a few minutes the stranger, after giving his pen many circular movements over the book, and changing his position several times, succeeded in writing his address in full, as follows: "*Mr. John Isaiah Hempfield, Hoss Head, Persimmon Post Office, Yellow county, Indiana.*" He pointed to this specimen of his "chickography," with pride, and seemed wonderfully pleased with the fulsome praise bestowed upon it by the gentlemen present.

Expressing a desire to get fixed up, the clerk showed him to the wash-room, when the two fops, who had endeavored to enjoy the Hoosier's greenness, were struck with an idea—about such an one as generally racks the bedulled brains of men—if men they can be called—of their stamp. Anxious to display their smartness, and to create amusement at the expense of another, the fop's seized the porter's brushes, and giving the crowd a knowing wink, as much as to say, 'we'll make fun for you,' approached Hoss Head.

"Shall we bwrush you, sirrah?" asked one, endeavoring to play the servant.

"Wall, now, by thunder!" exclaimed Hoss Head, as he dropped the soap from his hands, and ceased his ablution. "I always wor good at guessin'," but this beats all kreation. Look here Kurnell — addressing the clerk — "I no sooner seed these fellers to-night, than I guessed right out they war sarvants.'

The boisterous laugh which followed, was to the great chagrin of the fops.

"They jest look," he continued—every hit being heartily enjoyed by all but the fops—"as if they war'nt made fur nothin' else but to scrape the mud from a feller's legs, and do little chores round a tavern. I *thunk* that, when I first seed 'em; an' by thunder, war'nt I right, though? Brush me off? Sartainly! and (with a dignified air) mind you make a clean sweep, or I'll report you to the Kurnell, thar."

The fops, finding that Hoss Head had thrown the joke upon them, endeavored to recover; so they informed him that he could not be brushed unless he paid in advance.

"Pay in advance!" was Hoss Head's indignant reply. "Thunder and salvation! don't the tavern pay you for yur lazy, triflin' work? I reckon you think I'm kinder green, an' want to skin me, don't you?"

"Pon onah, we dwon't' replied one.

"We-ah spweak the truth," answered the other.

By this time, Hoss Head was victorious, so far as the spectators were concerned. While they could sport with the Hoosier's ignorance of "city manners," they could but despise the senseless dandies, who would make him an object of ridicule. Every "hit," therefore, that Hoss Head gave them, drew forth loud acclamations from the gentlemen present. This nerved "the gentleman from the country," and giving his head a toss which threw his hat to one side, he asked—

"Arn't they tryin' to skin me, boys?"

"Yes," came from a dozen.

"I thunk so, from the start, an' it sort o' riles me to cum across such critters. I've hearn tell of the cattle afore, and I was on the look out for 'em. 'Squire Jones told me afore I left hum, to look out for the tavern thieves when I got to the city, an' by thunder I've run agin two on 'em right at the start."

"Dwo you mean to insult us?" asked one of the fops, forgetting the part he had volunteered to play, and feeling that he ought to profess indignation on being called a thief.

"If the shoe fits, wear it," was Hoss Head's pointed answer.

"Did you apply the twavern thief to us?" asked the other fop.

"Sartin' I did."

"Then, sirrah, we will let you know-ah that we only asswumed the character of swervants. We are gentlemen, sirrah, and we inswist on your-a takin' bwack the obnoxious wappellation, or we'll seek redress."

"Yes, sirrah, we'll seek redress with our canes-ah," said his highly indignant companion, as he flourished a very slim specimen of a cane over his head.

"What!" exclaimed Hoss Head, drawing himself out to his full length and giving the diminutives before him rather a scornful look. "What! you want to fight, do you? Just clar a ring, boys, and stan' back, if you want to see me eat them two critters in half a minit. I can do it by any watch in this crowd. Just clar the ring."

"Stop, stop!" interrupted the clerk, who saw that matters were going too far. "We can't have any fighting here."

"Then larn your servants to be purlite," replied Hoss Head.

"They are not servants, sir, and do not belong to the house. They are not even boarders, and I assure you, sir, I never saw them before this evening."

"Don't belong to the tavern, and tryin' to skin me."

"I presume, sir, they only intended to play a harmless joke."

"That's all, pown 'onah," replied one of the fops, who saw that matters were assuming rather a serious aspect for himself and friend. "That was all we intwended, wasn't it Chwarles?"

"Pon onah, it was."

"Kinder pokin' fun at me, eh?" Wall, now I kin stand a joke as well as the next man on airth, and, Kurnell, I'll gin twenty-five cents all in silver, jest to carry them'ar men out of the house."

"I have nothing to do with them, sir, and you can act your pleasure," replied the clerk.

The fops surmising the intention of the Hoosier, started for the door, but he seized them both, and said:

"Hold on! it's better to ride when it costs nothin'. I've got to tell you a story, and larn you a lesson afore you leave this tavern," and grasping both tightly by the collar, he held them as if in a vice. The fops remonstrated, but Hoss Head, to the delight of the crowd, told them very mildly, that there was "no use talkin," for they could not go until they heard his story. They consented to remain if he would let go of them, to which he did not object.

Surrounded by such persons as are always found in a hotel

office, Hoss Head, with his eyes on the fops, told the following story:

"My old man, down in Yellar county, owns as sumptious a farm as lays in all them diggins. On that ere farm he's got an old horse, he calls Dick, as good natured a critter as ever rubbed his nose in feed, and all anybody could say of him, was, that he was right smartly common in his looks. One time, a rich feller, who lives sum whar in this town, was travelin' in his carriage, and broke down, right agin our farm. He concluded he'd go in the cars, and he left his hosses with the old man to take care on 'em, an' I must allow, that a purtier pair of critters never rubbed a britchin'. The old man put 'em in the barn-yard along with old Dick, and told 'em to make 'emselves to hum. Old Dick was monsus glad to have company, an' he cum runnin' up to 'em in a neighborly sort of a way, an' throwed his head over fust one o' their necks an' then the other, an' was as luvin' as any gal could want her beau to be. The city hosses did'nt appear to like this much, an they kind 'o drawed back, took a good look at Dick, and seein' he was uncommon ugly, they jest turned up their noses, flirted their tails and walked off.

"This sort 'o riled old Dick, for he knowed he was just as good a hoss as ever lifted a hoof, and after thinkin' to hisself awhile, he determined to have satisfaction on the two upstarts, who thought they war better than him. So he goes up to them an' turns his back to 'em just this way:" and here Hoss Head got down on all fours, with his 'hind parts' to the two fops. "After he had stood this way about a minit, he rared and kicked this way," and the same moment one of his feet was in the stomach of each of the fops, and they found them selves sprawling on the floor.

"Old Dick," continued Hoss Head, unmoved at what he had done, "keeled them over, and by the time they war up, he was thar agin, and he rared agin this way;" and the fops who had just risen and were making for the door, found themselves on their stomachs. "Our old hoss kept followin' of em up," continued Hoss Head, as he moved slowly backward on all fours, "until he got the city hosses, who could brag o' nothin' but the purty har on their hides, right by the bars, an' then he rared sort of this way, and sent both on em out o' the barn-yard a kitin'," and taking good aim, he gave the two fops a third and a harder 'hoss kick,' which sent them through the open door-way, on the pavement.

As soon as the fops could get up, they ran off, screaming murder at the top of their weak, feminine voices, which however, was not loud enough to alarm any one. The spectators of the scene nearly split their sides with laughter, as kick after kick was given, all heartily concurring in the opinion that Hoss Head was administering a just and well deserved punishment. After he had given the last and most fearful kick, the Hoosier resumed an erect position, and participating in the general roar of laughter, said:

"Wall, boys, I guess I larned them dandies, *that the best hoss doesn't al'ays show the finest har!*"

The event made Hoss Head quite a lion at the hotel. Invitations to drink were extended to him oftener than was desirable; wine was sent to him at table; he was conducted in a carriage through the city to see the sights, and when at length he departed for home, the landlord told him he had no bill to pay, and that he could consider his "hat chalked" for that hotel, whenever business or pleasure called him to the city. John Isaiah Hempfield Hoss Head expressed himself highly delighted with the Queen City, and all the people therein, except fops, and left the Western Metropolis a very highly tickled individual. The fops have not been seen since that 'ever memorable evening,' when, for a joke, they assumed the character of servants.

LITTLE LIZZIE; THE FLOWER OF THE BARRACKS.

A TRUE STORY OF CITY LIFE.

"Little Lizzie is absent again to-day," said Miss Martha Jones to her Sabbath school class, as she finished calling their names before entering upon the duties of the morning. "This is the second Sabbath of her absence, and I am fearful the sweet little girl is sick. Do any of you know where she lives?" she asked of the class.

"I do," responded one of the girls.

"Where?"

"In the Barracks, in Charcoal Alley, back of St. Xavier church."

"Have you been to see her?"

"No ma'am—I was a goin', but I see so many ugly looking people in the Barracks, it skeered me, and I did'nt go in."

"You should have persevered, child," replied Miss Jones, who was a fervent, pious Christian, and who labored zealously in the holy cause of Sabbath schools. "You should have persevered, child, for God is ever with His children to save them from harm. Always trust in Him. I fear little Lizzie, whom we all love, is sick, for she is fond of her Sabbath school, and would be here if able to come. I will go find her as soon as school is dismissed."

All Miss Jones had seen of Lizzie was in Sabbath school. The child was about nine years of age, and had been in school, and in Miss Jones' class, some six or eight months. She was always very poorly clad, but was so devoted to her school, listened so attentively to the sacred instructions there imparted, and enquired so seriously and frequently for religious advice, that no one could doubt she was endeavoring to be in word and action a Christian. So sweet was her disposition, so kind her heart, so pure her conduct, that all in the Sabbath school knew her but to love her. Miss Jones had often asked Lizzie about her parents, and where she lived, but received merely a tear for a reply. Finding the enquiries so affected her pupil, she did not press them, though she often wished she knew where Lizzie lived and could visit her.

No sooner was the Sabbath school dismissed that morning, than Miss Jones proceeded to Charcoal alley. It is a narrow, dirty avenue, noted for its extremely filthy condition, and no one ever passes through it unless forced by circumstances to do so. Miss Jones stopped at the entrance of the alley. She thought it could hardly be an avenue leading to the residence of any human being; but observing a large building about half-way up, which answered the description of "the Barracks," she proceeded. It was an unusual sight to see a well-dressed woman enter that alley, and it was no wonder those who resided near by lifted their windows and watched her with surprise and astonishment. I warrant that not one of them rightly divined her mission, or guessed the purposes of her heart—none presumed that she was a ministering angel of God's own appointment, seeking distress to alleviate it, or sorrow to destroy it. Oh! thou faithful Sabbath school-teacher! called of Heaven to plant seeds of ever living Truth in the hearts of the young—to train youthful minds to walk in the paths of Christianity—to feed his Lambs with the Bread of Life — thy task, though laborious and oft-times severe, is still a joyous one! In after years many will stand up and bless thee; and though the world knows but little of thy labors, and fails to cheer thee in thy pure charities, in Heaven, Angel of Earth, is thy reward!

Miss Jones proceeded up the alley until she reached the Barracks—and here, reader, we will pause for a moment while we examine the exterior of the building, which is one of many lately erected in this Western Metropolis, (all called "Barracks") by capitalists, ostensibly for the *accommodation* of the poor. The building on Charcoal alley is about one hundred feet long and thirty wide. It is five stories high, with a wide and spacious porch, the whole length of the building.

The edifice has but one stairway and one vault, and they are together in the centre; as might be supposed, a foul current of air continually passes from the latter through the former. There is one hydrant to each porch, and a trough for the slops. While one is running almost constantly, the other is generally filled up with rotten, decayed matter, which, of itself, would destroy all purity in the atmosphere.

A tenement in the "Barracks" consists of two rooms, one fronting on a porch, and the other in the rear of that. They are rented at from six to twelve dollars a month; the tenements of the lower story being let for the highest, and those of the upper story for the lowest sum named. The owner does not rent the house, but employs an agent at a per centum to do that work, and see that the property is not destroyed. The agent has unlimited power to control the premises, and is, in fact, the landlord. Though he may use every exertion to preserve the property, he but seldom repairs and never cleans it, and consequently it is always in a dirty, unhealthy condition.

The Charcoal alley Barracks contain nearly an hundred tenements, which are occupied generally by a low, ignorant order of people. Sometimes, honest, upright families are forced by circumstances to move into it; but so bad do they find their neighbors, so vicious, turbulent and boldly dishonest do they find those with whom they must have intercourse, that they remove as soon as possible.

Quarrels are ordinary affairs in the Charcoal alley Barracks, and a fight is an every day occurrence. Go there at any hour, and you will find some *woman* pouring forth a torrent of profane and licentious language, and perhaps see another under the influence of whisky, endeavoring to excite a "muss." Oh! what crimes have been committed within the walls of that building, and how much degradation, misery, and human suffering, has been witnessed there. In erecting it, the owner may have intended to accommodate the poor, but he has succeeded only in building a huge rendezvous for the lowest characters, a building which harbors and sends forth a moral pestilence, a house which is a nuisance to the neighborhood, and a disgrace to a Christian land!

It was in such a place as this, that Miss Jones, the Sabbath school-teacher, sought little Lizzie, in whom she felt so much interest. Many females would have shrunk from such a place, but Miss Jones, with her heart fixed solely upon her holy errand, thought only of the object of her search. As she stepped from the alley into the paved passage-way, which runs beside the building, she encountered about a dozen rough looking men, who were in the act of passing the bottle. They seemed surprised to see one of her gentility of appearance in such a place, but gave way, and she passed on.

"Be jabers an' it's a lady," said one, as she passed.

"An' a dacint one too, me life on't," added another.

"What may she be afther?"

"Seein' some dacint gintleman," replied another, with a peculiar wink of his eye.

"Och! none o' that, ye blaggard," responded the second speaker. "Don't yees see she is a dacint lady? Take the botthle, and stop wid it yees dirthy tongue."

That happy rebuke caused a roar of merriment from the crowd, and the bottle was immediately passed, and its inspirations made them forget the "dacint lady," whose appearance had surprised them. Miss Jones heard it all, but paid but little attention to it. She passed on by several tenements, until she reached the foot of the stairway, where she met rather a genteel-looking Irish woman, with a prayer-book in her hand, who was evidently going to church.

"Good morning," she said, addressing her.

"Good morning to yer ladyship," responded the other, making a curtsey.

"Can you tell me whether a little girl named Lizzie H—— lives in this building?"

"Is it little Lizzie yer ladyship wants, the girl wid the black hair an' the black eyes?'

"She has black hair and black eyes."

"Arrah, yer ladyship 'ill find her more dead nor alive. She's a good girl, yer ladyship, an' the meanest baste could say no ill forninst her."

"She is truly a good girl, and I am anxious to see her. Will you be kind enough to show me to her room?"

"Yes, yer ladyship, come wid me."

The conversation had attracted the attention of every family who lived in the first story of the Barracks, and while the men and women poked their uncombed heads out of the doors and windows and listened in silence, their children, ragged and dirty, gathered about the visitor and divided their attention between the conversation and an examination of her dress. A little boy slily abstracted Miss Jones' handkerchief from her pocket, and a girl stole her pencil from her waistband, while she was conversing. After Miss Jones had started up the dirty, filthy stairway, twenty inquiries were made among the women below, as to who she was.

"I reckon," said a corpulent old woman with a pipe in her mouth, "she must belong to some benevolence societies."

"She's a lady now, do ye mind that," said a bunchy Irish woman.

"A lady indade," responded a snub-nosed, red-haired specimen of womanity, "did yes ever see a lady talkin' to a Fardown? She's no more a lady'an mesel'."

"Ha! ha! you is very fun," said a lively French woman. But we will leave them to their arguments and proceed on in search of little Lizzie.

The stench in this stairway was so strong that Miss Jones was almost overcome with it. Her guide observed it, and immediately gave her opinion of hard-hearted landlords and their impositions upon the poor. In fact she kept her tongue running quite briskly until she reached the head of the stairway in the fifth story, when she lowered her voice, and said:

"Walk aisy, yer ladyship, for the noise of our futs may disturb the darlint."

The admonition was useless, for in a room near them a group of persons of both sexes were singing a licentious song over a jug of whisky, and at the west end of the porch two women were quarreling most violently. Several persons, either drunk or asleep, were stretched out on the greasy porch. Miss Jones followed her guide to the eastern end of the porch where she was shown into a room, the appearance of which made her very heart ache.

Not a particle of furniture was in the apartment, and on a bed of straw, in one corner of the room, lay Little Lizzie, pale and emaciated, her hands folded on her breast, and reposing apparently in a refreshing sleep. The Sabbath-school teacher kneeled by her side, and tears gushed from her eyes as she raised her soul in prayer to Heaven. Lizzie slept sweetly on, and her teacher not wishing to disturb her, arose and turning to the woman who had conducted her to the room, asked where were the parents of the child.

"If I must tell yer ladyship the trut'," was the answer, "they be in jail. The coonstable took 'em up yestherday, for takin' a dhrop too much, and batin' one o' their neighbors a little! Arrah! yer ladyship, what does the guvernment care for the poor?"

"But where is their furniture?—they certainly had some."

"There be black sheep in every flock, yer ladyship, an' there be thaves in this house. They plunthered the room last night, and yees can see, they took all but the bed unther the swate little girl."

Miss Jones was horror-struck at such baseness, but with a becoming presence of mind, she took immediate measures for the relief of her pupil. She paid the Irish woman to go instantly for a physician of her acquaintance, and to stop on her return and procure certain necessaries. The woman had no sooner left, than a crowd gathered about the window of the room, and amused themselves with commenting on the appearance of the apartment and the bad character of its occupants, as they supposed, to the chagrin of the lady who was present. From their remarks, Miss Jones inferred that little Lizzie's parents were of the basest kind, and that what the Irish woman had told her of them was really true. She spoke to none of the debased crowd at the window, but again kneeling by the bedside of her much-loved pupil, sought comfort in silent prayer, until the arrival of the physician and the return of the messenger. Their entrance awakened little Lizzie, and her eyes instantly fell upon her teacher.

"Oh! Miss Jones, have you come to see me?" she said, throwing her arms around her teacher's neck, as she bent over her to kiss her. "I have been so sick, and I wanted mother to tell you; but she would not. I prayed to our Saviour to let me see you before I died, and I knew he would do it. I am happy now."

"Thank Heaven that I have found you, my sweet child;" replied the Sabbath school teacher, though her tears almost choked her utterance. "You may get well now. I have sent for a doctor, and see, he is here."

The physician, who was much affected by the scene, now

stepped forward to examine his patient. As he took her wasted arm in his hand to feel her pulse, she, in a faint voice, said:

"You can do no good, Doctor, for I am dying now. I know it. I feel I shall soon be in Heaven. God has been good to me—he has answered my prayers, and saved me from the wickedness of those about me. And He has sent my kind Sunday-school teacher here, to help me over the dark river of death. I am ready to die."

"Is there no hope, Doctor?" asked Miss Jones, as she took little Lizzie in her lap and pressed her head to her bosom.

"None—none—none!" said Lizzie, her voice growing fainter at each word. "Don't cry, Miss Jones, don't cry. I am going to that Saviour who died for us all—I shall soon be happy in Heaven. I am happy now, Miss Jones—happy—happy—happy. Press me closer to your bosom—angels are coming to take my soul away—meet me, meet me in Heaven."

Her voice grew weaker with every word, and in a short time after she spoke her last, her pure spirit calmly took its flight to the world above, to join the angelic hosts of Heaven.

Miss Jones closed those once bright black eyes forever, and hugging the corpse to her bosom, gave vent to her feelings in tears.

It was a strange death-bed scene for the Charcoal Alley Barracks, and though hundreds had died there before, I fear that little Lizzie was the first who departed this life in that building with a pure heart and clean hands.

Miss Jones afterwards learned that her little pupil had lived a practical Christian life. Her voice was often heard in prayer, and day after day she would go from room to room in that den of degradation, rebuking sin, and endeavoring to persuade old and young to become Christians. She was often repulsed and often abused, but she continued to preach, nevertheless, until seized with that illness which caused her death. Her parents were very degraded, and often whipped her because she prayed, but she bore it meekly and without a murmur.

Her body was placed in a coffin on the day of her death, and removed to her teacher's residence. The next morning a large number of persons followed it to its last resting place. Miss Jones and her Sabbath-school class being the mourners. Religious services were performed at the grave, and as the minister, in touching language, portrayed the scene at the death-bed of the youthful Christian, tears flowed from the eyes of all present — tears to the memory of "LITTLE LIZZIE, THE FLOWER OF THE BARRACKS."

COURTSHIP:

OR, HOW A DUTCH WIDOW MANAGED TO GET A YOUTHFUL HUSBAND.

IN a little frame house near the eastern boundary of that portion of the Queen City known as "Bremen," lived once upon a time, Kathleen Von Steidle, as fair and lively a young widow as ever sighed for a second husband. Kathleen bore the seal of her ancestry in her stout, plump form. She came from a country where females are not treated as dolls, and where women consider it a duty to labor equally with the other sex; consequently she was stout and able-bodied. Her eyes were as bright as a bran-new krout spoon; her cheeks, delightfully round, would compare in plumpness and rosy tint, with the favorites of the orchard; her nose hung from between her eyes like a crimson tassel; her neck was thick and as straight as a wooden water pump; her waist which had ever scorned the pressure of whale bones and brown linen, was as symmetrical as a water barrel; her ancles stout enough for a Hercules, and her feet, patterns for a patent brick machine. In truth, there was none of that sickly, repugnant delicacy in Kathleen, which is seen so much among the women of the day, and which unfits them for the duties of life. She was a stout, well-made woman, calculated to battle life in whatever shape she should meet it.

Kathleen was a widow. Four years previous she had been made so, and at the time of writing she had again many suitors for her hand. She was no Hindoo, and did not believe in burying herself alive with her dear departed Gotlieb. She had done him all the good she could while he lived, and after his death she believed it to be her bounden duty to love and comfort some other individual of the masculine sex. These opinions Kathleen had often expressed, and hence the suitors.

But Kathleen was not to be caught in a trap. She knew that the hymeneal state could only be happy by mutual love, and she rejected every offer where she could not feel her heart yearning to the one who made it.

"I knows 'em all!" she soliloquised one day. "Shake wants to marry me mit mine house. He no gits me. Shon dinks I make money while he trinks lager-pier all der vhile. He gits fooled. Hermann pees a goot man, but goot Himmel!

he pees more sour as der krout vot Old Spikes send me vhen I lend him monish!" And Kathleen shook her head. She proceeded thus to scan the merits of her beaux, until she reached the very last on the list.

"Well den, I likes none of 'em, any more," she said, as she ripped open a head of cabbage — "I vish Frank was mit 'em. Ah! mine Himmel, vat a goot boy mine Frank is. He pees so burty. Vy don't Frank say, 'Kathleen, let's go to der 'Squires, an' git married?' He say not'in' at all, all der vhile, " and heaving a sigh, Kathleen went into a deep thought. The Frank spoken of was a young man of twenty-three, and really a handsome fellow. He had been but a short time from Fatherland, and was still imbued with all those habits which won Kathleen to Gotlieb in another clime. He appeared to have quite a fancy for Kathleen; called to see her often; got her to do his mending; listened attentively to her kind advice; but further than that he said nothing.— Several times the widow thought she caught him casting sly glances of love at her, but she was not sure enough to accuse him of it.

In truth Kathleen loved Frank, and took various opportunities of hinting the matter to him, but Frank had not lived long enough to understand a hint, and his stubbornness in this respect, provoked her very much. Frank's frequent visits, however, convinced her that his affections were assailable, and she determined to besiege his heart, and if possible to capture it.

One evening, just after she had come to that conclusion, Frank visited the widow. He sat down opposite her, and, lighting his pipe, he assumed his usual quiet position, and said nothing further than to answer her questions as briefly as possible. The widow now determined to lay siege.

"Frank," she asked, with a pretty smile, "vat you come here so much for?"

"To get mine clothes mended," was the short reply.

"Ish dat all?"

"Yaw."

"Vy you no get 'em mend down town to your poard house, eh?"

Frank's reply was a shake of the head, and an uneasy whiff of his pipe.

"You no likes der womans down dere, Frank?"

A shake of the head

"I tinks so," continued the widow, who noticed that she had cornered the young man. "You like to come, live mit me, Frank?"

"Yaw."

"Vell, come along."

This prompt invitation seemed to astonish young Hans.—He raised his eyes, looked a moment at the widow, and then casting a glance at the only bed in the room, gave a long sigh, and again became transfixed.

"Vat you tinks, Frank?" asked the widow.

"Tinks?" asked Frank, in reply.

"Yes, vat you tinks ven you looks at der bed?"

"I tinks not'in'."

"Not'in', Frank? I knows vat you tinks."

"Vat?"

"You tinks dat bes von goot bet, an' you likes to sleep dere, vat you say, Frank?"

"Yaw, dat ish it."

"Vell, you can, all der vhile."

"Vhere you sleep?" asked Frank, somewhat astonished.

"On der floor, mit der quilts."

"Nix," was the emphatic negative to that proposition.

"How we fix it den, Frank?" pressed the widow, who confident that Frank was smitten, but too bashful to break the ice, drew her chair close to his.

Frank could not conceal his embarrassment. The truth was, he had never been in love until he had seen the widow, and, being entirely inexperienced in such matters, he did not know how to proceed. As the plump Kathleen for the first time sat close by his side, he felt a strange sensation, which greatly increased his embarrassment. He was afraid to move, and even forgot to whiff his pipe, the stem of which he almost severed between his teeth.

"How we fix it den, Frank?" repeated Kathleen, letting her head drop carelessly on her lover's shoulder. Frank quivered at the touch, and his eyes rolled almost convulsively. He could not have spoken if he would.

"You sprakin not'in', Frank," she continued, taking his hand in hers; "and, mine Himmel! you shakes like mine little tog vhen he's got der sherks. Vat bes der matter mit mine Frank?" she urged, putting her arm around his neck, and giving him what in common parlance is called a hug.

A bright glow gradually lighted up the countenance of the young lover. He felt as he had never felt before. The fond hopes of months were now being realized, and so unexpectedly, that he could scarcely believe it. He heard every word addressed to him, but was unable to lisp a syllable.

He even imagined he was dreaming, and to make sure, passed his arm around the fair Kathleen's waist. There was no mistaking its pillowy softness, and in his ecstacy he dropped the pipe from his mouth and exclaimed—

"Goot Himmel! dat ish mine Kathleen!"

The widow now considered her triumph complete; and as her speechless and pipeless lover clung to her, bright visions of a youthful husband and a happy future rejoiced her heart. After the first ecstacy of love was over, however, she was reminded that Frank had not yet popped the question. Knowing the inconsistency of man in general, she determined to consummate the match that very night.

"Frank," she said, after due consideration; "Frank, you come to poard mit me, how we fix it about der bed?"

"Poard?" asked the lover in reply.

"Yaw. Don't you want to poard mit me? Dere is Shake, an' Pete, an' Shon, an' Mike; dey vant to live mit me, but no poard."

"Nix poard?"

"No. Shake say, 'Kathleen you got only von ped; I like to live mit you—vot shall ve do?' I say, 'not'in',' den he say, 'Let's go to the 'squire an' get married,' an' I say, 'I marry nopody but mine Frank.'"

"Dat ish goot," replied the lover.

"Vell?" asked the widow with much earnestness.

"Vell," was the stupid response.

"Shall we go to der 'Squire, Frank?" asked the widow, finding that she must pop the question herself.

"Yaw."

"Vhen?"

"In der mornin.'"

"Oh, mine Frank! mine Frank!" exclaimed the widow, overjoyed at the happy result.

The next day, the two were made one, and those who knew the "frau," declared she was far more devoted to the youthful Frank, than she ever was to the deceased and forgotten Gotlieb.

THE NEW LEAF:

OR, A NEW YEAR AT THE CROSS-ROADS TAVERN.

"New Year's comes but once a year, boys, an' as old Fifty is 'bout expirin' into etarnity, old Tim can afford to stan' treat, all 'round. Come up, ev'ry mother's son of you, and give the old year a partin' drink!"

Such was the language of old Tim, landlord of the "Head of Washington," to a bar-room full of customers, early in the last evening of the year 1850. The "Head of Washington" is an old tavern, and I might say, that it is firmly fixed in the memory of thousands who have patronized it. Scores of distinguished men have eagerly sought its comforts, and gladly accepted its hospitality. Weary travelers, borne slowly in the stage-coach, day and night, through a frosty atmosphere, have hailed its glowing fires and warm meals with joy. The poor wayfarer, with all his earthly possessions on his back, has often entered its doors downcast, and left them enlivened in heart. Aye! the "Head of Washington," kept for years by old Tim Walker, at the cross-roads, near

G——, in a Western State, has comforted many a sorrowful heart and afforded good cheer to many a weary soul. Nay, more. There, in the bar-room of that old tavern, more than one now distinguished man has first displayed his "larnin'," and first made his mark among his fellow-men—and there, in after years, has he been compelled to mingle familiarly with those who assisted to elevate him to fame, but who had gone down, down, while he ascended. There public measures have been discussed, great enterprizes projected, and important movements set in motion. There in that same bar-room, ministers have prayed and exhorted, patriots vented forth their devotion to their country, and travelers related thrilling adventures, to eager ears. And *there*—truth compels the assertion—*there* have hundreds of men, with noble forms, stout arms, and sound minds, imbibed feelings, and engendered habits, which have proved their total ruin. Oh! thou old tavern at the cross-roads! while many remember thee with pleasure, hundreds curse thee for their destruction!

Like all landlords in rural districts, Tim Walker was a "big man" among his fellow citizens. His house, the only place of resort in the village, was visited by all, and upon holidays, especially, the villagers assembled there, *en masse.* On the occasion above alluded to, the last evening of the year 1850, the bar-room was crowded with a merry throng, who had commenced the celebration of the new year ere the knell of the old one had been pealed by the hand of time. Tim was a "jolly old soul," and the sight of so many gathered together in anticipation of a holiday, cheered his heart, and induced him to give the invitation to "all hands" to take a drink, free of expense. A second invitation was not necessary, for in a moment "all hands" save a few, were at the bar, glass in hand. And it was not a little amusing to observe how the various grades clustered around that bar. First, and nearest to the landlord, stood the 'squire of the township, with a stomach equal to Falstaff's, and a plump, red nose, which glistened in the cheerful light. He was the leader of the first plattoon, which embraced closely the counter, and there was something in all their looks, which betrayed an eagerness to sip the inspiring liquid. Next to them, and just able to reach the glasses on the counter, were a sturdy-looking set of men, who, though not so eager, were anxious to join in the general drink. Behind them, were still others, and they looked on and laughed, and appeared careless as to whether glasses reached them at all, and indeed their chance for a drink did at one time appear rather doubtful, so eager were those who had reached the counter before them. Around the fire, and farthest from the bar, were a knot of individuals who were evidently disposed to let others do their drinking. But when old Tim said, "drink all round," he meant it, and his dram touched not its glass, until all in the bar-room stood liquor in hand, and awaited a signal from him to drink all together.

"Now, boys," said he, as he prepared his dram, "who will give the toast?"

"Bill Crawford!" shouted a dozen voices.

"Bill Crawford 'tis, then," was his reply. "Come, sonny," said he, to a tall young man, whose face seemed almost bursting with the liquor bloat, and whose scanty clothing was in rags. "Come, sonny, get on to a cheer, and sing it out."

"I guess the 'squire had better do it," replied Bill Crawford, the individual addressed, as he stepped on to a chair, with his glass in hand. "When it comes to a 'bout, Bill's in, but 'squire's got more larnin' than was ever packed in the hull family of Crawfords, and he's the chap what ougth'er gin the toast."

"The 'Squire," "the 'squire!" shouted the crowd.

"Thar it is," continued Bill. "'Squire you're in and this little chicken's out. Drive on with your wagon, 'squire."

This was followed by merry appeals to the 'squire for the toast.

"Gentle*men*," responded the official, as he took off his hat and wiped his face with a yellow and red mixed cotton handkerchief, "Gentle*men* and fellow citizens: I fear you are reposing heavy responsibilities upon me, forming as you do, too stupenduous opinions of my capabilities. I'll however, endeavor to satisfy your thirst for something good. This is New Year's Eve, gentle*men*, and I will give you something appropriate. I will give you a verse, which was sung at my cradle, by my patriotic father, years ago. It goes —— be you all filled and ready?"

"Ready!" was the response.

'Well then, here's the toast:"

"Apple-sass and ginger-beer,
New Year's comes but once a year—
So here's to you—here's to me—
Merry, merry we will be."

A shout followed the toast, and down went the liquor. Old Tim was glad to see all so merry, and he rubbed his hands with glee.

"Boys, make yourselves at home," said he, "for you are all welcome to the 'Head of Washington' to-night."

This called forth another shout, and then the 'squire treated, and then somebody else treated, and so the treat went round to all those who were able to stand it, and, as is generally the case, to some who were not. The more liquor drank, the more jovial the company, and songs were sung, jokes passed, and quite a happy feeling prevailed. All seemed merry but Bill Crawford. He was considered the most ready wit of the neighborhood, and stood unequalled there in spinning yarns, and singing songs. But this evening he appeared sad and demure, and not a smile crossed his generally merry countenance. He volunteered to assist Old Tim, and taking a place behind the bar, busied himself in keeping its fixtures in order. In vain was he called upon to sing a song or tell a story—he invariably, as with the toast, forced some one else to do it for him. His singular conduct caused some comment, but was soon forgotten in the hilarity of the evening.

Soon the sound of music was heard in another part of the old tavern, which proved more attractive than even the bar. The dining-room had been cleared of its immense tables, and under the direction of Mrs. Walker, a portly busy-body, arranged for the usual New Year's dance. From the day she had become landlady of the "Head of Washington," she claimed it as a special privilege to invite her friends to welcome the New Year, in a pleasant dancing party. The dining-room festival was so enticing to the inmates of the bar-room, that most of them proceeded to join the dancers. Even old Tim, himself, leaving the bar in the care of Bill Crawford, proceeded thither, as he jocosely remarked, "to shake a foot with the gals."

The dining room of the "Head of Washington" is about thirty-five feet long, by fifteen in breadth. Its walls and ceilings are as white as chalk, while its smooth floor is as unstained as the falling snow. On this occasion, all the looking glasses and pictures about the tavern were arranged upon the walls of the dining room, to give it a holiday appearance. Chairs and benches were placed around the room, and at one end a pine table, with a stool upon it, was set for the special use of the fiddler.

The ball was a kind of "free blow," Mrs. Walker, in *selecting* her company, having invited nearly every person in the neighborhood. The guests were not slow to come either, and at the time when the sound of the fiddle was first heard, nearly all the seats were occupied.

The musician was an old negro, whose only name was Bob, and who had been the village barber and dancing master from its earliest settlement. He almost worshipped his fiddle, and gloried in the clear, strong manner in which he "called the figures." No monarch ever ascended a throne with more avidity than he mounted the pine table that night, and no despot ever sat in his chair of state, with more dignity, than did Bob on the fiddler's stool.

"Is your voice clear to-night," asked Mrs. Walker of him, as he was tuning his instrument.

"Clar!" was his reply. "Clar! Is dar any mud in de moon-shine? If dar is, dis niggar's voice aint clar. Jus' wait till I tunes up Old Benjamin, (his fiddle,) an' den I'll show you wedder dis voice am clar!"

This satisfied Mrs. Walker, and taking a sort of dignified strut through the room—such a strut as a landlady only can give—smiling to this guest and to that one, she finally seated herself opposite the musician, and gave him a knowing nod of the head, which was the signal to begin.

"Pardnah's for de cotillion," yelled Bob, as he furiously run his bow over his fiddle strings.

The floor was soon filled with eager dancers, and on receiving another nod from Mrs. Walker, Bob set them in motion. And such music as came from that violin! I have heard Ole Bull on his single string and his diamond-set fiddle, but never heard him produce the rich, full, and melodious sounds which came from old Bob's instrument. It is an orchestra complete, and needs no accompaniment save the "clar" voice of its owner. And that voice was musical, too, as it gave forth, in merry strains, the figures about as follows:

"To de right and lef all four,—tee-dum tee-dum — De balance now—deedle-dum deedle dum—Ladies will you change—high-die die-do—Promenade across de room—bee-ye bee-ye—An' now come back agin," etc.

People may talk as they please about the inferiority of the African race; but if there is not music in a negro, there is certainly none this side of heaven. At least the company no doubt thought so, as Bob, beating time with his feet, produced such inspiring sounds from his instrument, and sang the "figures" so delightfully to the air he was performing. The dance went on, and the bar-room was deserted, except at the intervals between the cotillions. While the music was going, the girls were more attractive than the decanters, but the moment old Bob laid aside " de fiddle an' de bow, " stimulants were sought in the bar-room.

I need not relate the events of the evening — tell how 'squire Higgans sat up to the widow Spriggans — how affectionate the young married couple were in public; making the girls blush and the boys giggle — how Sally Scruggs got jealous of Molly Muggs, and tripped her up, while she was dancing with Bill Snipes, her beau — how Mary Spurrs broke one of the looking-glasses in displaying her ugly face in it — or how Mag Surly mistook a shadow for a seat, and set herself flat on the floor, right before the whole company.

Neither need I tell how Bill Snipes suffered with his new tight boots—what a dash Bill Thompson cut with his new shirt collar—how Dick Murphy, having more of the "ardent" about him than he could carry, fell into the fire, and came near burning himself up—how Joe Turner pulled nearly all the hair out of his head, and would'nt dance because he was in love with Mrs. Doxy, and could'nt get her, as she already had a husband, or how Dick Handscrabble insulted Miss Terry by asking her if the old year would'nt leave her an old maid.

The dance went on. All were happy while the fiddle played, and joy seemed to reign over the festive gathering. The hour of twelve approached, and preparations were made to welcome the New Year in a becoming manner. Mrs. Walker, the landlady, had her own notions about this ceremony, and if not consistent in any thing else, she was in this. The New Year had always been received with a certain ceremony, at her annual parties, a ceremony she had concocted the first year of her landladyship, and to which she would hear of no alterations or amendments. It was this:

At ten minutes before twelve o'clock, the company took hold of hands and formed themselves into a circle. They were to join man and woman all the way round, and if there were more men than women, or *vice versa*, the odd ones were sent out of the room as black sheep. The circle formed, old Bob slowly and solemnly walked inside of it, and then all getting upon their knees, he played a solemn requiem to the expiring year. While playing, he kept his eyes upon the clock, and the moment the large hand came within one minute of twelve, he ceased playing. A dread silence then prevailed until the clock pealed the meridian of night, when the violin instantly struck up a lively air. The company then jumped to their feet, and retaining hold of each other, moved briskly around the room, shouting "a happy New Year!" This was a strange ceremony, but not inappropriate or uninteresting.

On this occasion the circle had been formed, the company were on their knees, and Bob had just commenced the requium, when a startling incident took place. Bill Crawford, the lively joker, the merry singer, and the never-failing drinker, came slowly into the room upon his tip-toes. His face bore an ashy hue, while his large black eyes had an unearthly, ghastly look. At each step he would place the fore-finger of his right hand upon his lips and say in a soft whisper, "Hist!" His strange appearance startled all in the room, and even the musician's fiddle fell from his hands with the requiem half finished. Not a soul stirred, or scarcely breathed, as that ragged toper, with his wild, unnatural look, approached the center of the room, and solemnly knelt on his bended knees.

"Hist! hist!" said he, "the Old Year's agoin'," and with us, is on its way to ruin. The devil is after Bill Crawford, the drunkard—he is—he is—he's coming in the door—he knows me—he's got me by the hair—help! murder! help!—save me from death!" and thus shrieking, the poor man, his face assuming the most horrid shapes, fled to the farthest corner of the room, where he buried his head in his hands, and uttered the most agonizing groans.

The utmost consternation pervaded the company. Many, alarmed at the horrible sight, fled from the house; while all the females who remained shrieked as if they thought the Judgment Day was at hand. The only man present who appeared to retain his presence of mind was old Tim, the landlord. Mounting a chair he coolly said:

"Make more noise, won't you all? Can't you see that nothin's the matter, only Billy's got the man-an'-the-poker agin?"

This served somewhat to quiet the fears of the company, and old Tim instantly turned his attention to the afflicted man. With two or three others he approached the crazy drunkard, for the purpose of removing him to a more suitable place. The moment their hands touched Crawford, however, he shrank from them as from a viper. His face was still ghastly pale, while large drops of sweat stood upon his brow. He trembled from head to foot, and fixing his glaring eyes upon the landlord, he exclaimed,

"Go away you devil! Your hands are hot, you burn me—oh, my God, take the devil away. I'll drink no more, if you don't take me now! Oh, murder, murder! I'm burning up—my head—my feet—my hands—my body, is all on fire!—Good Lord! water! water! water!"

"Bill, don't you know me?" said old Tim, I'm the landlord."

But the suffering man heeded not his words. The most dreadful exclamations, followed by terrible groans, still came from him, while he trembled from head to foot. He was finally seized by four stout men, and though he resisted with the strength of a maniac, and uttered the most piercing shrieks, he was carried to the bar-room and laid upon the counter. An effort was made to force liquor down his throat—a good antidote for the disease when properly administered—but he resisted with all his might. Suddenly, that resistance ceased, his jaws became fixed, his eyes ceased their rolling, and he lay motionless and still.

"There's no use workin' any longer with him," said Tim, the landlord, "for poor Bill's drinked his last drop—*he's dead!*"

He spoke the truth—the toper had drawn his last breath. This was his third attack of the *mania-apotu*, and it had hurried him away. He took his departure with the expiring year, and oh! how dreadful was his death.

No more mirth was witnessed in that house that night. Toper as he was, degraded as he had been, no one was more liked about the village than poor Bill Crawford. He possessed a liberal heart, and was ever ready to oblige those who asked his service, and to discommode himself to be useful to others. But he loved the bitter cup—could not resist its fascinations—and drank himself to death. Sad, indeed, was the entree of the New Year, at the old tavern at the cross-roads! It brought sorrow, fright, and consternation, and the horrid scenes of that night will never be removed from the memory of those who witnessed them.

The terrible death of Bill Crawford affected no one more than old Tim, the landlord. After surveying the corpse silently for some minutes, during which, big tears rolled fast down his cheeks, he said—

"*This night I turn over a New Leaf—No liquor can be bought at the* "*Head of Washington*" *during the New Year.*"

Old Tim was true to his vow. But a short time after poor Crawford's body had been laid in its last resting place, on New Year's day, every drop of liquor in the bar of the old tavern at the cross-roads, was given to the soil to drink. The landlord became a temperance man and a temperance advocate, and now the village of G——, mainly through his exertions, stands prominent among temperance localities.

Mrs. Walker, is still alive, and since the night of Crawford's death, has given two more "New Year welcomes." She declares they are far more happy without the use of ardent spirits, and that she is glad her husband abolished the bar. She often relates the circumstances of Crawford's death to habitual drinkers, who chance to stop at the old tavern, and advises them to do on the next New Year, if not sooner, what her husband did that evening—"*Turn Over a New Leaf!*"

MRS. O'CALLAHAN'S SPLASH:

AND HOW MONS. LA FORCE RECEIVED IT.

Mons. La Force is a French gentleman and a teacher of music. He possesses all the grace and vivacity for which the original frog-eaters are celebrated the world over, and being always *a la mode* in his dress, polite in his attentions, and agreeable in his intercourse with others, it is no wonder he is a favorite among the ladies. Where are the Frenchmen who can not make themselves attractive to the feminine sex?—Though they may be as ugly as a rough stone fence, their general acquaintance with the artificial means of adorning the person, their refinement and good taste, give them an advantage which those of the same sex, of other nations, do not possess.

Mons. La Force is in love for about the one hundred and twentieth time. He is smitten with the charms of a belle to whom he is engaged in giving instructions in music—"bootiful moosic." He calls on her often, and manages to impress the heart, as he delights the senses and refines the mind.

Monday last was Monsieur's day to call on his lady-love. How he did primp, and fix, and fuss, before the looking-glass, ere he took his departure. This curl was arranged, that curve in the cravat gracefully stationed, every defect in his apparel carefully hidden, and all disagreeable odors removed by a free application of the most delightful perfumes.

"Bootiful! bootiful! — fascinate ze ladee, ze sweet ladee!" he exclaimed, as he surveyed himself for the last time in his mirror. "Ah, ha! I captivates; I swear, zis time, my love to ze bootiful ladee."

With a small bundle of music in one hand, and his delicate cane — if a polished and highly ornamented switch can be called a cane — in the other, Mons. La Force proceeded toward the residence of his bewitching pupil, and lady-love. He was on Spring street, within a square of his destination, and his heart began to experience those sensations which ardent lovers are apt to feel when approaching the object of their affections — in fact his heart commenced beating "pitty-pat," when a roar, much like that of a cataract, fell upon his ears, and the next moment he found himself completely drenched with dirty, greasy water.

"*Mon Dieu!* vat is ze matter?" he exclaimed, the moment he recovered from the shock. "Who do zis to me? — Ah! oh! vat s'all I do? My toilet ruin — my perfoom gone, an' I smell like — like — like — ze bootcher s'op. Ah! oh! I kill myse'f wiz ze suicide."

"Are yez hurt, darlint?" sung out a voice from a porch in the third story of the house, in front of which Mons La Force was bewailing. The Frenchman, casting his eyes upward, discovered that the interrogatory came from Mrs. O'Callahan, a middle-aged Irish woman, of massive form, who stood on the end of the porch, resting her head upon one of her huge red arms, and clasping a wash-tub with the other. Though she was looking at him very unconcernedly, Mons. La Force could not but see at one glance, that she and the wash-tub were the causes of his misfortune.

"*Ah, ha! vous bete, monstre,*" he exclaimed; *vot for you kill me wiz ze tub? Vot for you pour ze water on ze shentleman, eh!*"

"Howly Mary, an' its mad I believe yez are," was Mrs. O'Callahan's reply. "I did n't know but the soods had cracked yer head, yez kept up such a wailing. It ain't a bit hurt yez are, thin?" coolly asked the woman.

"Hurt, you say, Madame?" asked Monsieur, as he cast his eyes over his stained and wilted apparel. "Ah! look at ze chapeau, ze boozom, ze bootiful pantaloon. Ah, Madame! vhy you do all zis?"

"Why didn't yez get out uv the way whin I tould yez too? Tell me that, now, if yez can. It ain't mesel', a poor woman that I am, that is to waste me time on the likes uv yez. I tould yez the wather was comin', an' Mrs. O'Callahan niver waits for the divil's own. Och! begone wid yez, now."

"You do zis perpose, eh? Ha, Madame you von scoundel, you von dog. I sue you wiz de court—I makes you pay ze money for my poor chapeau, my poor pantaloon, my boorty boozum. I get ze gens d'armes, ze police, to take you to ze"——

"Och! but yez are a fool, darlint," coolly interrupted Mrs. O'Callahan. "Go home wid ye, an' put on some thry clothes, if yez has thim, an' whin yez comes this way agin, look out for Mrs. O'Callahan's wather. Do yez mind that!"

"Vat ze name? vat ze name?" cried the music-master, as the old woman strolled slowly along into her apartments. Her only reply was a defiant shake of the head as she closed her door between them.

"Oh! vat s'all I do?" continued the Frenchman. "I sue ze, Madame, by the Court, but *mille tonneres*, I no have ze name.

Ah! *mon ami*," he exclaimed, turning to a stalwart son of Erin, who stood in the door of the lower story of the same building, complacently smoking his "dudeen," and enjoying the Frenchman's trouble. Ah! *mon ami*, you tells me ze name?"

"Is it me yer spakin' to?" asked Patrick.

"Oui, Monsieur, vat is ze Madame's name?"

"The woman's name is it ye want?"

"Oui, Monsieur, ze ladee wiz ze tub."

"Shure an she is a poor woman," continued Pat.

"Oui, Monsieur, ze name—ze name?"

"An' ye want to know it?"

"Ze name! yes, Monsieur, ze name!"

"An' is it bad ye want to know it, me old boy?"

"Let me tell ze von littell sing, Monsieur," said the Frenchman, confidentially, as he approached the Irishman, the very picture of dispair and distress. "I get ze Madame's name, I sue her wiz ze Court, and, ah ha! I makes her pay ze—ze—ze—vat you call him? ha!—ah! yes, ze costs."

"And ye'll make the poor woman pay the costs, will ye?" asked Patrick.

"Oui, Monsieur, ze costs. I have you so—so—so—so—ah! yes, sopeeny, as von gran' vitness. You come to ze Court—you swear wiz ze hand up—an' Monsieur, you gets ze money for zat. You tells me Madame's nàme now, eh?"

"An' its informer ye'd make uv me thin?"

"Form—form—form," muttered the somewhat puzzled music-master, "*in*form, ah! yes, Monsieur, you inform ze Court, and gets ze money?

"Out wid ye thin, ye dirthy spalpeen," shouted Pat, as he took his dudeen out of his mouth. "It's mesel that'll niver inform against a poor widdy. Git the name the best as yez can, wid yer monkey face, for I'm not the boy to tell ye that it was Mrs. Callahan who doused the dirthy wather on ye."

"Zat's it! zat's it!" shrieked the Frenchman, as he heard the name; clapping his hands and jumping for joy. Ah! ha! I got ze name now. Callahan—Callahan—Callahan—I remember zat so very well—Callahan—Callahan—Callahan."

"And who in the divil tould ye?" asked the astonished Irishman.

"Ah! it is ze Madame's name, Monsieur," was the reply. "I go to ze Court straight away off. I get ze gens d'armes to come catch ze ladee, an' you, *mon ami*, s'all be von gran' vitness. Adieu, Monsieur."

With a polite bow, the music-master took his leave, returning in the direction whence he came. In the exuberance of his joy in ascertaining the name of the female who had so suddenly and carelessly destroyed the best of his toilet, and caused him even to forget for the time his lady love, he seemed to have overlooked altogether his sad plight, and distressing appearance. It is to be presumed he hastened to the Police Court, where, laying his complaint before the Judge, he succeeded in obtaining a warrant for the arrest of the unmerciful Mrs. Callahan, and "wiz ze Court," made her "pay ze costs."

THE LOST BALLOONIST.*

BEING A BRIEF NARRATIVE OF A NOVEL EXPLORING EXPEDITION.

I had advertised to make my fourth ærial voyage from the city of N——, in north-eastern Ohio. Up to that period I had adopted ballooning as a money-making experiment, though I must confess that each ascension so charmed me, that with three ærial voyages I had become ambitious to distinguish myself as an æronaut. My fourth ascension was

* On the second day of October last, a Mr. Winchester, made his third or fourth ascension with a balloon from a city in Ohio. His balloon was not fully inflated, and he was forced to ascend with but a small quantity of ballast. Yet he expressed his determination, notwithstanding his limited experience, to go higher and farther than any æronaut had ever done. He has not been heard of since. This sketch is a supposed account of his voyage.

advertised to take place on the second of day of October, 1855. On the day previous I read in the newspapers an account of the return of Dr. Kane and his daring companions from the Arctic regions, and a brief detail of their sufferings and privations in endeavoring to penetrate those dreary regions of the north, never looked upon by the eye of civilized man. The query immediately entered my mind, "could not a voyage to the Artic regions be made with greater success, less danger and less suffering, in a balloon?" The idea seemed to possess me entirely, as I could not drive it from my mind. No matter with whom I conversed, or about what I was conversing, a sail to the Arctic regions haunted me continually.

In the air, the voyager would be free from those obstructions which have defied the ingenuity of man, was the argument which presented itself to my mind. Once in the proper current, the æronaut could fly in hours, the distance that ships cannot accomplish in months, and it appeared to me, that with good luck, I could reach the latitude of 32 deg. 30m.; the farthest point made by the Kane expedition, in less than forty-eight hours. I knew, from observations made at previous ascensions, that at the hight of about two miles, there was a constant and swift current of air from the S. S. W., and once in that current, I was confident I would be borne along at the extraordinary speed of from one to two miles a minute. I could apprehend danger from two causes only. One was an explosion of the balloon, from an expansion of the gas in the very cold atmosphere, and the second, inability to keep from freezing to death. The first I thought could be avoided, by taking with me a small quantity of ballast, which would enable me to ascend with my balloon only half inflated, and the second I was willing to risk, with such precautions as circumstances would allow me to make.

As I have heretofore stated, the subject was constantly in my mind. I could not sleep for it, and I arose on the morning of my proposed ascension from N——, with the firm conviction that Providence designed I should penetrate, by this novel means, the unknown regions, and be the first to reveal their condition to the civilized world. The conviction seemed to nerve, nay, inspire me, and I resolved to make the voyage that very day!

My thoughts and feelings were a secret with myself. I had not breathed a word about it to a soul, not even to those dear to me as life, and I was determined that the secret should ascend from earth with me, and if I perished, perish with me. I made no preparations whatever, save to provide for personal protection against intense cold, firmly believing that Providence would guide and direct me, and save me from an untimely death.

I never left *terra firma* without bidding my family and intimate friends an affectionate farewell, and receiving their wishes for a safe return. This I did, because they, not I, apprehended danger. After my first ascension, I was satisfied that the balloonist encounters no more danger, or runs no more risk than must be met with in every other mode of conveyance; but my friends thought differently. On this occasion my feelings were peculiar. I knew not whither I was going, or how long I would be absent, yet felt confident that I would one day return, crowned as the great adventurer and discoverer of the age. My hand may have betrayed a nervousness in the parting grasp, but my heart was firm.

I placed in the car the clothing I had prepared, ten pounds of food, and only twenty-five pounds of ballast. When my balloon was about half inflated, I found it would lift the weight and myself with ease, and, to the surprise of my attendants, I made instant preparations to ascend. Stepping into the car, I said:

"I intend to go higher and farther than any æronaut has heretofore gone. Let go."*

My order was obeyed, and my ærial ship floated gently upward, taking a northeasterly direction. The earth never looked more beautiful to me than it did then. It appeared like an enchanted basin, glowing with loveliness upon every hand. Forests dwindled down to tiny groves, lakes to silvery pools, and villages to mere dots upon the landscape. Long after N—— had faded from my view, I sat leaning over my car, my thoughts entirely engrossed with the enchanting scene. It was not till I approached Lake Erie, that my grand design again entered my mind. I looked at my barometer, and found I was at the hight, and in the current of air I desired to reach, and I then busied myself in arranging the contents of the car for the night. I was sailing swiftly, fast enough to satisfy myself that my calculations made the night previous would be fully realized.

I had scarcely reached the lake when a layer of clouds shut the earth out from my view, and I saw no more of it that day. As night advanced I became chilly, and at an early

* These were the words uttered by Mr. Winchester just previous to his last ascension.

hour in the evening so cold that I prepared at once to shield myself from the frosty atmosphere. My preparations were novel. My car was of circular shape, made of willow, the exterior covered with India-rubber cloth. I fastened a Buffalo robe I had prepared for the purpose over the top of the car, which excluded the air, and made me a complete prisoner for the time being. It was so fastened, that in case of necessity I could unloosen it in a moment, and be free to manage my balloon. I pulled on the garments I had prepared, partook of stimulants, wrapped myself in a buffalo robe, and lay down in my car.

That dreadful night! Language can not depict my feelings. There I lay, sailing in mid-air, shut out entirely from the world, and drifting, God only knew where! Several times was I tempted to descend, to relieve myself of the dreadful anxiety which tormented my mind, but faith in the idea that I was fulfilling a design of Providence, induced me to resist the temptation. I was at the mercy of Heaven, for if I ascended any great distance, my balloon would assuredly explode, and if I descended, injury, if not death, was certain.

My intention had been not to sleep, but many hours had not passed before slumber would have been welcome to my troubled mind. How long I was in that condition, I can not tell; it seemed an age to me, and I began to think that daylight would never come. At last I fell asleep.

When I awoke, I felt much refreshed, though my limbs were stiff from the intense cold. I could hear the wind sweeping with tremendous fury over the earth, and I determined at once, light or dark, to endeavor to ascertain my location. With difficulty I raised myself on my knees, to unfasten the covering of my car. I found it frozen so stiff that I could do nothing with it. I hid my faoe in my hands and implored the aid of Heaven. As if directed by Providence, I thought of my knife, and the next moment I endeavored to make an incision into the robe. This I found to be a difficult undertaking. The robe seemed to be covered with a thick body of ice, which retarded my progress very much. I labored away, however, picking out the ice by small pieces, feeling that my existence depended on my success.

I must have been an hour making an aperture large enough to thrust my head through; for I frequently shrank from the biting atmosphere which came through it, and which affected my system most strangely. When the hole was large enough, I suddenly thrust my head through it. The effect of the atmosphere was such as to almost destroy my sensibility, but courage and determination supported me. Wonderful! wonderful! indeed was my position. The air seemed filled with frosty particles, which sparkled like silver in the twilight haze. Neither earth nor sky could be seen, while the atmosphere seemed almost destructive to life. I gave but a single glance, and then shrank back with horror into my car.

Death seemed imperative. My balloon was beyond management. If I could have succeeded in reaching my valve-rope, it would have been impossible for me to open the valve, against the icy lock that had been placed upon it. I could do nothing but lay and await my fate. I endeavored to close the hole in the top of my car, but was unable to do so, and it was not long before I became utterly powerless. While lying in this condition, I felt the car rushing through what seemed to be water, and as the wind whistled terribly through

6

the rigging of my ærial ship, I was sure that my progress was being impeded. I listened. At first I thought the car was dragging upon the earth, but was soon convinced it was not so. I at last came to the conclusion that I was encountering icy obstacles in the air, and I expected to have my balloon torn to pieces, and to experience a rapid fall to the earth. I prayed for it.

By degrees, I felt those sensations, which exposure to intense cold is sure to bring, until I became drowsy, and finally fell asleep. How long I lay in this condition I know not. My return to consciousness, found me lying by a fire, surrounded by a strange looking people, whose appearance enabled me to recognize them at once as inhabitants of the Arctic Regions. They looked upon me with wonder and astonishment, though evidently pleased with the success of their efforts to resuscitate me. How long I have been with them, I can not tell, as there seems to be no daylight here, and I have been unable to gather any information of these people, further than that I came down from Heaven. I am now but barely able to move, and have written this account to relieve the monotony of my prison hut, and with the hope that I may be able at some time to dispatch it to the civilized portion of the globe.

How far north I am, I have no means as yet of determining, but I have good reasons for presuming that I am nearer the North Pole than Dr. Kane was. Still firm in the faith, that my expedition was instigated by Him who ruleth all things, and that it will finally be successful, I have determined, as soon as I am able, to make such investigations as circumstances will permit.

FIRST LOVE:

OR, JEREMIAH TRIUMPH'S OPINION OF CITY GALS.

"JERRY, gin us your 'sperience with the city gals," said old 'Squire Jones, to his nephew, Jeremiah Triumph, as they were in the hight of enjoyment at an "apple-cutting," at the old 'Squires, in a North-Western county of Ohio.

"Yes, Jerry, tell us about the city gals," exclaimed a dozen voices, and Jerry was soon surrounded by fifteen or twenty as plump and fair maidens as ever graced a farmer's household.

Jerry was naturally talkative, but, since his return from the city, he had preserved a mysterious silence, on the above subject, save occasionally throwing out a hint which induced his friends to believe he had fallen in love with somebody's daughter while away from home, and had been "crossed," or met with some other equally great misfortune. Many efforts had been made to bring Jeremiah to a confession, but the fatherly persuasions of his uncles, the matronly inducements of his aunts, and the seductive arts of the girls had all failed, up to the present occasion, to get out of him the story of his love.

To the above request, Jerry merely put on a sober face, crossed his legs, rested his chin upon his right hand, turned his tobacco in his mouth, looked into the blazing fire, and solemnly shook his head. Not a word would he say. At last, Molly Frazier, as sweet a being as ever lifted a milk-pail, placed a stool beside Jerry, and seated herself upon it. She then laid her head upon his lap, and bringing her large, lovely, blue eyes in full view of his, she said:

"Jerry, do tell us about the city gals, just for my sake."

Jerry was stirred. Those blue eyes, staring him in the face, and that lovely form leaning so fondly on him, moved him. Changing his quid to the off side of his mouth, and smiling quite happily, his voice almost trembled, as he replied,

"I reckon."

"I knew you would!—I knew you would!" exclaimed Molly, attempting to rise.

"Hold on a little," interposed Jerry, as he caught her around the waist, and gently held her fast. "I reckon there is one condition, Molly, afore I tell it."

"What's that?" asked the surprised girl.

"That you lay right thar where you are, till I get through."

Molly blushed; but taking the terms in good part, she, "jist to obleege the folks," assented.

The company now all gathered round Jerry, placing the apple-baskets in such position that while they listened they could peel and split the golden fruit without interrupting the narrative. All ready, Jerry commenced:

"Fust love," said he, "is al'ays reckoned etarnal. Like mustard weeds, when it once gits in a patch, there's no gettin' it out. You may plow, an' you may hoe, an' you may jerk it up by the roots—but jist as sure as growin' time comes, it will spring up an' shoot, in spite of you."

"That ar' a fact," interposed the 'Squire, giving Aunt Tabitha a knowing look.

"I knows it, sartin," was the good wife's reply, as she wrung the core out of a good sound pippin. "I al'ays contended that there war but one love, and that war the fust. Aint I al'ays said so, gals?"

"Yes, mum," was the general response.

"How is it, then," inquired Molly, "that folks sometimes get married a second time? Don't they love the first time?"

"Laws only knows," replied Tabitha. "It's my opinion that thar's no love in a second weddin'; an' I *know* that one man's enuff for any woman's life-time."

"Aye, an' I never could see what a man wanted with more'n one wife. One's as many as I can manage," replied the 'Squire, with a knowing look, which caused a burst of laughter, in which the good aunt took part.

"I reckon," said Molly, after the laughter had subsided, "those who marry the second time don't love their first wives."

"That's it," replied Jerry, as he twirled one of Molly's ringlets in his fingers. "Bekase a man marries a woman, it aint any sign he loves her. Some marry for money, some for spite, and some just to nat'rally settle down, and be at rest. But fust love, it's a root what can't be dug up; a tree what'll never die."

"That are true," replied the 'Squire; "but, Jerry, what about the city gals?"

"I war just a goin' on to tell about 'em," replied Jerry, heaving a sigh. "I war never in the city but wunst, an' you know when that war. The drovers bought our hogs, an' they offered me two bits a day an' found, to help drive them to Sinsinnati. I hadn't nothin' special to do, an' thinkin' it war a good time to go to town and see city sights, I took 'em up, put on my best wamus, my cow-hide boots, an' started."

"Laws! I remember the time jist as if it war this morning," remarked Aunt Tabitha. "We all got up when the hens begin to crow, to git you an airly breakfast, an' to see you off. Right smart of hogs you took with you."

"Yes, an' a time we had of it, afore we got to town. I didn't think of nothin' then but hogs, and the gals didn't trouble me a bit," ejaculated Jerry, with a mournful countenance.

"Didn't you love no girl then, Jerry?" inquired Molly.

"Nary a one."

"Not one?"

"Now, Molly, you needn't ax that agin; you know I kinder set up to you, but you al'ays went from meetin' with Jim Downs."

"But I never loved Jim, an' you know it."

"An' you never loved *me* nuther," was Jerry's reply, giving Molly a very meaning look.

"You don't know that," answered the coquetting little witch, placing her hands over her eyes.

Jerry was confused—confounded. He felt his heart beat as it never had before, and as he gazed on the handsome form of Molly, his tongue refused to give utterance. He seemed to fall into a reverie, from which he was aroused by the 'Squire, who, after the young folks — they understood Molly—had enjoyed a good titter, sang out —

"What on airth's the matter with you, Jerry? Aint you never goin' to tell us about the city gals?"

"Yes, yes," was Jerry's confused reply. "Can't you gin a feller time to think? Let me see. I war talkin' about the hogs, warn't I, Molly?"

Molly nodded assent.

"Wall, we druv the hogs to town, an' sich a town! Thar wer nothin but houses and people from one end to t'other, an' the streets wer so crowded, they had to squeeze by one anuther, jest as we do out here at big meetins. An' the gals! you never seed the beat in all your born days. You couldn't look no whar, nor turn no way, without runnin' right agin a dozen on 'em. An' golly, how purty they war. They had all sorts of purty fixin's about 'em, an' went sailin' round so, that they made me think of the angels, what the new preacher talked about at the Baptist meetins the Sunday afore I druv the hogs to town. I couldn't help lookin' at 'em, an' come mighty nigh losing some of the hogs on account of it.

"We druv the hogs down to the pens," continued Jerry, after a moment's pause, "an' then sez I to the boys, I'm goin' to see the gals. Sez they, be keerful, Jerry, or some on 'em will bite you. Sez I, I don't keer if they do; an' gosh! I just thought then that I wouldn't keer if them gals would chaw me all up into nothin', they war so purty. I went down to market, an' thar I stopped. It was jest arter sundown, an' thar war an amazin' sight of people in the streets. An' sich gals! you ought to jest have seed 'em, Uncle 'Squire—it would a made your old eyes glisten without specs. Bimeby one of them gals stopped right in front of me, an' she looked right square in my eyes. From the top of her head down to her feet, she war streamin' with ribbons, an' the gold on her jest spangled right out. Her cheeks war like the peaches on the corner tree, an' her eyes war equal to any fox squirrel's. Gosh! but she war purty, an' I do declare to gracious, that if I hadn't seed her walk, I'd a took her for one of the wax figures we seed in the show."

Jerry now stopped, perhaps to rest, or maybe it was to think. Aunt Tabitha had become so interested in his narrative, that she had deserted the apples and naturally taken to her knitting, while the 'Squire had allowed his specs to drop clean over his nose without knowing it. The young folks, particularly the girls, were listening with breathless anxiety; none more so than Molly, who still, as per agreement, lay quietly in Jerry's lap.

"As I said," continued Jerry, his eyes thoughtfully fixed on the blazing fire, "she looked right at me. It war then I felt my heart turn a somerset, an' I thought I war sinkin' right through the airth. *That war furst love!* I s'posed the gal had fell in love with me, onsight, onseen, an' she war so purty I could a tuck her in my arms, an' packed her right off to the preacher's an' got married without axin' a word. She kept a lookin' at me, an' I kept a feelin' more so. At last, sez I to myself, sez I, 'Jerry, she's a waitin' for you to pop the question — now or never!' So I straightened up, an' kind a brushed my har', and steppin' up to her, sez I 'How-de-do, mum?' 'De-do?' says she, an' she kept a lookin' me right in the face. I war kind a stuck right thar, and I commenced coughin' jest to show I war n't bashful. —

She kind a throw'd back her bonnet, an' put her face close up to mine, till I thought she war a goin' to buss me right thar in the road, with all the people about. I kinder spread out my arms, to gin her a hug, when she holler'd, '*Take that for your imperdence, Mister Hoosier!*' an' she give me such a whack about my ears, that I thought a clap of thunder was a strikin' about."

Jerry was here interrupted by an outburst of laughter from the young folks, which seemed to displease him very much.

"Taint no laughin' matter," he continued, as soon as he could obtain attention. "That war my first love, jest think of that, an' though the gal treated me all-fired mean, its my downright opinion that I kin never love another. I think on it day an' night, an' it worries me terribly."

"Why laws, Jerry," interposed Molly, "I should n't believe you'd think well of any city gal, after that."

"I can't help it, Molly. Though it's my opinion that all city gals are mighty mean, *first love you know is endurin'*."

"You don't mean to say you will never love any body else?" inquired Molly, as she patted him softly on the cheeks.

"Yaas, I'm sartain I wont—that is, so long as the first love lasts, Molly. I think," he continued, looking steadfastly in her eyes, "*my first love extends only to city gals.*"

A general shout followed this meaning expression, and before the apple-cutting party broke up, it was quite evident that Jerry had forgotten his first love in a fond affection for Miss Molly. Is not Jeremiah Triumph's first love about as enduring as most persons,—lasting until something better turns up?

I AM TOO LOW TO BE REDEEMED:

OR, THE FATAL TERMINATION OF A RUNAWAY MATCH.

THE watch-house in Cincinnati is situated in the basement of the City Building, fronting on Ninth street, between Plum and Western Row. It is composed of three departments or rooms, as follows: — The first or front room is the roll-room, where the police gather, at roll-call hours, to answer to their names, and receive instructions. From this you pass into the male prison, which contains twelve cells. These cells are made of strong iron grating, fastened firmly into a heavy stone pavement. The only furniture in each cell is a heavy, thick plank, so fixed that it will serve for either a seat or a bed! Farther back is the female prison, containing six cells made precisely in the same manner as those in the other room.

It is mournful to visit this prison at any time, for you can never do it without observing some poor wretch, whose misfortunes or folly attract your attention, and excite your sympathy. The gruff tone of the keeper, as he abruptly answers the questions of those imprisoned, at first sounds harshly indeed; but when you know, as reporters and policemen know too well, that, with rare exceptions, neither compassion nor interest can permanently affect those there confined, you are ready to pity the keeper's troubles, as well as the miseries of the prisoners. Many a sad tale has been related in that watch-house, and I have seen stern watchmen, who, in the performance of their out-door duties seemed heartless and hardened, affected to tears by the sorrowful, painful, stories of the inmates.

One summer evening, I heard that a female had attempted to commit suicide by leaping off one of the ferry landings into the river, but that a watchman had rescued her and taken her to the watch-house. It was too good an "item" to be lost, so I hastened to the watch-house to learn the truth of the story. I was shown to the unfortunate female, but found myself unable to get any information from her in regard to her rash conduct. Indeed she sat almost motionless, her long, black tresses hanging loosely over her shoulders, and her eyes fixed intently on the floor. She was apparently about seventeen years of age, with handsome features, and a most lovely countenance. All I could do, or those who were with me, failed to elicit an answer from her.

At last, watchman ———, an old policeman, and one too, who had not been hardened by his intimacy with crime and vice, entered the prison, and as soon as he saw the girl, he recognized her.

"Julia," said he, "what are you doing here?"

She knew his voice, and as soon as she heard it, tears gushed from her eyes, and she buried her face in her hands.—Tears came from the watchman's eyes, too, as he approached her tenderly and affectionately, and said:

"My God! has it come to this!"

"Oh!" replied the poor girl, her voice almost choked with sobs, "had I taken your advice, one short year ago, I might have been saved; but now, oh! now, it is too late — *I am too low to be redeemed!*"

I shall never forget the anguish with which those words were uttered — they sank deep into my heart, and often indeed they have touched my memory, when I have seen vain, foolish girls taking the initiatory steps to inevitable ruin.

The girl being unwilling to converse in our presence, the watch-house keeper, and myself withdrew, and left her alone with the watchman. Their interview was a long one, and when he left her and came to us again, he was much excited. He said it had been the most painful scene he had ever participated in, and asked us to sit down while he related the unfortunate girl's story.

Abcu a year ago," said he, "I was telegraphed from the northern part of the State, to be on the look-out for a runaway couple, with the information that the man was believed to be of bad character, and had evil designs upon his young but willing companion. About the time of the arrival of the train, I took my station in the depot, and almost the first female I saw step from the cars, was this girl, accompanied by that notorious thief, Long John. From the description in the dispatch, I knew them to be the runaway couple; and as he handed her into a hack, I stepped up and insisted on taking a seat there also. Long John knew me, and at first seemed inclined to leave; but afterward, without demanding any explanation from me—for he knew he could not get one—jumped in and ordered the driver to proceed to one of our fashionable hotels. Sure of my game, I made no advances until we arrived at the hotel, when I told the girl as she stepped from the carriage that she was my prisoner, and must remain such, until the arrival of her father. I shall never forget the sweet, innocent expression of her face, as she replied, "But we will be married before father comes."

"She looked for her intended husband but he had gone. Long John, though a bold and desperate thief, dreads the vag-room, and he knew I would put him there if he gave me any trouble. I took the girl into a room at the hotel, and told her who I was, and gave her the true character of her lover. She disbelieved me at first, but, poor soul! I thought her heart would break, when waiting vainly, hour after hour, for his return, she began to realize her true condition. I called the housekeeper to console her, and left to telegraph my success to her parents.

"I was not absent over half an hour, but on my return I found I had been out-generaled. Long John, determined not to be beat, must have loitered about the place, for the housekeeper told me I had not been gone five minutes before he entered the room. The girl flew to his arms, and he immediately carried her to the door of the hotel, placed her in a hack and drove off. He did it all within a minute's time, so quick indeed, that he was off before the lady I had placed there, sufficiently recovered from her surprise to give an alarm.

"I searched the city thoroughly that night, in pursuit of the fugitives, but could see or hear nothing of them. I saw the father the next day. He was a fine-looking old gentleman, and said he would not have objected to his daughter's marriage with her lover, had he not had cause to doubt his honesty. When I told him the truth, it rent his heart most sadly. He said he had money in plenty, and a fortune should be mine if I would save his daughter from the clutches of the villain who had seduced her from her home. Day after day, we continued in search, till the old man was reluctantly forced to give it up, and, broken-hearted, returned to his desolate roof.

"A month ago, I received a note through the post-office, stating that a lady friend desired to see me, at the ——— House in Covington, and that I must not fail to call at the hour named. I went, and found the lady to be this same girl Julia. But oh! how altered! Care had taken the place of innocence upon her countenance, and grief apparently filled her heart. With tears in her eyes she received me, and her first expression was that made to-night—"Had I taken your advice, I might have been saved, but now it is too late—I am too low to be redeemed!"

"She told me she had found my description of her lover too true. He had postponed their marriage from day to day, and by degrees informed her of his villainy. With all his faults she could but love him, and with the hope of persuading him to desert his evil ways, and become a man respected among men, she had clung to him and proved a faithful mistress. Gradually he appeared to lose his affection for her, until that time, when she was often the subject of his abuse. She could bear it no longer, and had sent for me to ask my advice as to what she had better do. I immediately advised her to return to her parents, but to that she would not listen. She said her character was gone, her name was a reproach among her father's neighbors, and too many would take pleasure in increasing the sorrows of her heart, and the affliction of her parents. Indeed, to every proposal I made for reform, her reply was, "I am too low to be redeemed!"

"I left her after I had gained her consent to have an interview with her father. But that night Long John came near being caught while robbing a house in Covington, and had to make tracks. She foolishly followed him, and I have not seen nor heard of her since, until to-night."

"But what induced her to attempt suicide?" I asked.

"She has just told me," he replied, "that her villainous lover was killed in a street affray at L——, and without a protector of any kind she had returned to this city with the firm intention of drowning her sorrow in a life of the deepest degradation. She has been here only one week, and life becoming a torment to her, she determined to-day to seek peace in the grave! "Poor girl!" he continued, with a sigh, "life must be a burden to her—she is really to be pitied."

I indeed felt so, and suggested to him to see if he could not persuade her to return to her father, and if he could, to make such arrangements as would secure her a speedy departure. After much persuasion she consented to accompany him on the early train, next morning, to her long deserted home. She returned that night to the vile house where she had been boarding, for the purpose of packing up her apparel, and preparing for her journey. As soon as her kind friend, the watchman had left her there, her depraved companions commenced taunting her about her foolish attempt to drown herself, and made sport of the tears of anguish which gushed from her eyes. She hurried to her room, and the next morning, when the watchman called for her, he found her *dead!*

A knife guided by her own hand, had ended her earthly existence.

A note directed to the watchman we have mentioned, was found in her room. It read as follows:

"Forgive me, kind sir. I should like to see my parents, but oh! I am too degraded. My only peace is in the grave, for I now feel bitterly and keenly, that *I am too low to be redeemed.* Farewell, forever,

JULIA B——."

Thus terminated the life of one poor girl, who, contrary to the wishes of fond and affectionate parents, suffered herself to be allured by the pleasing appearance and the gay deceptions of a stranger. How many, alas! like her, have been deceived in the same manner, and led from one degree of degradation to another, till they, too, found they were "too low to be redeemed!"

Such is the story of one inmate of the watch-house. Others as sad might be told, if we could but read the hearts and trace the paths of the hundreds who have been confined within the iron cells of the city prison.

HANS VON SPUTTLES:

THE LAST OF THE WOODSAWERS.

SOME one has denominated history, a record of the past in which great men are set up as mile-stones, to denote the progress of a nation or people. But few of the humbler classes, no matter how deep their sufferings or how great their wrongs, are ever honored with the care, laborious thought, or deep research of the historian. It is too true that historians — those who collate the facts of the past, and publish them for the enlightenment of the present and future generations — generally judge of an event by the character or standing of those engaged in it; often giving great importance to trivial acts of a monarch, while they overlook entirely the more important performances of those moving in an humble sphere. But the present day has developed a new order of historians — those who record, in the ever-living pages of the newspaper press, facts as they occur, and give to the world a true and faithful history of the men and things of the day. Such historians are not influenced by the *position* of an important character, and whether that character be monarch or subject, senator or wood-sawer, he receives all the attention his acts deserve. Professing to belong to the latter class of historians, the writer of this believes no apology necessary, for calling the attention of the reader to the most important scenes in the life of an individual who bears the name which heads this sketch, and who followed so humble an occupation as that of wood-sawer.

Hans Von Sputtles was a native Dutchman, a lineal descendant of a noble family who lost their titles and wealth, because they could not muster flesh and blood enough to combat a certain monarch, who chose to take unto himself, the lands on which they dwelt, and all the privileges thereof. — His youthful ears were often regaled with stories of the wealth and greatness of his ancestors; for, in truth, these were about the only acceptable things his father, who was very poor, could bestow upon him. Hans loved to hear those stories of departed greatness in his family, though they were ill substitutes for a full dish of krout for dinner, or a much-loved pretzell for supper. Hans lived and grew up amid those stories, and though when a man, his countenance betrayed the slim fare of his father's table, Hans had the glorious satisfaction of knowing that noble blood flowed through his veins.

Hans Von Sputtles was well nigh thirty years of age, when he found money enough in his purse to enable him to carry out the long-cherished object of his heart, viz: to emigrate to the land of money and liberty, ease and freedom — the land of Columbia — the land of the brave and the free. Hans emigrated, and, like all emigrants, found that a sail across the big water was "a hard road to trabbel." After various narrow escapes, and without any food in his stomach or money in his pocket, or the slightest knowledge of a trade in his head, he was landed a stranger in a western city.

There he found an old friend from Fatherland, who not only recommended him to a then profitable employment, but gave him instructions in the business, and provided him with the necessary tools for operation, viz: a saw and buck.

No language can describe the emotions of Hans, when he first hung his saw upon his buck, and placed his buck upon his back, and started out in search of employment. He had learned a sufficiency of English to make a bargain, or at least to state his terms, and he confidently expected to be a rich man, before many more seasons of cabbage were numbered with the past. He had not proceeded far, before his eyes were rejoiced by the sight of a load of wood piled up near a curb stone. His heart beat as he approached it, he walked around it several times in hope of attracting the attention of its owners, and at last found himself obliged to make application for the job. Setting down his buck, with his saw in his hand, he knocked at the door of the house opposite the wood pile. A female responded to the knock, and she no sooner appeared, than Hans aiding each word by unmistakable gesticulations, said:

"Woot—saw—how—mooch—two, tree pieces, hey?"

"Do you want to saw the wood?" asked the female.

"Yaw," was Hans' response, "yaw! — nix sprakin der English—saw woot," drawing his saw up and down, in explanation.

"How much will you charge?" inquired the female, saying it, too, at the top of her voice, laboring, as she did, under the prevalent mistake, that speaking louder, makes language easier of comprehension to those who, with difficulty, understand it.

"How mooch? one, tree pieces — hey?" asked Hans, holding up first two and then three fingers.

"Two pieces," was the ready answer.

"How mooch?"

"Yes, how much will you charge?"

"Woot—how much?" asked Hans, aiming to get at the quantity of wood.

"Yes, the wood—how much will you charge?" was the answer, which rather stumped the wood-sawyer. His bill of prices had been fixed at eighty cents for a cord, fifty cents for a half cord, and thirty cents for a quarter of a cord; but his instructor had neglected to give him the size of a pile of each of those quantities, and as Hans could not make the woman understand, it puzzled him to fix his price. After surveying the pile of wood for some moments, and muttering to himself in his mother tongue, he concluded to be on the safe side, so he replied:

"Tri-fatal tollar."

"Gracious!" replied the female, who knew there was but half a cord—"too much—can't pay it — go away," and shaking her head, she was about closing the door, when Hans asked,

"How mooch?"

"Fifty cents," she replied.

Hans shook his head, and said "too mooch little," which seemed to exasperate the lady, and she shut the door in his face.

Hans was "stuck." After a long pause, he looked down to the wood pile, turned over a few sticks, looked up at the windows of the house, and not seeing anybody, walked away, came back, examined the wood pile again, looked at the windows again, and finding he could not attract attention, concluded at last to saw the wood, and run the risk of getting ample remuneration for his labor. How he sweated over each stick, and how faithfully and patiently he labored at the job until it was completed, and with what care he picked up the splinters and sent them to keep company with the wood, and how nicely he scraped the sawdust from the pavement with his nail-covered soles! He had no sooner completed the work than the woman appeared at the door, and gave him half a dollar, and he went away pleased and happy. Such was Hans' advent into a profession (all occupations which can not be dignified with the title of trade, are called "professions") to which he afterward became devoted.

Hans flourished in his business. A few days' experience improved his English and his aptness with the saw. He worked hard, made money, saved it, and in a short time became quite independent of the world. Though never formally admitted into any of the gangs who claimed the exclusive privileges of the wood market, or perambulated the streets in pairs in search of a chance job, the "profession" all knew Hans; and many even of the oldest, envied the neat proportions of his buck, and the easy and expeditious, if not graceful manner in which he ran his saw through the largest, hardest, and most unruly sticks of wood. More than a dozen endeavored to enter into partnership with him, but Hans was determined to "go it alone."

All occupations have their seasons of success and adversity, and the humble business of wood-cutting is not an exception. At least, so Hans Von Sputtles found it. He had labored at his business probably a year, had filled a stocking with bright silver coin, and was a happy man, when "the trade" experienced a shock which ruined it entirely, and made Hans Von Sputtles the very last of the wood-sawers. The cause of the shock Hans could not divine; but, that his business was going down! down! down! he could but observe. Though wood was as plenty and sold as rapidly as ever, jobs became wonderfully scarce. Wood-sawers, terrified at the appearance of the trade, and the evident approach of famine, threw down the saw and the buck, and in flocks sought refuge in other occupations. In a few days the wood-markets were cleared of them, as if a fatal epidemic had swept their ranks. Now and then, a solitary sawer might be seen slowly pacing the streets, with buck on neck and saw in hand, in quest of employment; but all bore a melancholy countenance, for work was not to be had. Though people purchased wood, none wished it sawed; and from house to house, and door to door, the poor sawers were turned away. Even Hans Von Sputtles' reputation did not save him from the general calamity, and even his offers to work for almost nothing were rejected by the purchasers of cord-wood.

Hans was "stuck," the second time—badly stuck; but, like a true Dutchman, resolved never to give up. He could not conceive the cause of this sudden change in the minds of the people, and his pride forbade him to make any inquiries. So, day after day, our hero—for certainly a hero he had become—threaded the busy streets of the city in search of employment, returning home each evening with no more money in his pocket than he had when he started out at early morn. It pained his heart to draw, week after week, from the fund in the old stocking, to pay expenses; but this he was determined to do, rather than be driven from the occupation which was the choice of his heart. He had faith in the hope that a better day would come for the wood-sawing people.

One bright morning in May, Hans Von Sputtles found himself the only wood-sawer in the main wood-market. No saw but his glittered in the refulgent beams of the sun, and no buck but his graced the shoulders of any mortal in that vicinity. In vain did he look for a companion, one fellow of his class, to relieve the lonelinesss of his heart, and cheer his drooping spirits. Hour after hour he stood, like a statue, upon the curb stone, while hundreds came and purchased wood, but none gave him the welcome call. Once, twice, nay thrice, he ventured to ask for a job, but the wood-purchasers either laughed or scoffed him away. Hans could stand it no longer, and leaning against a lamp-post, he soliloquized as follows:

"Hannes, vot pes der matter mit you? You pes willing to work hardter as nottin; you trinks no schnapps, only von leetle tram, dwo dimes vonce a tay; you pegs no greese for der saw, put gets him from Gertrude, vot does der cooking at der poarding house; you pes a nobleman, Hannes, and you comes all der vay from Fáderland to git rich by sawing der shentleman's vood—and yet Hannes, you gits nottin to do. Pes your peard too long enough, or dosh him kraut make him look too much ugly, Hannes? Ah! Hannes, tere pes some-tings mitin your face, or mitin your pelly, or mitin your heart vich make you mooch badder dan you dinks, you Hannes. You make der beeples mad, Hannes, und you skeer der wood-sawers avay, Hannes, und you play der Dible mit us all, Hannes. Ah! Hannes, I dinks all apout it now—you got too mooch money in your stockin', Hannes! You get rich too fast, Hannes! You too means, Hannes!—der beeples no like you Hannes, und saw mit der own saws!

This last reflection threw Hannes into a deep study. What his thoughts were, must be conjectured, but recovering from his reverie, he seemed to bring his mind to a desperate determination. He walked rather hurriedly away, turning neither to the right nor the left, but pursuing a straight cut down street.

As he reached the intersection of two of the main business streets, his attention was attracted by a singular sort of noise. Looking westward, he observed a crowd of people surrounding the base of a huge wood-pile, and from that pile the hissing, roaring, singing sound seemed to emanate. He drew near with mingled feelings of wonder and fear, and as he approached, the crowd welcomed him with shouts and opened a way for him to enter. Hans Von Sputtles was struck with astonishment at what he beheld. Near the edge of the wood-pile was a machine, small in its proportions and rough in its construction. A horse which evidently belonged to the *genus* "crowbait" peered his head loftily from the top of the machine, while he flirted the remnants of a tail from his posterior parts, as if proud of the movements he gave the wonderful apparatus. Not far from the motive power stood a sort of a table, in the center of which was a circular saw, whirled almost with the speed of electricity, by means of a belt attached to the horse power. By that table stood or moved an "everlasting Yankee," who applied the wood to the saw, and shouted to his horse as the sticks were severed with the rapidity of lightning, and sent flying into the air.

For the third time in his wood-sawing career, Hans Von Sputtles was "stuck." As he seated himself upon his buck beside the machine, with his rusty and greasy Dutch cap upon his head, his mouth opened to its fullest extent, and his eye fixed in wonderment upon the *Horse Wood-sawing Machine*, he presented a picture worthy of the most talented artist. He there beheld the demon which had ruined his occupation, and had slain, as it were, the whole race of wood-sawers, leaving but himself to tell the story of their fate. The horse — the crowbait horse, seemed to have an instinctive knowledge of the presence of Hans Von Sputtles, and after making a desperate tug in the traces, came to a dead halt.

"Hell-yo," shouted the Yankee attendant to the animal; "what are yew abeout, now, old Stub Tail. Deon't smell another sawer, neow dew ye?"

"Mine krout!" exclaimed Hans, aloud, being the first words he had spoken, and which attracted the attention of the Yankee.

"Well, I'll swow, there *is* a sawer," continued the Down-easter. "Where *did* yeou come from old s-k-e-u-l-l cap? Just from Jarmany, eh? Kinder takin by surprise, at this invention? It's an amazin' piece — can cut more wood than ten t-h-e-o-u-s-a-n-d such critters as yeou. Just see the timber fly neow — get up! yeou Stub Tail!"

But Stub Tail refused to "get up." He rested his head

over the side of the machine, and casting mournful glances at the sawer, positively refused to lift a foot.

"Mine krout!" exclaimed Hans, the second time.

"Deon't set there a cussin' and swearin' like a sinner, who deon't intend to work eout his salvation," said the Yankee. "Stub Tail kin smell the grease on yeour etarnal cap, and dang the stroke will he make till yeou are gone. I did think I'd driv' the hull craft of yeou to t'other side of the corporation, but as the razor-strap man would say, "there's one more left of the same sort."

"Mine krout!" exclaimed Hans, for the third time.

"N-eow, stranger, I know yeou feel kinder hurt, but I can't lay idle to please yeou—that's a fixed fact, as Deacon Brown used to say when axed if the Congressmen would spend most of their time in making l-e-o-n-g speeches. N-eow Old Skull Cap, you've got to tramp. Stub won't budge while yeou are in smelling distance. Pick up your insignificant teools *and* toddle, yeou last of the Woodsaw*ers*."

Hans understood the command too well, and being too harmless even to contend for his rights, he left without a murmur, merely exclaiming, "mine krout!" as he passed out of the crowd. But he did not go far without stopping. At the nearest corner he again seated himself upon his buck, and looked long and steadfastly upon the scene of the Yankee's labors. He saw the immense wood-pile diminish before the horse-sawing machine as a mountain of snow before a Midsummer's sun. It was not until the last stick of the pile had been cut in twain, by a single touch of the saw, that Hans wended his way homewards.

The next morning Hans Von Sputtles, the last of the wood-sawers, was found dead in his bed. In his dying moments he had placed his buck for a pillow under his head, and hugged his much-loved saw to his bosom. He died a martyr to an humble and a laborious occupation, and a victim to the labor-saving genius of the everlasting Yankee Nation.

CHRISTMAS AMONG CHRISTIANS.

Bright glowed the coal in the grate of Mr. Goodly's parlor on Christmas evening. The Christian holiday was about closing, and as had been his custom for years, Mr. Goodly had gathered his family around the cheerful fire to review the events of the day. Mr. Goodly was a pious man, and unlike too many of his neighbors, properly appreciated this sacred anniversary. He believed it to be of all others, a day when the Christian should rejoice in the goodness of his Maker, and manifest his thankfulness by doing all in his power to make those around him happy. Consequently, Christmas was always joyous at his home, and he and his kind wife and their affectionate children anticipated it with pleasure.

The morning of that day had scarce dawned, ere Mr. Goodly and his wife were awakened by the merry prattle of their smaller children. They raised their heads and listened. The little ones, as soon as sleep had forsaken their eyes, had slipped down stairs to see if Santa Claus had visited them during the night. Now a whistle was sounded, then a drum beat, a doll covered with ecstatic kisses, books clutched with glee, as each was taken from the little stockings hanging by the fire side. The stockings empty, brisk but soft footsteps were heard upon the stairway, and the little ones came rushing into their parents' chamber. Need I attempt to tell how the hearts of those parents rejoiced as the little innocents spread, with stammering language, the gifts of Santa Claus, before them? No, for no pen, however gifted, could describe that joy.

As soon as this welcome clamor was over, the family assembled around the family altar, for the morning devotion. The father opened the Holy Book and read of the birth of the Redeemer. Then he turned the pages over till he came to another chapter appropriate to the occasion. He read of the sufferings, the crucifixion, the burial and resurrection, of Christ, our Lord. Santa Claus and his gifts were forgotten even by the little ones, and all listened with reverence to the Divine words as they were repeated by the father's lips. Laying the Holy Book aside, the father arose from his chair and impressively addressed his little family circle. Then they united in singing and prayer. Oh! what a delightful sight it is to see a Christian family gathered around the domestic altar, with their hearts united in devotion to the Most High. No nicely decorated altars, no gilded robes, no empty forms of prayer, no ecclesiastical dictation, no terrible threats are necessary there; but united in love, the hearts of all bow meekly before the Throne of Grace, and send pious thoughts to Heaven. Angels may well hover over such a scene, and murmur "peace on earth, good will to all men."

At the breakfast table all the children found a sum of money beneath their plates, to be laid out as they should see proper, during the day. With such a beginning, and with a visit to church in the forenoon, and a reunion at a good old-fashioned Christmas dinner, the day passed pleasantly with the Goodly family; and at night, when they again assembled around the domestic hearth, the coals within the grate were scarcely brighter than their smiling countenances.

"My dear children," said Mr. Goodly, "another Christmas has come and gone, and that we may know whether all have performed their duty to God and themselves, it is well we should tell what we have been doing through the day. Each can profit by the other's experience. Listen first to me."

Mr. Goodly then went on to state that after he had left his family in the morning, he visited his place of business, when the men in his employ congratulated him with a "merry Christmas." He gave them a holiday, and presented each with a Christmas gift, which he said he knew gladdened their hearts. He returned home, stopping on his way to see if several poor families, whom he knew, were having a merry Christmas. His purse was open to all, for, said he, "he who giveth to the poor lendeth to the Lord." He visited church with his family, and was much profited by the sermon. The Christmas reunion at the dinner table was especially gratifying to him, and though somewhat dyspeptic he could not avoid eating a hearty meal. Indeed he had been happy, very happy, all day long. He concluded by saying that his purse was empty, but his heart was full.

Mrs. Goodly, a homely-looking woman, whose large, blue eyes teemed with kindness and love, then told how her time had been occupied. She was at home nearly all the day, dispensing Christmas gifts to children who came and "caught" her, and dispatching delicacies to those who were sick, and as she knew, unable to procure such things. " With the exception of a visit to church, " said she, " here have I been all day long. And here I would always stay, for if the mother can not find happiness at home, where can she look for it? Here I am queen over a kingdom, and my subjects (pointing to her children) are so obedient that peace never forsakes my dominions. Heaven has truly smiled upon us, and this day my cup of happiness is full. May we never be wanting in gratitude, to our kind Heavenly Father. Mary, have you made any one happy to-day? "

This query was addressed to the oldest child, a young lady of eighteen years of age, whose plainness of dress added a charm to her beautiful person.

" I was not at Church, mother, " she promptly replied, " but I have a good reason for it. After leaving home in the morning, I purchased a few presents for the children of my Sabbath school class. Several I presented, and I assure you they made their little hearts glad. I finally came to the residence of Jane Handy, that poor little girl whom I brought home with me last Sabbath, that I might clothe her comfortably. I expected to find distress there, but oh! mother, what I saw was dreadful. The child's mother was prostrate upon a bed, suffering in the last stages of consumption — the father lay insensibly drunk upon the floor, and three little children, all as sweet as Jane, lay clustered around their mother, to shield themselves from the cold. Not a morsel of food, not a drop of medicine, not an ounce of fuel was in the room. The pillow was wet with the tears of that mother, who, helpless in her bed, saw starvation staring her and the children in the face. Mother, I saw all at one glance, and the scene so touched my heart, that I wept. Little Jane crawled out of bed, and threw her arms about my neck, kissed me, and asked me if I had any thing to eat, for she and her ma, and her brother and sister were starving. Oh! her pale, innocent face looked so sweet that it made me think of the cherubim of Heaven.

"I approached the bedside of Mrs. Handy, and asked her what I could do for her. 'Nothing for *me*, my dear,' was her reply, 'for I shall soon be in Heaven, but relieve, if you can, the sufferings of my poor little children, not one of whom has tasted food for three days.' I told her to be of good cheer. I could and would relieve not only the distresses of her children, but her own, I kissed her thin, cold lips, which brought a smile to her face, and seemed to enliven her spirits. She called me an angel, and said she knew God had sent me to her. She told me that her husband had long been a victim of intemperance, that he was a very wicked man, and abused her most dreadfully. She bore with him patiently, but he had at last broken her heart, and she was now dying from suffering and anguish. She dreaded leaving her children in the sole care of that debased man, and begged me to promise her, if she died, that I would see they were properly cared for.

"I promised her that her children should never suffer if I could prevent it, and giving her all the Christian consolation I could, I excused myself for a few minutes, while I proceeded to procure something for them to eat. My first thought was to call on Father, but as that would take too long, I determined to do the work myself. I purchased groceries and fuel, and had them sent immediately to the house, where I also soon returned, taking with me Dr. Davis. If ever I felt like working, it was then, and I soon had a glowing fire and a warm meal in the lately destitute house. Our good physician aided me much, and his medicines so revived Mrs. Handy that she sat at the table with her children. I made them as comfortable as possible, engaged a nurse for Mrs. Handy, and then bade them farewell until to-morrow. Their sweet smiles and fervent kisses as I left them, more than repaid me for all my trouble—they filled my eyes with joyous tears, and made my heart dance with inexpressible delight."

"And thus," said Mr. Goodly, "Heaven blesses all who administer to the wants of their unfortunate fellow creatures. William, my son, what have you been doing to-day?"

William was the oldest boy, a lad some fourteen years of age, and a student in one of the public high schools. He had listened attentively to his sister's story, and more than once during its recital had brushed a tear from his full black eyes.

"I have not accomplished as much as my dear sister Mary," he replied. "As I was coming home last evening, I saw little Jimmy Perkins, the drunken widow's son, crying on the corner and he said he cried because he was hungry. I told him I would give him some money this morning; and when he called here to-day, I gave him the bright half dollar I put away three months ago, and told him to buy bread with it, and take it home. He clapped his hands when he received it, and ran home as fast as he could. In the afternoon I saw him again, and again he was crying. He told me he was still hungry, for his mother had made him buy whisky with the money I had given him. This information aggravated me so that I told him he ought not to have obeyed his mother.

Then I thought that was wrong, so I took it back, and told him he ought to pray for his mother. He said he did'nt know how to pray, though he had often tried to learn at Sabbath school, when his mother used to let him attend. You do not know how bad it made me feel to hear him talk so. I conversed with him a good while, and then took him to a bakery and bought for him five large loaves of bread, and a lot of cakes. From the way he commenced eating them, I thought he was nearly starved. It was not my fault, father, that the half dollar was spent for rum."

"Not at all, my son," replied Mr. Goodly, "but what did you do with the balance of your money?"

"I have it yet, father. I was so fearful that more might go for rum, that I kept it tight in my pocket. I thought of giving it to one of my school-mates, who told me yesterday he was afraid he would have to leave school, as his parents could not afford to furnish him with books; I have money enough to buy him all the books he will need the next year."

"That is a happy idea, my son, and I am glad you have such a love for your school-mates. So frequent are the changes from rich to poor, and from poor to rich, and so great are the opportunities for even the poorest man to ascend to fame and fortune, in our beloved country, that your young friend may, if he lives, be able sometime to return the kindness you contemplate. "Ellla," he continued, addressing the next youngest, a girl about ten years old, "Ella, what have you been doing to-day?"

"I gave all my money," she replied, "to Mrs. Thompson, our wash-woman, to buy a tombstone to place on the grave of that pretty babe of hers, we all loved so much. I heard her say she was not able to purchase one, and it grieved her very much. She was so glad when I gave her the money, that she wept. I had enough to buy the tomb-stone, and if I live till next Spring, I expect to cover it often with pretty flowers, after it is placed on the grave."

"Sweet girl," said Mr. Goodly, "the memory of that babe will never leave you. But what did my Johnny (a bright little fellow, six years of age) do with his money?"

"I spent it, Pa," said he.

"What for, child?"

"For thugar takes."

"And what did Johnny do with the sugar cakes?"

"I dib 'em to the wood-thawer, and tell him to take 'em to hith 'ittle boy."

"What made you do that?"

"Tause ith ittle boy thay ithterday, he neber hath any ood things; and I know if I dib him ood things he love me." And the little fellow's face beamed with smiles as he gave the ready answer.

The two younger children were sound asleep, one upon its mother's lap and the other in its father's arms.

"Thank Heaven," said Mr. Goodly, as Johnny finished his reply, "we have all been able to accomplish some good to-day. May every Christmas find us thus disposed to commemorate the birth of our blessed Redeemer."

In this manner the Goodlys spend each Christmas day; and so should every Christian family who would prove their faith by their works. If their example was more generally followed, Christmas would not be the day of debauchery it now is, but one of peace and love.

AN INCIDENT IN THE LADIES' CABIN.

OR, HOW A GOSSIP'S TONGUE WAS SILENCED.

A GOSSIP upon a steamboat! Did you ever see one there? She is as much out of place as a fish is when out of water; for if any place in the world should be free from a tattling tongue, it is the cabin of a steamer. The people congregated there are strangers to each other, some from near and some from distant lands; some traveling for pleasure; others on business, and others perhaps on melancholy errands; but all look to the steamboat cabin for social recreation and pleasure, while being borne forward upon the bosom of the waters. The etiquette of the drawing room is laid aside, for the more genial sociability of home, and though this sociability may afford food for gossip, there is no place on earth where a tattler would appear to greater disadvantage than in the cabin of a well regulated steamboat.

Last Spring I was one of about a hundred cabin passengers on the superb packet, Golden Era. We were descending the Upper Mississippi, at a time when low water and sandbars made traveling tedious—and the trip was monotonous, until an incident occurred in which all took an interest.

Among the females was a married woman of some thirty-five years of age, whose jaded appearance, rambling eyes, and toothless mouth, indicated the gossip. On the evening of the first day out, she entered into conversation with two sisters, who were from Minnesota, and, with their brother, on their way to Michigan. The sisters were young, intelligent, modest and pretty.

"Aint you awful lonesome?" asked Mrs. Chatterbox, as I shall call her.

"Not very," replied the older of the sisters.

"Well, I am," continued the gossip. "I've traveled considerable in steamboats, and I have never seen such a gawky, close-mouthed set of gentlemen in my life, as these on this boat. Not one of them has come in here to say a word to the ladies, all this blessed day."

"O, you are mistaken, madam," replied the younger sister. "My brother has several times been in here, and"—

"Talked with *you*," interrupted Mrs. C. "But that's the way with the men: they are always selfish, and when they are traveling, they don't think of the ladies. My husband's just the same way. When he is traveling, he never thinks of talking to anybody but me."

"Indeed," said both the young ladies, smilingly.

"Yes, it's true, but I never approved of it; I think that when people are traveling they ought to make free. I like to see it."

At this point the conversation was interrupted by the brother of the two young ladies entering the cabin, accompanied by a fine-looking young gentleman, to whom he introduced his sisters. Mrs. Chatterbox fell back, remaining, however, within hearing distance. After some minutes of conversation, the stranger proposed that the four should proceed to the upper deck, where it was more pleasant, and where they could, in the bright moonlight, look upon the majestic scenery which lines the upper Mississippi river.

The proposition was readily acceded to, and the party proceeded on deck.

From the workings of Mrs. Chatterbox's countenance, it was plainly to be perceived she was disappointed. She had expected an invitation to accompany the little party on deck, and had "hoped on" until they had disappeared from the cabin. She threw herself into a rocking-chair, and remained there some time in deep thought.

An hour rolled away, and the promenaders had not returned to the cabin. Mrs. Chatterbox could restrain her tongue no longer. Taking her seat beside a quiet middle-aged lady, she said—

"Did you ever see such impudence?"

"What?" asked the lady.

"Did you see those two men who walked right into our cabin a while ago?"

"No, I did not observe them."

"Well, they walked right into *our* cabin, and commenced talking right away with those two upstart girls who occupy No. 26. The girls didn't seem a bit bashful about it, but laughed and prated away, and at last went on deck after dark with the two men."

"But is not one of the gentlemen their brother?"

"Laws only knows. But suppose he is, ain't this a pretty time for young girls to be trolloping about on deck?"

"Not if they are under the protection of their brother."

"Protection, indeed! who knows if he is their brother? I've heard before of relationship being trumped up while people are traveling. I tell you what it is, I don't believe a *gentleman* will come into the ladies' cabin after supper. It aint polite, and its unreasonable. I don't know how you feel about it, but I think it's an insult to us all, and I have half a notion to complain to the Captain about it."

At that moment the party returned to the cabin. Mrs. Chatterbox "looked daggers" at them, but to her great dismay and horror, the two gentlemen seated themselves, and remained in conversation with the ladies until the chambermaid gave unmistakable hints that it was time to retire. This increased Mrs. Chatterbox's rage, and she declared that the first thing she would do in the morning would be to complain to the Captain; she could not be insulted in that way without resenting it.

The next day, Mrs. Chatterbox and the young ladies were the great objects of interest in the ladies' cabin. The sisters received several visits during the day, each one arousing more and more the indignation of the gossip, and accelerating the movements of her tongue. As a matter of course, the sisters were aware of her indignation, her suspicions and her threats; all of which they, like women possessing noble hearts, entirely disregarded.

When supper was announced, Mrs. Chatterbox was the first, as usual, to rush to the table. She was seated in what may be termed an eligible position for observation, and had cast a glance down the table, while sipping her tea, when she suddenly threw her head back, and fixing her eyes upon two persons opposite, with an expression of horror, said to a lady sitting beside her, and loud enough to be heard by a number—

"Just look at that! One of those girls has allowed that strange fellow to see her to the table. Such conduct," looking and speaking to the Captain, "is outrageous, and for one, I wont countenance it."

Saying which, she arose from the table, and in a most excited manner proceeded to her state-room. Her conduct was so well understood, that it caused only a smile, and she failed to make the impression she expected to.

"She must be in want of a beau," remarked a gentleman at the table.

"And she shall have one," responded the individual who had so politely gallanted one of the sisters to tea.

It was after 9 o'clock that evening when Mrs. Chatterbox again made her appearance in the cabin. It happened that the young gentleman above alluded to was there at the time, and he immediately offered her his chair, which she indignantly refused. Allowing her to seat herself, he addressed a remark to her, which she abruptly answered, but not noticing her stiffness, he continued pressing inquiries, and in less than five minutes was engaged in a lively conversation with her. At once she seemed to have forgotten the events of the day, and was apparently charmed with the polite attentions and interesting speech of the one beside her.

After conversing about an hour, the gentleman spoke of the delightful evening, of the charming moonlight views from the deck, and offered to escort her to the promenade above, if she was so disposed. She immediately accepted his invitation, and on deck they went, to the great delight of all the other lady passengers. Eleven o'clock came, and they did not return. At twelve o'clock they were still promenading, and so extremely agreeable did Mrs. C.— find the company of her gallant, that it was near one o'clock, when they again made their appearance below.

Mrs. Chatterbox was not a little surprised to find all the lady passengers up and in the cabin.

"Well," said one, as she entered, "it is an outrage for a gentleman to come into the ladies' cabin."

"I think so," remarked another, "and then for ladies to encourage it, too."

"And not only encourage that," followed a third, "but to promenade on deck with a gentleman at such a late hour."

"I feel indignant at such proceedings," remarked a fourth, "*and I intend to complain to the Captain!*"

"I wish," said Mrs. Chatterbox, her eyes flashing with anger, "*that people would learn to mind their own business.*"

She stepped into her state-room, slamming the door after her. She appeared in the cabin but once or twice afterward during the trip, and then it did not take more than ordinary observation to perceive that her tongue was completely silenced. She had been caught in her own trap.

SNOB JOHN.

A LOCAL EDITOR, or Reporter of a city daily newspaper is thrown into all shades of society, all classes of the community. Fashion and poverty, intelligence and degradation, honesty and corruption, virtue and villainy, are the subjects of continual investigation with him — made so by the duties of his vocation. From the description of a brilliant festival, "which he has had the honor to attend," he descends into the meanest hovel, to gather the particulars of a "horrid occurrence," or a "revolting spectacle." There are no spots into which Reporters are more frequently thrown, in pursuit of "items," than drinking-saloons, those tempting places of refreshment, where men congregate to while away an idle hour in social conversation, and sip stimulating fluids until excited to an unnatural flow of spirits. In those most frequented, the Reporter is sure to hear some news, or to be put upon the track of an item. And how often is it the case, that in these gilded palaces of pleasure, he commences a story which ends in a far different place! How often amid

"The sound of revelry by night,"

does he witness the poor inebriate, whose only comfort is burning liquor, and whose "sudden death" he will be under the painful necessity of recording the next day? How often does he see men there, full of life, glee and humor, whose wives and children are starving over their restless needles? How often does he hear the cruel boast of the seducer, that his victim is degraded beyond redemption, and afterward to witness the ravings of that victim in a cell of the watch-house? I have traced many a sad story from the coffee-house to the grave, but none more sorrowful than the following:

The patrons of the W——— Restaurant, on Fifth street, all knew John Smith (I give him that name), the pert little shoemaker, who was always to be found there after dark, unless otherwise particularly engaged. He had the reputation of being one of the cleverest men in the world, and in truth he never hesitated to "treat the party," when he had the funds to do it,—was always full of fun and ready to tell or play a joke. He was commonly known as "Snob John," and was a great favorite with the frequenters of the W—— Restaurant. He was a hardworking man,—that is, he worked full ten hours every day, until he made enough ahead for a spree, and then his shop missed his presence, until many days after his funds had run out. I say many days, for he was such a clever fellow, so full of fun, that his sprees were prolonged by the purses of kindred spirits, who could never be without him in a frolic.

I always supposed "Snob John" to be a jolly old bachelor, who could sing with truth,

> "I care for nobody,
> Nobody cares for me,"

and was determined to sail down the stream of life as merrily as possible, without infringing upon the happiness of others. I was, therefore, not a little surprised when a friend of his informed me, that John was a husband and a father, but "as the old woman was sorter cross, he didn't often go home." From that time I could not entertain so good an opinion of him as before,—his mirth appeared devilish, and his wit stale, flat and unprofitable.

Last Christmas Eve, the W—— Restaurant was crowded with frolickers, celebrating the sacred anniversary with debauchery and blasphemy. In one of the upper rooms a party of ten or twelve persons were having a jolly time over the "luxuries of the season," and the best of the bar. Among them was "Snob John," in fact, he was the prince of the party, for his humor made them lively, his jokes kept them merry. They were all in the happiest mood, when a little, ragged boy, about nine years old, opened the door of the room, and with shivering limbs, unobserved, approached "Snob John." Timidly laying his hand upon his arm, he whispered:

"Father, Mother wants you."

The father, unlike the rest of the party, was not in the least surprised by the appearance and conduct of the child. But, without a change in his countenance, he rose up, seized the little fellow by the ear, led him to the door, gave him a kick and bade him go home.

"Is that your boy?" asked one of the party, of Snob, as he returned to the table.

"My boy," replied the shoemaker, with a forced smile, "he knows who his mother is, but the D—l couldn't father him."

"I thought he called you father?"

"So the scamp did, but you'll all understand, when I tell you that he lives in Gas Alley, and that his wench of a mother, when she wants money, sends him to me, and tells him to call me dad."

"O ho! then you've been down *there* lately?" inquired another, with a knowing nod of the head.

"Why, yes," replied Jack; "I couldn't help calling on *her*,—vidders, you know, are very tempting."

This called forth a shout of laughter, and Snob John, having convinced his companions that the child was not his son, went into a long disquisition on love, particularly the love of "vidders," as he termed them.

After the door had been closed in the face of the little boy, he burst into a flood of tears, and remained on the stairs weeping, until his conduct attracted the attention of two gentlemen who were passing through the hall below. In answer to their inquiries he stated that his mother, who was suffering, had sent him after his father, who had not been home for many days, and had just cruelly abused him. The gentlemen were affected at the child's simple story; and at once concluded to conduct him home in order to learn the truth of his statement. He seemed anxious they should go, but still was afraid that his mother would not like it. It was not until after the gentlemen looked into the room, and assured the boy, from what they saw, that his father would not go with him, that he consented. One of the gentlemen wrapped him in his cloak, to protect him from the freezing air, as they wended their way over the ice-covered pavements, while the unfortunate child told them that his mother was very poor and sick, that his little sister was dying, and his mother had sent him for his father to save her life. After a lengthy walk they arrived in the dismal neighborhood of the Gas Works, and turning into Gas Alley, came to a building dilapidated through age and misuse. The boy led the strangers into an upper room, telling them that there was where he lived; and as the little fellow entered the doorway, tears rolled down his cheeks, and he walked lightly, as if afraid to disturb the dying slumbers of his little sister.

The gentlemen were horror-stricken with the scene. In that cold room not an ember sent forth its grateful heat.—There was no furniture, save an old table, two or three stools and a bedstead, while a tallow candle, fastened into the wall, cast but a faint and dismal light around the room. Leaning over the bed, was a delicate woman, whose eyes were fixed upon an object before her. She neither observed nor heard the quiet entrance of her visitors, and they staid their steps as she gave vent to the following bitter exclamations:

"O, God! spare my darling Clara but a few hours longer —John will come and see *her* die. He does not love her mother any more—he has made his home so miserable, that he never visits it—but he always doted on Clara—he called her his darling girl. O, John! John! your daughter is dying! she has asked a thousand times for her papa, and you can not be so cruel as to stay away! Good God! my child is dead!" and giving a shrick, she fell upon the floor.

The two visitors flew to her assistance, and lifted her upon the bed. While one attempted to comfort the boy, the other went for a physician. Both succeeded, and soon Mrs. Smith was revived and placed beside a bright fire which had been kindled in the meantime. Medicines were administered, but they afforded no relief. Her heart was bleeding,—broken from negligence, suffering and woe. She looked around the room again and again, and asked for John, but he was not there. The physician and the two visitors endeavored to console her, but in vain. Before daylight she breathed her last, pronouncing with her dying breath the name of her negligent husband. She was placed by the hands of strangers on the bed beside the angelic form of her *starved* daughter. The gentlemen who had witnessed this sad scene, could not refrain from tears. They made every arrangement necessary under the circumstances, and while one took the now lone boy home to be properly cared for, the other started in search of the husband. "Snob John" was found at the W—— Restaurant, but so drunk from the night's debauch that it was impossible to communicate the news to him, and therefore, without consulting him, the strangers had the wife and daughter decently interred.

Careful inquiry led to a knowledge of the following facts. "Snob John" had been a kind and affectionate husband, until he became addicted to the use of ardent spirits. As he advanced through the different stages of drunkenness, he became less careful of his family, and at last deserted them altogether. The wife strove hard against poverty, and day and night plied her needle to save herself and children from a miserable death. She would occasionally appeal to her husband through their son, but received only such answers as he gave on Christmas Eve. She had toiled on, suffered on, till through sickness, unable to purchase even food, she sent her child for the last time, through the chilly blasts of a winter's night, to beg her husband for bread to save his family from starvation. John came not; the daughter sank exhausted into the arms of death, and the mother died of a broken heart.

Such was the fate of the family of the merry, the witty, the jovial "Snob John," whose credit was as good as a banker's at the W——— Restaurant, and whose company was always sought by the frequenters of that splendid saloon.

But the end was not yet. Not many days after, I was attracted to one of the cells of the watch-house by what I supposed to be the ravings of a maniac. Looking into the cell, I observed that the distracted creature was "Snob John," suffering under that most dreadful disease, the *mania-a-potu*. In his ravings he frequently called for protection from his wife and child, who, he imagined, were assaulting him, and repeatedly declared that he had not drawn a sober breath since their decease. From the watch-house he was conveyed to the hospital, where a wretched death ended his miserable existence. He died an unrespected pauper, all his friends having deserted him, as he had deserted his family, in time of need.

WEARING THE BREECHES:

OR, WOMAN'S RIGHTS ILLUSTRATED.

"Sit down, Mr. Thompson, I tell you, *sit* down!" These words were uttered by a plump, pert, and tidy-looking woman in Esquire Rowekamp's office, one afternoon. She had been arrested for assaulting one Miss Blossom, and the trial was about proceeding, when she gave the above command. The gentleman addressed was her husband, a man who presented a rather shriveled-up and fidgety appearance. He held a little babe in his arms, and was standing near his wife. It appears that all the parties being present, the Magistrate had inquired of Mr. Thompson, whether his lady was ready to proceed, and that gentleman having arisen, was about to respond, when his "better-half" addressed him as above.

"Why, my dear," was his answer, "the 'squire had just asked me—and—and—and—I—my dear, ———"

"Mr. Thompson, *sit down!*" interrupted the wife, this time stamping her foot quite emphatically upon the floor. Your wife needs no spokesman. If the 'squire wishes an answer let him address the individual interested."

"I beg your pardon, madam," said Esquire Rowekamp, with a smile, "but it has always been our custom, when a lady was accused, and was accompanied by her husband, to address ourse——"

"It may be your custom, sir," interrupted the accused, "but it is founded upon unjust and tyrannous social relations, which must sooner or later, be dissolved under the rising and burning sun of progress."

"That may be, madam, but here we must conform to the custom of the day. Your husband, no doubt, understands law better than you, and———."

"My husband understands no such thing, sir. We discard the tyrannous customs of the day, and Mrs. Thompson, I will let you know, sir, enjoys the same domestic rights and privileges that her husband does."

"Be that as it may," said the 'squire, "I can not stop to argue with you. If you do not wish your husband to answer for you ——"

"I tell you again, sir, that I can speak for myself. I am not to be intimidated by the fact that *custom* forbids me to speak."

"Well, then, madam, I will ask *you* if *you* are ready for trial."

"I am, sir, most certainly."

"Have you an attorney?"

"I—I—I—went down to see—lawyer Brown," stammered out Mr. Thompson, slowly rising from his seat, and keeping his eyes steadfastly fixed upon his wife, said eyes opening wider and wider, with each word uttered. "He wasn't—he wasn't in, and he—he—he——"

"Mr. Thompson, what do you mean?" cried the wife,

jumping from her seat, and giving her husband a most vigorous look. "Did you go for lawyer Brown after I had forbidden your doing so?"

"Why, my dear, I—I—I—thought that we—we—ought to have a lawyer," said the husband, apparently much frightened.

"Ought to have a lawyer," exclaimed the wife, "*ought* to have a lawyer, when you know I have been reading Blackstone these three years?"

"Blackstone, my dear?"

"Yes sir, Blackstone, the key, as it were, to all law—the foundation of all legal pleading—and the great fountain of all adjudication. I know more about law now, than one-half of the lawyers, and Mr. Thompson, you ought to have been aware that counsel was not necessary in *my* case. I am surprised at your stupidity, and I hope, sir, you will take your seat, and not display your ignorance again."

The spectators, who had, out of gallantry, suppressed their merriment until now, here burst into a loud peal of laughter. Even the 'squire, as dignified as he is in the Magisterial chair, could not resist an urgent desire to give a "haw haw!"

Fire flashed from the eyes of the lady, and turning to the laughing Magistrate, she said, "Was I brought here to be insulted by these heathenish men?"

"Not at all, madam," was his reply; "but as you see proper to make yourself ridiculous, you must—"

"Sir, you are no gentleman."

"Come, come, madam, we have had enough of this nonsense. I have gone as far as my duty would permit me, to accommodate you; but as you have seen fit to unsex yourself in so public a place as this, I find I must drop my gallantry and use my authority. I *command* you now to keep silence."

"While these remarks were being addressed to Mrs. Thompson, she several times interrupted the speaker, but he succeeded in keeping her pretty quiet until he got through. Then she said, I will speak if I choose."

"I command silence."

"You won't get it from me!"

"Then I will imprison you for contempt of court."

"Do it, if you dare."

"I dislike to do so, but I must have order in court."

"Then keep your mouth shut."

"Constable Housman, take that lady in"—

"No, no, don't 'squire, cried Mr. Thompson, who still held the baby in his arms. "She'll be still, 'squire—won't you, my dear?"

"Mr. Thompson, you are a fool," she replied. "No I won't be still—I can suffer as a martyr in the cause of right! Man has power now—he rules—but the time is coming when poor down-trodden woman will break the bonds of slavery, and claim and enjoy all her natural privileges."

"That's true," half groaned Mr. Thompson.

"I do not wish to deal severely with you madam," said the Magistrate, but justice can not be dispensed without order. I shall therefore proceed with the trial, hoping your good sense will prevent you from interrupting the proceedings again."

"Yes, that's it, my dear," said the husband nodding first to the lady and then to the Magistrate.

Mrs. Thompson, whose vexation appeared now wrought up

to decided anger, took no notice of either, beyond a scornful look at the Magistrate, and a searching one at her husband.—At this juncture the baby, which still lay in the arms of Thompson, commenced crying.

"Bye-bye-bye," sang its kind father, as he tossed it gently on his lap; but neither the tossing nor the "bye-bye" soothed the child, nor tended to stop its crying. Mr. Thompson then hugged it to his bosom, while he rocked to and fro on his chair; yet the child persisted in crying.

"My dear," whispered he to his wife, "the darling wants to come to you."

"I cant take her," she snappishly replied; "but it won't do to let her be crying here. Take her out of doors and walk with her."

Out went Mr. Thompson and the baby, to the great relief, no doubt, of the wife and mother, and to the no small amusement of the spectators. Mrs. Thompson then asked for pen, ink and paper, which being supplied, she announced her readiness for the trial to proceed.

Miss Blossom, the prosecuting witness, was now called to the stand, and being duly sworn, proceeded to testify. She was rather a venerable Miss, perhaps thirty-five or forty years of age, tall and slender, and presented generally a decaying appearance. Her nose was long and sharp, her little grey eyes dull, her cheeks sunken, and her chin almost as prominent as her nose. A flow of ringlets around her neck, might have given her a youthful appearance, had not their color differed materially from the hair on the top of her head. Her dress was a glaring muslin-de-laine, the skirt covered with flounces edged with black lace, and the waist all dotted with fancy buttons and ribbon bows. She had a bonnet on her head, but it could scarcely be seen for the flowers and ribbons which adorned it, while, slung upon her left arm was a bag capacious enough to hold an ordinary library. During the time she had been in court, not a smile had brightened her rigid countenance, though her eyes had been almost constantly fixed on Mrs. Thompson, the person against whom she was to testify. It took her some minutes to arrange herself in a suitable position as a witness, (wishing, like all old maids, to show to the greatest effect,) and as many more to adjust her dress, her curls, etc.

"What is the ground of your complaint?" asked the 'Squire, for the fourth or fifth time, before he could get an answer. At last she replied:

"I have been a member of the Anti-Despotic and Woman-Elevating-Society, (of course the real name of the society she mentioned is not given,) for fifteen years."

"Fifteen years?" asked Mrs. Thompson, writing down the words.

"Yes, fifteen years, coming next St. Valentine's day."

"Remember," said Mrs. Thompson, "you're under oath, and I am writing it all down."

"I don't care if you be, for my word can't be impeached by the likes of you."

"You'll have to answer for that, my lady," replied Mrs. Thompson, evidently cut at the remark.

"Ladies, ladies!" said the 'Squire, "this will never do.

"Mrs. Thompson, you must not interrupt the witness."

"Let her tell the truth, then," coolly replied the accused.

"Proceed, Miss Blossom," said the officer.

"Well," said she, "as I was saying, when I was most ungraciously interrupted, I have been a member of that philanthropic association fifteen years next Valentine's day. I never asked to be promoted to any of the high stations, for I always was (fingering her ringlets,) a modest girl."

"Girl!" significantly exclaimed Mrs. Thompson, who still continued to take down the evidence.

"The members," continued Miss Blossom, "kept persisting in giving me an office, for, as they said, I was deserving of it. So at last I, by hard work, overcame my modesty, and consented to serve as President, providing they'd elect me. Well, things went on in that way, till election day, and then the Society had a meetin'. I was nominated, and the Society was about to —— "

'My dear," said Mr. Thompson, in rather a loud whisper, as he leaned over the railing of the bar, having slipped in unperceived, "my dear, will you take the baby now?"

"Mr. Thompson," was her reply, "don't you see I'm engaged? Leave the room instantaneously." Not daring to disobey, Mr. Thompson went out much faster than he came in.

"The Society was about to elect me by acclamation, when Mrs. Thompson"——

"This lady here?" asked the Magistrate.

"Yes, this lady here," replied Mrs. Thompson, before Miss B. could primp her mouth to answer the question.

"She got up," continued Miss Blossom, "and told them that if they elected me, I'd break up the Society, for I was nothing but a nasty, mean, good-for-nothing tattler."

"That's true," exclaimed Mrs. Thompson, still taking down the evidence.

"Now," said Miss Blossom, "I always was sensitive, and I must say the remarks of the lady cut me to the quick. In the excitement of the moment, I repelled the charge by telling her she had better go home and nurse her baby. From what you have seen here to-day, you may judge I insinuated the truth. With that she came right up to me, and with the open hand struck me in the face. That is what I call an assault, and for which I ask the interference of the legal authorities."

"Is that all?" asked Mrs. Thompson.

"If I am obliged to answer, yes."

"Didn't you pull my hair?"

"Yes — in self-defense."

"Didn't you scratch my face?"

"Yes — in self-defense."

"Didn't you tear my bonnet?"

"Yes — in self-defense."

"Didn't you call me a hussy?"

"Yes — in self-defense."

"Didn't you jump on me like a wild cat, and utter such shrieks as to cause nearly all the ladies to leave the room, and break up the Society for the time being?"

"Yes, yes, yes," impatiently responded Miss Blossom, "I did all that *in self-defense.*"

Here the magistrate put a stop to the examination of Miss Blossom by Mrs. Thompson, and called for the next witness. But it appeared that Miss Blossom, believing the testimony all sufficient, had brought no one with her to corroborate her statements. For the defense, Mrs. Thompson offered herself as a witness, and became very indignant, indeed, when Esquire Rowekamp informed her that she could not testify in her own behalf. She then wished to plead her own case; but this privilege the Magistrate also denied her. She was about expressing her indignation, when her husband again again made his appearance, and almost in a whisper said to her:

"My dear, will you take the baby now?"

"Mr. Thompson," she replied, impetuously, "why do you persist in thus obtruding yourself upon my presence? Take the child and go home."

Mr. Thompson, with the babe in his arms, left the office for the third time, and with more reluctance than ever. Fearful, however, that his dear wife might get into trouble, he went no further than the door. After trying in vain to stop the defendant's tongue, the Magistrate briefly summed up the case, found Mrs. Thompson guilty as charged, and offered to fine her only a small sum if she would plead guilty and allow the proceedings to rest with him. This she refused to do, and he therefore required her to give bonds for her appearance before a higher Court, and to keep the peace in the meantime. This she also refused to do, stating that she would stand on her natural rights if she died by it.

Not wishing to commit her to jail, and knowing her husband to be an honest and law-abiding man, the Magistrate dismissed her, with the expectation of having her bonds secured at an early day, and glad to get clear of her at that.

Miss Blossom complained somewhat at this, but the Magistrate telling her that she also was liable to a fine, and that he would have imposed one on her, had she not redeemed her acts by breaking up "the Society," she appeared more contented, and left the office without even claiming her witness fees.

The last seen of Mrs. Thompson that day, she was walking thoughtfully homeward, *followed* by her husband, still hugging and trying to pacify the crying baby, and presenting a picture of the "good time coming," when the women are to wear the breeches.

OLD MAG:

A STORY OF THE ICE-HOUSE

THE Old Ice-House! once a depository of Winter's creation, is now a tenement of human beings. Instead of the pure, clear ice, it now receives lumps of degraded, miserable humanity, and is known as the abode of evil doers.

A prominent inmate of the old ice-house was a female of some forty years of age, known as Old Mag. She was a pitiable wretch. Her great pleasure was the bottle, and to satisfy the cravings of her disordered and degraded appetite, she would resort to the vilest conduct. She occupied a room by herself, would never allow any one to enter it, and was extremely close-mouthed regarding every thing connected with herself; though often, while intoxicated, she would heap curses upon a certain name, but so indefinite were her mutterings that nothing could be gained from them, except the surmise that she was a deeply injured woman. That she possessed intelligence, and that she had seen better days, could be readily discovered by her conversation, but that she was debased to the lowest degree, was evinced by every sentence from her mouth. She was alike feared and detested by her house-mates, and even the police, who had frequently come in contact with her, feared alike her fist and her tongue.

About a month ago, Old Mag died. For four or five days she had remained shut up in her almost dungeon room, and although her neighbors heard her alternately groaning and cursing, and had cause to believe that she was dangerously ill, no one had courage to attempt to enter her room. The police of the ward were at last informed of the circumstance, and, as in duty bound, they entered Old Mag's apartment.

"What do you want here?" she asked, with an oath, as the two policemen entered, at the same time making an effort to rise.

"We come to see what is the matter with you—are you sick?"

"Sick? what is it your business if I am? Get out of my house, you infernal dogs."

The policemen, supposing that Mag was in much better condition than they had been led to apprehend, turned, and were about to leave, when the old woman thus addressed one of them:

"Hold on, Bob; I am sick—sick as the D—l, and I want to talk with you. Put the dogs out, fasten the door, and come here."

Of all vocations in the world, that of a policeman is the least desirable. He is continually brought in contact with crime of every kind; becomes intimate with the haunts of iniquity, familiar with the most degraded of his race, and often, very often, an unwilling witness to the most terrible scenes. The policeman whom Mag addressed, had been in the service many years, and had always endeavored to perform his duty as a man and a Christian. He had no other feeling than pity for the poor wretches whom he was obliged to arrest, and instead of applying abusive epithets toward them, as is too often done, would use every persuasion to induce them to reform. He had often arrested Old Mag, but never abused her, and the result was, she respected him, and would never misbehave in his presence. He obeyed the sick woman's summons. Propping up the unhinged door, he approached her. She lay in one corner of the room, upon the bare, damp floor, and when the light of the candle he held in his hand shone full on her face, he saw at once the poor woman was not long for this world.

"Why, Mag, you are very sick," he exclaimed.

"Yes," she replied, her voice now faint and feeble, "I am dying."

"I will send for a physician," he said, moving toward the door.

"No, no, come back," she exclaimed, throwing all her energy into an effort to stop him; and succeeding in this, she feebly continued, "It is too late — I am dying, I tell you. Time is now precious—sit down—I have something to tell you."

The watchman could see in those eyes that she spoke the truth—that she was in reality dying. He seated himself on the floor beside her, brushed the hair from her face, took off his coat, placed it under her head, and bid her go on.

"Bob," she said, "I did hope that I would die alone. For three days have I lain here helpless, and I have prayed that I might die before my condition was discovered. Oh, God! how I have suffered. The agony of ten thousand deaths would not compare to the remorse that has racked my brain the last three days. I tried to pray—pray as I used to, before crime! crime! crime! stained my heart and hands. Good Heaven! why was I ever born?"

"Be calm, Mag," said the watchman, who saw that former impressions were about to be fulfilled, "you have not long to live, and should prepare to meet your God."

"Bob, you are a Christian, I know," she continued, "I always told the infernal dogs that infest this house that you were, and now that I am dying, after having prayed day and night that I might die alone, I know that God has sent you here to receive revelations for years locked up in my breast. And, oh, God! how those secret thoughts have burned in my soul. I have drank, drank, and drank, until I became a loathsome object in the sight of man, to destroy the torture within my breast, to remove the gnawing at my heart, but the more I drank the more dreadful was my punishment. Would to Heaven that this hour had come years ago—would it had come when innocence was mine—for, oh! I once was innocent—once was respected—once was loved. Don't you believe it?" she asked, raising herself upon her elbow, and staring the watchman wildly in the face.

"I do, indeed, Mag," was his reply.

"Mag! Old Mag! that's what they call me now. Ha! ha! Old Mag! whisky for Old Mag!—ha! ha!" and thus screaming, her head again fell back upon the floor, and she lay as if dead. The watchman brought some water and bathed her face, and she soon became conscious again.

"I was once a decent woman, Bob," she continued, "Twenty years ago last Wednesday, saw me one of the happiest wives and mothers in Ohio. Don't you believe it? Can you imagine that Old Mag—wicked Old Mag—was ever beloved and respected? You've been to D——?" The watchman nodded assent. "You've noticed, then, that lovely spot on the hill, just back of the town — that superb house with its pleasant garden and enticing groves ?"

"Yes," replied the policeman.

"That once was mine," she screamed, "and curse the day that I was induced by sin to leave it. Oh ! sir, Old Mag is a victim to the basest wrongs. I was contented and happy in my own house, the wife of a fond, doting husband, and the mother of a cherub babe, when a monster, in the shape of a man — a devil — wound himself, like a serpent, around me, and crushed me. Oh ! that I had resisted then—oh ! that I could have died, then. Oh ! commit crime once, and death alone can relieve the constant punishment of your conscience."

The agony of the poor woman, as she thus expressed herself, wrung groans from him who sat beside her. He saw he had a duty to perform, and he hardly knew how to do it.—Crime lay hidden in that woman's breast—she was dying—and he must learn her secret. He could not interrupt those harrowing thoughts of what had been ; and he could not withdraw her mind from the guilty past to the present. He had listened to every word she had uttered, but as yet he had received no satisfactory information. At last he asked her—

"And who was this man, Mag that was the means of destroying your happiness ?"

"Who was he ?" she said, with a ferocious expression upon her face, "go to the lake of fire and brimstone and inquire. *I sent him there !* Ha ! ha ! he ruined me—he stole me from my husband and my angel child—he dug their graves—he deceived me—he deserted me—he poisoned my heart—he maddened my brain—and I, yes I, Old Mag of the Ice-House—I murdered—ha ! ha ! ha !—I murdered him !"

"Murdered whom?" asked the watchman, using every effort to attract her attention.

She rose partly up, seized the watchman by the shoulders, and placing her face directly in his, hissed forth a name, and then fell back, never to speak again.

The watchman called in his comrade, and took immediate steps to have the body removed for interment. The name she had whispered with her dying breath rang in his ears.—He had heard it before, but could not recollect when and where. On referring to his note-book, he found an old extract from a newspaper, which explained the whole mystery.

"The body of J—— S——, whose sudden and mysterious disappearance has caused so much excitement in this community, was found in the canal last evening. The investigations of the last few days, render it certain that he was murdered by Matilda H——, the female with whom he formerly lived, and whose wrongs are familiar to our readers. The woman has fled, and as the sentiment of the community is decidedly in her favor, no one is willing to pursue her. Thus has a series of wrongs, commencing with the seduction of a young, handsome and respected wife, and the suicide of her husband, ended in the terrible murder of the seducer by the hands of his victim. Heaven have mercy upon the half-crazed, degraded and miserable murderess."

A comparison of dates, etc., made it certain that Old Mag was the woman alluded to in the above paragraph. She must have fled to the Ice-House, immediately after committing the crime alluded to, and sought death in the sure poison of the bottle. Well might she exclaim, 'Once commit crime, and death alone can relieve the constant punishment of conscience.'

THE LITTLE OLD MAID'S STORY;

AS RELATED ON THANKSGIVING DAY.

THANKSGIVING was about closing, as the family of old Mr. Thompson was gathered around the domestic hearth. Children and grand-children had come from a distance to bow again at the family altar, and to participate in the annual happy reunion. In the morning they had assembled around the old Patriarch, who they knew lived "in the fear of God," and endeavored to "keep his commandments," to hear from his lips once more, a chapter from the revered family Bible. They had joined him in prayer and thanksgiving, and united with him, in singing praises to the Most High. Together they had attended church, reviewed the events of the past year, and renewed their vows for the future. They had once more sat together at the Thanksgiving table, and while partaking of the dainties so carefully prepared, feasted on the joys of family love and devotion. In fact, Thanksgiving Day had been spent happily, as many others had, in the old homestead of Mr. Thompson, and in the evening all had gathered around the hearth, as was their custom, for a "good old family talk."

At the right sat "Old Mr. Thompson," the head of the little flock, robust, though aged, and a happy smile playing upon his still unwrinkled face. Next to him, upon her little chair, cushioned years ago, with her own hands, rocked the good matron, who had devoted her life, not to the frivolities of the world, but to a mother's duties. By the joy which beamed from her still unfaded eyes, one would judge that as she looked around her, she felt proud of those she had reared with so much care. The children and grand-children formed the circle around the family hearth, and a rosy smiling circle it was.

But at the left of the fire-place sat one, to whom I ask particular attention. All called her Aunt Mary. For years this house had been her home, and yet her full history was not known to them. It was apparent that she belonged to that class of much-abused females known as old-maids; I say much-abused class, for, despised as they are by some, ridiculed as they are by others, condemned as they are, as sour, crabbed, queer, old-fashioned, and foolish — who are more attentive to the sick, more kind to the afflicted, more ready at all times to obey the calls of the distressed, than old maids? If there is a misfortune in a family, the old maid is the first to offer consolation; if there is a bereavement, the old maid is the first to sympathise; and if volunteer aid is required, she is the first to tender her services.

Then they are always so clean and neat, so prim and so tidy. They are as regular in their habits as the sun, and as careful of their example as the most devout minister could be. They waste no time, but are ever busy with the house-cloth or the needle, for the benefit of themselves or others. Old maids may be ridiculed in the ball-room, and among the silly and gay; but at home, whether it be in the sick-room or the kitchen, they are models for the younger of their sex.

Aunt Mary occupied the left of the circle, and though,

she had performed most of the labor incident to getting up a Thanksgiving dinner, depriving herself of attending the morning service,—she sat with the hearth-broom in her hand, ready to remove the smallest particle of dirt which might fall upon the bricks, so thoroughly cleaned by her. Like most old maids, she was shriveled and little; but beneath a shade of melancholy she had a sweet and tender expression of countenance.

After an hour or two had been spent in conversation, the old gentleman turned to her and said:

"Aunt Mary, while seated just where we are, and as we are, at this hour last Thanksgiving Day, you remarked that you were once in love; and to the pressing inquiries of the children, you promised, if your life were spared until the next Thanksgiving Day, that you would relate to us the whole story of your life. Thank God! we are all seated here again, as we then were, and the time has now arrived for you to redeem your word."

Aunt Mary had evidently forgotten her promise, but now immediately prepared to make it good. After brushing up the hearth, and arranging her dress with much exactness, she commenced relating—

THE LITTLE OLD MAID'S STORY.

"I almost regret my promise," she said, "for the story has been so long locked up in my bosom, that it ought to remain there. But I will tell it, and with the hope that it will not only prove interesting but instructive, particularly to the children, who are yet ignorant of the cares and sufferings of life.

"It will be just thirty years next March since my mother

died, leaving me an orphan at the age of sixteen. Two years before, I had lost my father, which bereavement almost broke my heart; but when my dear mother, who loved me so affectionately, was laid in the cold, cold grave, I prayed for the privilege of following her there. The world was a blank to me, and for months my only consolation was tears, bitter tears.

"The memory of those days still touches my heart, and I recur to them only when necessary. Mankind is doomed to many evils and much suffering, but I can conceive of no situation in life more pitiable, more sad, more worthy of condolement than of a girl, on the verge of womanhood, deprived of both parents, and cast upon the broad world without a protector. Oh! the aching of an orphan girl's heart. What tongue can relate, whose pen describe them?"

Here Aunt Mary paused a few moments, while with a neatly folded handkerchief, she wiped a tear from her eye. Bitter memories were passing through her mind.

"I knew of no relative living, and you can imagine the dreariness of my heart. I had been left, however, sufficient property to support me, and a neighbor and his wife, who had for years been intimate friends of my parents, offered me a home with them. They became my protectors and did all in their power to allay my anguish. They were kind, very kind to me, but with all their kindness they could not supply the place of the departed. I found in them, however, friends for a season, and I at least became to a great degree reconciled to my sad fate.

"With full confidence I placed my property in the possession of my volunteer guardian, to use it to the best advantage for my interest.

Two years passed away. I had formed many pleasant associations, and began to think there were yet some joys in store for me. Among my young associates I was quite a favorite, and they insisted on dragging me into society more than my inclinations sanctioned; for my affections were still in the grave, and though the grass grew long o'er my mother's mound, oft in retiracy the tears of sorrow coursed down my cheeks. 'Oh! my mother, my dear, dear mother,' I would exclaim, 'could I only look upon your sweet face again, and hear your affectionate voice, my poor heart would be relieved. There is no one who can fill your place.'

Aunt Mary again paused to brush away tears, and the drops from other eyes in the little circle told plainly how interested all were in the story.

"The third year of my sad bereavement," she continued sorrowfully, "brought additional troubles. For some months I had noticed, that the family in whose house I had found a home, seemed daily to grow colder in their intercourse with me. My inquiries as to the cause always received evasive replies, and at last, near the closing of the third year of my orphanage, I was requested to find another home as soon as convenient. The reason given for this request was a desire on their part to reduce materially their expenses. I complied with their wishes, again moving among strangers, and feeling as sensibly as ever my own loneliness. Nor was that all. A week thereafter, I ascertained that my voluntary guardian and pretended friend, had cheated me out of all my property."

"Is it possible?" exclaimed old Mr. Thompson, astonished at the development.

"Indeed, it is too true."

"Swindle a lone orphan! that is outrageous," exclaimed the old gentleman, while his eyes flashed fire.

"Indeed it is," responded the eldest son.

"So I thought," continued Aunt Mary. "The way he managed to swindle me was this: He persuaded me to dispose of my little estate and turn it into cash, informing me that I could loan the money to much better advantage than I could rent the property. After he had obtained the cash, I naturally gave it to him to loan for me, being entirely ignorant of such business. He took it, and afterward denied having received it."

"Did you not take his notes?" was asked.

"No. I did not even know that it was necessary, and if I had have known it, I had such confidence in the man, that I would not have asked it."

"Why didn't you sue him, child?" inquired Mrs. Thompson.

"I did, but not without encountering many difficulties. I applied to several lawyers to undertake my case, but finding I was without money to fee them, they refused to have anything to do with it. After I had given up all hope, however, a kind-hearted member of the bar, who had heard my story, called upon me, and agreed to conduct my suit without a fee. He expressed but little confidence in my success, but was determined to try it, let the result be what it would. I entered suit, but only to find that the law, though designed to dispense JUSTICE, affords no protection to lone and penniless orphans."

"'Twas too bad," interposed the old gentleman.

"I was now thrown upon the world, without friends and

without money. My utter destitution, however, nerved me, and I diligently undertook to earn my own living. Opportunities soon presented themselves, and for three years I lived the life of a city needlewoman. Robbed as I had been by those who pretended to be my best friends, I had confidence in no one, and kept entirely aloof from the world. Indeed I soon found that the poor needle-girl was not the orphan with property. Many of my former intimate companions now scorned me, and passed me in the street, without speaking to me, because a pretended friend had swindled me out of my subsistence. Such is the pride of poor human nature. I toiled on, however, at my needle, earning barely enough to keep body and soul together. Sometimes I nearly starved, and often I was almost induced to throw aside my work, and lie down to die. It is a dreadful life, and I am satisfied that most needlewomen in our large cities are as badly off now as I was then. I was paid a reasonable price for my labor, but it was my inexperience in the kind of work I was forced to take from time to time which caused me to suffer. But now, needlewomen receive but a bare pittance for their toil, and from what I observe, God only knows how they live. But few, very few seamstresses, I warrant, have partaken of a Thanksgiving dinner to-day. Heaven have mercy upon their employers!"

"Amen!" was the response of more than one.

"Three years, I said, I labored as a needlewoman," continued Aunt Mary. "During the third year I formed an acquaintance with a young man, to whom I soon became much attached. He seemed to realize my condition, sympathized with me so heartily, and treated me so kindly, that he soon won my heart. To make a long story short, I was in love," and Aunt Mary heaved a deep sigh.

"Yes, in love. For the first time since my mother's death, there was joy in my heart—joy because I had found a being upon whom I could place my affections. The world became new to me; and happy in the present I anticipated great pleasure for the future. "Would that my story ended here," continued Aunt Mary, with the strongest emotion depicted upon her countenance; "but the orphan girl has still further sorrows to tell. My lover deceived me! He cruelly, basely deserted me.

"Oh! it chills my blood to recur to those days, days of the deepest anguish. Disappointed, ruined, and desperate, I determined to relieve the world of my presence, and in despair sought death by suicide. Rushing to the river, I plunged in, when you, grandfather, (addressing the elder Mr. Thompson,) rescued me from a watery grave. You brought me to your house, revived and endeavored to console me. You know how I despaired for months, how cautiously I received your kind proffers of friendship, and how long it was before I again became reconciled to life. I was at last convinced that kind Heaven had cast me among Christians, on whom I could rely. I became one of your family, and have remained with you until I have become 'Aunt Mary,' not only to your children, bnt your children's children. With the exception of an occasional recurrence to my early days, I am now and have for years been happy. This house has proved a home indeed to me, and 'Aunt Mary's' earnest desire is that she may end her days with you."

Tears flowed down the cheeks of the "little old maid" as

she concluded her story. Her heart was full. The children, large and small, gathered about her, and assured her that she should never sorrow as long as they could contribute to her happiness. Their affection eased her heart, and, with her tears still flowing, she said:

"I know it, darlings, I know it. Aunt Mary appreciates your love and is happy."

Even the "old folks" were moved to tears, tears of joy, the old man called them, at Aunt Mary's deliverance from her sorrows and an untimely death. Mr. Thompson asked:

"Have you ever heard of the fate of your dishonest guardian and perfidious lover?"

"Not until lately," was Aunt Mary's reply.

"God seems to have punished them both. The former became a drunkard, lost all his property, died a pauper and was buried by the authorities, not a mourner following him to the grave. The other was shot down in the streets of a Southern city, for making improper advances to the sister of the person who caused his death."

"Heaven truly hath avenged thee, Aunt Mary," said the venerable head of the family: "and from her story, children, learn this—that dishonest or dishonorable action brings sorrow not only on the injured, but eventually on him who commits the injury; and that he who administers comfort to the poor and distressed, will find his reward, both upon earth and in Heaven."

THE HOG DROVER'S VISIT:

OR, BILL JENKINS' FIRST IMPRESSIONS OF THE QUEEN CITY.

A FEW years ago, when nearly all the pork-packing for shipment in the West, was done at Cincinnati, hundreds of hogs were purchased miles away, and taken to Porkopolis in droves, on foot. This was practiced to such an extent that hog driving in the Fall of the year became a regular business, and many were the farm hands who annually calculated on buying a new "rig out" for the Winter, with the receipts of a "drive" to Cincinnati behind a lot of porkers. Railroads have monopolized this business now, so far as Ohio and Indiana are concerned, but from Kentucky, hogs are yet brought to this market in the good old way. How much the drivers receive I never had the curiosity to inquire, but they certainly are deserving of more than ordinary wages. It is no light job to trudge over a muddy road, day after day, urging on the hogs continually with a whip or a switch, yelling "so-boy" constantly at the top of one's voice, now running like all fury to head a spry hog, which has taken a notion to go the wrong road, and again helping a lazy fellow along, by wrapping his tail around one's hand, and giving him a boost with the knee and arm together. It is a laborious work, and I am not surprised that drovers are rejoiced when they arrive at their journey's end, or that, having the hogs safely penned at the slaughter-houses, and receiving the cash for their services, they grab the money tightly, and walk through the streets of the city, as if they intended to buy the whole place, before they took their departure.

Bill Jenkins' first visit to Cincinnati, was as a hog drover.

"You see," said Bill to the folks after he had got home, "I never had ben to the darned town afore, and know'd nothin' of how they suck'd the dimes out of a critter. But Uncle Josh, who's ben to town with hogs heaps of times, had sorter gin me an idee, for when I started with the hogs, he sez to me, 'Bill, keep yer eyes skinned, or the critters in Cincinnati will skin you afore they do the hogs.'"

"'I'm bright,' sez I to Uncle Josh, and then, Uncle Josh kinder winked to me, as much as to say, 'you don't know nothin' about it.'

"Well, I went on with the hogs, you know, and a pesky time we had with 'em. That black, spotted critter raised by 'Squire Sidebottom, was so lazy that we had to wollop him every step. He's a plaguey ill-mannered hog, and I come mighty near being the death of him afore we got half way thar. As 'twas, I pity the feller what eats his meat, pickle or no pickle. Well, we druv the hogs on an' on, tell we cum right down to the river, an' thar was the town of Sinsinnaty, not more'n twenty rods from us. Jemeny! but its a smashin' place. The houses are built all along, and the roads are just as clean as a stable floor. It must a took a mint of money to fix every thing so stylish. I stood and looked ever so long, and I thought I could look to eternity, and not see half of the things. Purty soon a steamboat, big agin as our barn, cum along puffin' and blowin' worse than a skeery bull. We all turned too an' druv the hogs on to her, an' then we got on ourselves. In a jiffy we war on t'other side, and then we druv the hogs right squar through the town. Lawrdy! you oughter just have seen the place. There was more'n 'nough people than it would take to lam all Mexico, and the busses and wagons couldn't be packed on Uncle Josh's plantation. It kept me dodgin' all the time, an' the only wonder is that the hogs warn't all killed afore they got to the pens. I *was* a little skeered I tell you, and from the way the critters squeeled, I guess they war too.

"Directly I seed two hogs goin' off from the drove, an' as a matter of course I goes arter 'em. I chased 'em clear up a lane, an' heads an' turns 'em back agin. I was a drivin' 'em along to the drove, when a feller sez, 'Hey, you, what you going to do with them ar hogs?' 'Take 'em to the drove,' sez I. 'Drove,' sez he, 'them's my hogs.' 'Your'n,' sez I, remembering Uncle Josh's talk about skinnin" 'I ain't so green as you might make out.' 'Well, you leave them hogs alone,' sez he, 'or I'll bounce you.' That ar sort of made me riley, so sez I to him, 'bounce and be darned.' This appeared to tickle a hull lot of fellers who was standin' round thar, and one on 'em sez, 'Go it, Kaintuck.' I give the two hogs a whack, which sent 'em squeelin' on to'ards the drove. I run arter 'em, and was just laffin' to myself to think how I'd stood up to the city feller, when cha-bang! sumthin' took me side the head. It sorter laid me out, an' the first thing I know'd that darn'd chap was a drivin' off the hogs agin.—'Hello.' sez I, singin' out to the top of my voice, 'Hello, fotch back them ar hogs.' 'Go to grass,' sez he. This sort of raised my dander agin, an' I started arter him. I hadn't gone more'n ten steps, afore two fellers laid hands on me.—'Stan' back,' sez I, determined to whale every thing of my inches. 'Hold on,' sez one on 'em, pintin' to a piece of tin on his coat, 'hold on,' sez he, 'don't yeu see, we're watchmen?' That sort a cooled me down, and sez I to 'em, 'don't you see that feller drivin' off them hogs?' 'Sartin,' sez he to me, 'and they're his hogs.' 'I can whip,' sez I, 'any man what sez that.' At that a hull crowd had gathered round, and some said, 'go it, Greeny,' and some said, 'go it, Kaintuck.' I told 'em just to draw back, and form a ring, an' I could whale 'em all, one at a time. Just then, the boss of the drove cum up, an' sez he, 'Bill, them aren't my hogs!' 'Nough said,' sez I, as I walked off to the drove, mighty glad the boss had cum up, for I know'd I'd had hard work to have fit all them chaps.

"Well, we druv along till we cum to the pens, though I was monsus careful all the way not to run after any more hogs, because, thinks I to myself, the boss may do it. After the hogs were all in the pens, the boss paid us off, and I was so afeered of some of 'em a stealin' my money, that I slipped behind the corner of a fence and put mine in the toe of my boot. With all the boys, I went down to the White Bear Tavern, whar we had been reckonin' to stop all night. It is a powerful big house—bigger than any meetin' house I ever seed. The landlord sez, 'how are you boys,' shook our hands as if he'd know'd us for all our life time, and then writ our names in a book bigger than the old Bible. We laid 'round the house till we got supper, continued Bill, and then we all went down to the Museum. I 'spected it would be as dark as all fury goin' down thar, but what d'you think? They had lanterns stuck on the top of posts, all the way down the road, and a feller could see just as well as if the sun was shinin'.

There was ten of us, an' as good lookin' chaps as you'd sec any whar. A nice lookin' man what was stoppin' at the tavern, told us to look out for the skinners, an' we sez to him we would. But he was so all-fired afeered about it, that he said he would go down too. 'Now,' sez he takin' us all into a room whar nobody could hear, 'now, boys,' sez he, 'it'll never do for you to show your money down thar, or some of those plaguy skinners will hook it from you.' All on you just gin me a quarter-apiece and I'll buy the tickets! 'All right,' sez I, and 'all right' sez all the boys, so we all gin him a quarter. 'Now,' sez he, 'we'll go.' 'Nuff sed,' sez the boys, and as I sed afore, off we started. Well, we hadn't got very far, before that very chap what had the quarters, broke and run up a dark alley. We hollered to him, but he never sed a word, and he never cum back. The boys sent me back to the tavern to ax about it, and the landlord sed he was sum darned sharper that had swindled us out of our quarters. You may reckon the boys war mad when I told 'em on it; and you may reckon I thunk sum of Uncle Josh about that time. The boys cussed a little about it, and then we all determined to go to the Museum and pay our own quarters. The feller cheated us purty, but as I told the boys, thar war no use cryin' over spilt milk; they sed so too, and so we determined to keep our eyes skinned for the futur'. Down to the Museum we cum, and Jemmy! you ought to jest have seed it. It wor a terrible big house, and candles war put in all the winders. There war no puttin' a light under a bushel thar, no how; so them folks go accordin' to Scripture a leetle bit, I reckon. And then the music! It beat the Felicity Band all holler, and had two drums. It made a feller feel all sorterish, kinder as if he war rich and would never want another cent till he died into Etarnity. I forgot all about bein' skinned out of the quarter, and so did all the boys. The folks war rushin' down to the show like all forty, and sez I to the boys, 'hurry up the cakes now, or the first thing you know, the Museum will be chuck full.' 'Hurry up the cakes,' sez they, and hurry up the cakes we did. We squeezed along, keeping all on us together, till we cum up nearly to the door. 'Twenty-five cents a piece, gentlemen,' sez a man standin' thar. 'Twenty-five cents a piece,' sez I to the boys, and you ought to seed how we forked over the quarters. We then squeezed along agin, till we cum to the door, an' I tell you it war squeesin'—a kind a squeesin' the girls would'nt like, and a kind a squcesin' that cum pesky near skinnin' us. We kept hold each other's arms, determined not to be lost, for thar's no knowin' what'd become of us, if we didn't stick right up to one another.

"We cum to the door. 'A quarter,' sez a man standin' thar. 'A quarter, sez I, what fur?' 'If you want to get in, sez he, you must pay.' 'We did pay sez I;' 'you can't cum the giraffe over me, sez he, so pay or get out of the way.' That sort a' riled me, an' sez I, 'we paid that feller standin' right thar.' 'Whar?' sez he. 'Thar, sez I, pointing right to the chap. But by Jemmy! what do you think? why the chap wasn't thar at all—he'd got the quarters and run. 'By thunder, boys,' sez I 'they've skinned us agin. That war ten quarters gone clean fur nothin'.' I felt kinder mad and kinder sheepish, an' so did all the boys.

"A good many of the folks around thar sed we was green, an' they laughed, too, which sort o' riled us, an' made us feel purty much like fightin.' We stood back a leetle out of the crowd, to talk about things. Sum reckoned one thing and sum another, till we all cum to the conclusion we'd see the Museum, if it tuck the last cent. 'Git yer quarters ready,' sez I, an' every feller rammed his hands into his pockets. And Jemmy, you ought to have seed us jest at that time. We all stood right stock still, an' looked right at each other, as if we war jest about tumblin' in our graves.

"We war skeered clean out of our boots, for while we had been talkin' an' considerin' about matters, sum of the tarnation thievin' chaps had got their hands in our pockets, an' stole every darned cent. Not a livin quarter was thar in the whole crowd of us, an' thar we stood tremblin,' for we spected next to be robbed of our shirts. 'Hello, boys!' sez I, let's move for home.' 'It's greed,' sed the boys, an' away we all started fur the river. My feet never stopped till I got clear away from the darned thievin' place; an' I tell you I was monsus glad when I got into old Kaintuck agin.

"I tell you," continued Bill, after he had stopped to take breath, "that town aint no place for decent folks. I know'd as soon as I seed it, that the folks could'nt build sich fine houses, an' have such mighty purty taverns without stealin' a little. Its properly named *Sin-sin-natty*, for it has got more sin in it now than Sodam an' Gonnorrow ever had. I war thar once, an' should I live to Etarnity, no airthly mortal would ever get me to go thar agin."

AN APPETITE FOR LAW:

OR, GRIT TO THE BACK BONE.

Deacon Jones, of N——, in the State of Ohio, who lived and flourished about ten or fifteen years ago, was full of pluck. It was his boast that he never undertook a thing but he carried it out, and his neighbors were so well satisfied of this, that on ordinary occasions, they, like Davy Crocket's coon, just came down, when they saw the grin. With this, the Deacon ought to have been satisfied; but such was not the case. Like an ambitious warrior, a great victory only gave him a desire for a greater one, and he often sought difficulties and encountered them, just to show his neighbors that he could successfully combat them.

The Deacon's natural ally was the Bar; his favorite battle field, the court-room. Like most selfish or turbulent men, his delight was to fight his antagonist through the interminable paths and mysterious depths of the law, feeling quite certain that he could use some of those many tricks which have been manufactured for the purpose of teasing Justice, to overthrow his opponent.

The Deacon soon obtained a vicious appetite for this kind of business. He was out of his element unless "in law;" and being a man of abundant means, he was always able to gratify this strange passion to his heart's content. It mattered not how much the prosecution of a case cost him—he would sacrifice twice or thrice the amount involved, and carry his suits to the highest courts, that he might gain the victory. The best legal talent of the neighborhood was always his, for he never grumbled at *their* fees; and—I regret to say it—in these degenerate days of the Bar, lawyers look more to the amount and certainty of their fees, than to the justice of the cause they agree to defend. With time and money to spare, with the best lawyers on his side, and his own close observation of the proceedings in courts, is it wonderful that Deacon Jones soon became invulnerable in lawsuits?

Yet many were foolish enough to battle with him; but always to their heart's sorrow, and to the great relief of their pockets: Always? No, not always; for the Deacon was once beaten, and the particulars of that fight are worth recording, not only as a warning to future generations to beware of the "uncertainties of law," but to exhibit in its proper light, the "clear grit" of Deacon Jones.

Lawyer P———, of the town of N——, a gentleman who has since been elevated to the Bench, was the "regular" attorney of Deacon Jones. The Deacon liked the lawyer, because he was shrewd, learned and candid; and the lawyer liked the Deacon because he paid promptly, and was a good customer.

One morning, about ten years ago, as the said lawyer was at his before-breakfast labors, he was called upon by the Deacon.

"Good morning, Mr. P———," said the Deacon, as he entered the office. "Glad to see you so early at it, for I've got a little work for you to do."

"Indeed," was the attorney's reply, "why Deacon, I have been of the opinion that your success in all your lawsuits had frightened every body so badly, that no one has now the courage to dispute with you."

"But you see you are mistaken. There are still some headstrong people left in the world, Mr. P———. I've got another suit on hand."

"Well, what is it?"

"It aint an individual,—I think I'm done with that class of suits. My neighbors have found to their sorrow, that I am always right, and I think there is very little danger of any of them forcing me into law again. I've now got into a fight with the authorities."

"Indeed!"

"Yes, you see, they have been trying to gouge me. In looking over my tax bill, I found they had charged me thirty cents too much, and I refused to pay it."

"*Thirty cents?*" asked the attorney in astonishment.

"Yes," coolly replied the Deacon.

"Why, is it possible, you intend to dispute that small amount in court?"

"Possible! why certainly it is, and, by the Jehocs, (a favorite expression,) I've already started the ball a rolling.— You see, I dont care about the thirty cents—that's nothing —it's the principle of the thing, I'm after. Now, who is in the right, the tax-gatherer or myself? That is the question I wish decided. If I'm wrong, let the court say so, and if I am right, I am determined the world shall know it."

"Well, this is rather a small business, Deacon, and I don't care much about having any thing to do with it, and honestly, if the party was any body but yourself, I believe I would positively refuse."

"O, but I must have you this time, Mr. P. I commenced the case myself, yesterday, and made a pretty out of it. We had a trial before Esquire G——, and by Jehocs, I was thrown. I appealed, of course, and now we must fight in earnest."

"Ha, ha! so you have been whipped, have you, Deacon?" laughingly said the lawyer; "that will probably teach you to stick to your attorney, hereafter."

"No, you can't say I was whipped. You know 'Squire G—— always had a spite at me, and he just wanted to give me trouble. But, let's to business."

"Well, give us the points of your case."

This the Deacon did, carefully explaining how and where he expected to make a "point." The lawyer listened to him patiently, and after he had heard the Deacon through, he unhesitatingly said—

Well, I advise you to stop where you are. You are entirely wrong, and can never gain this suit in the world.

The Deacon knew better, however, and insisted on continuing the suit; and after some persuasion, succeeded in inducing his attorney to consent to take care of the case, though that worthy declared he would loose it beyond all doubt.

Well, the case was tried, and notwithstanding the utmost skill and tact of the attorney, the Deacon lost it. Yet he was not satisfied. He obtained a new trial, engaged additional counsel, and gave the tax-gathering authorities another hitch. He had great confidence in the saying, "the third time is the charm," and now he was sure of victory. *Again he was loser.*

But few good lawyers can stand more than three defeats in one case, and it was so with lawyer P———. Finding that no expense, toil or trouble, could bring his client to a sense of his own interest, the Deacon's lawyer now threw up the case, and positively refused to have anything more to do with it.

The Deacon expressed his regret that one who had always been with him in law, should desert him at this trying moment. In vain did Mr. P. endeavor to convince Deacon Jones that he was throwing money away, and that he might dispute eternally without obtaining any other result in that case than such as had been meted out to him. The Deacon declared he would never surrender as long as the law left "a load in his pouch," and if he was not successful in the fourth, and the last possible "hitch" he could get, it would not be his fault. He paid P——'s bill without grumbling, and then sought after counsel for the last grand struggle for thirty cents.

Deacon Jones appeared to have trouble to get things to suit him for the fourth tussle. Time and again the case was continued or postponed at his request, and for months he did but little else than consult lawyers, examine law books, and study the decisions of courts.

Time rolled on. The case had departed from even the memory of lawyer P——, though he was frequently in the court upon whose docket it was entered. One day his eye caught Deacon Jones' as he was settling an account with the Sheriff, and approaching him, the following conversation took place:

"Good morning, Deacon," said the lawyer, "I should like to know what business you have with the Sheriff?"

"O, paying a bill," replied the Deacon.

"Not an execution, I hope. I thought you were never troubled with such things?"

"I hoped I never would be, but it seems they have headed me at last."

"In what case?"

"That little affair about my taxes, you know."

"I knew it," said the lawyer, really gratified at the intelligence; "I told you from the very start you would be beaten, and your perseverance in the case has surprised me not a little. But Deacon, the costs must be pretty heavy, are they not?"

"Only one hundred and seventeen dollars," coolly replied the Deacon.

"Which you are forced to pay just for disputing thirty cents. I guess you will follow your lawyer's advice next time, Deacon."

"Well, I don't know as I will; I now see the point on which they beat me; and I know that if I had it to go over again, somebody would be paying these cents. I tell you what it is, Mr. P——, I would like to give them another hitch, and I will give you one hundred dollars if you will get the case opened up again!"

This proposal was made in all sincerity, but the lawyer most respectfully declined. Other attorneys, however, accepted the proposition, but failed, as the case had reached its limitation. After all hope of a renewal of the fight had been extinguished in the Deacon's heart, he acknowleged that he never expected to gain the suit, but merely wished to satisfy his appetite for law, and to convince the adminstrative officers of the local government that he was "*Grit to the back bone.*"

VISITING THE SICK:

OR, A NEIGHBORLY CALL UPON AN OLD BACHELOR.

Bob Grubbs is a confirmed old bachelor. He occupies rooms in the retired locality of S—— street, which rooms, during his occupancy, have not been entered by a single neighbor. True, the ladies of the vicinity have been possessed of a great anxiety to see how the old fellow lived without a wife, but Bob always managed to upset their little stratagems to gain a neighborly admission. He vowed himself an inveterate hater of neighbors, declared they never performed a good act, but they expected another in return, and swore—for the old dog, like most of his class, could swear—that the only way to enjoy peace and quietness at home, was by rejecting all communication with one's neighbors. Bachelor Grubbs accomplished his object. Within one month he freed himself of every importunity, and was not even applied to for the loan of his newspaper. As may be supposed, however, he by so doing, excited an ill-feeling, particularly among the neighboring ladies. They looked upon him as a man who had lost all human feeling, and to whom life was a curse rather than a blessing. Vast indeed was the number of conjectures made as to his past history, and countless were the lashings he received behind his back, from tongues vibrating in delicate little mouths.

At last old Grubbs was taken severely ill. He might have died without help, had not a fortunate presentiment enabled him to call in Cuff, an old negro, who was always at his service either as waiter or nurse. The old bachelor was very sick indeed; at one time his physician almost despaired of his recovery. But old bachelors are always tough, defying the inroads of time, and ever ready to give the Grim Monster a hard tussle when he comes prowling around. Grubbs had no notion of dying, and he didn't die. He said he would get well, despite the forebodings of his physician, and the poison administered in the shape of medicines.

Though he did not once think of his neighbors during the severity of his sickness, they thought much of him. The frequent visits of the physician alarmed them; and learning from the doctor that his patient was really in danger, the ladies, with their usual kind heartedness, determined to forget his past gruffness, and tender their sympathies and services in behalf of the dying man. Old Grubbs was just beginning to feel that he was recovering; was able to enjoy a "sit-up," and indulge in a few luxuries, when the first of those who desired to pay him a visit during his illness, tapped on the door.

"Hello! the doctor again," grumbled the patient, after taking a sip of gruel. "He is very attentive, now that I am getting well. Just like the whole profession, make their visits as often as possible to increase their fees. Cuff, go to the door; let the doctor in, but mark ye, not a word about throwing those medicines into the fire."

Cuff obeyed, but as he opened the door and discovered two ladies, instead of the physician, he rolled his eyes and immediately exclaimed,

"Gor a mighty! what's dat?"

"How is Mister Grubbs, to-dav?" asked one of the ladies.

"Massa berry sick—dat is, he's—he's—gettin' well now, ladies."

"Ah, indeed! convalescent, is he?"

"Yes, 'um," replied Cuff, doubly confounded by the language. "He's convarted—he's got religion—got it todder day when de doctor fotch him much cal'mel, he t'ought he's gwyn' to die."

"Then he was really dangerous?" continued the lady, smiling. "We heard so, and fearing that, in his forlorn condition, he would not receive proper attention, we concluded to give him a neighborly call."

Cuff knew his employer's sentiments in regard to neighborly visits, and, not wishing to offend the ladies, did not know what to do. They, however, did not wait for his decision, but entered and proceeded directly to the adjoining chamber. Grubbs heard their movements, and knowing they would surely enter his bed-room, and catch him *en dishabille*, weak as he was, made a pitch for the bed. He succeeded in getting into it, and covering up, after a fashion, before the ladies reached his presence.

"In bed — poor fellow!" exclaimed Mrs. Smith to her neighbor, as she entered the chamber.

"Bless us! what an atmosphere," responded Mrs. Brown. "Enough to suffocate a person. I don't wonder that the poor man is at the point of death."

"Hush! softly! may be he is sleeping, and if so, we must not disturb his slumbers. I will see," said Mrs. Smith, as she approached the bed side. Tenderly removing the cover from the old bachelor's face, she inquired, "Are you asleep, Mr. Grubbs?"

A soft snore was the response, the sick man not daring to trust his temper, under the circumstances, and hoping to "possum" the ladies away

"Poor man, he looks sadly. He must have suffered intensely," continued Mrs. Smith.

"I don't wonder a bit," replied Mrs. Brown, "for I really believe I shall faint in this atmosphere. I must hoist a window."

"Massa'll kotch cold by dat," interposed Cuff, who had not yet recovered from his surprise.

"Not a bit of it," replied Mrs. Brown, "I believe in fresh air. Half the people are killed by being shut up in close rooms during illness. How in the world do you stand this atmosphere?"

"Massa lay down to it," responded Cuff, with a grin.

"Impertinence!" indignantly replied Mrs. Brown. "I wonder the man aint dead, being under your care. What do you know about making beds and keeping the house to rights? Every thing is upside down, and ———, but I forgot; we were in a bachelor's house. What can we expect."

"Really, Mrs. Brown," remarked Mrs. Smith, "you are right, and the wonder is, the man is not dead. We have been neglectful of our duty as neighbors. Had we laid aside our prejudices, and visited the poor man, as was our duty, we might have saved him much suffering. Ah! here comes Mrs. Jones. Good morning, Mrs. Jones. I am really glad you have come, for there is work here for us to do."

Mrs. Jones was another neighbor woman, and had taken the privilege of entering without knocking.

"I seed you comin' in," she said, "an' I sposed there was sumthin' up, so I slipped on my sluffs, an' just come over.—Is the man dead?"

"No," replied Mrs. Brown, "but we wonder greatly that he is not. Did you ever smell such an atmosphere?"

"It's downright orful," exclaimed Mrs. Jones.

"I am nearly fainting," said Mrs. Brown.

"And I'm just ready to drop," followed Mrs. Jones, as she leaned languidly upon a chair. "But whar's the woman of the house? She haint desarted the man."

"Bless you, there is no woman," continued Mrs. Brown. "Grubbs is an old bachelor, and will not have a woman about his house."

"Massy sakes!" exclaimed Mrs. Jones.

"And during all his illness has had nobody about the house but this ugly-looking nigger," pointing to Cuff, who stood grinning in the corner.

"Gracious mercy!" exclaimed Mrs. Jones, throwing up her hands, while she fixed her eyes on Cuff.

"Don't stand there grinning but stir around and help to put things to rights," said Mrs. Brown to the servant. "Dear me! how can men live to be old bachelors? Such a house and such an atmosphere."

Just at this moment Mrs. Smith, who had seated herself at the bedside, ready to sympathize with the unfortunate sick man, the moment he should waken, discovered a slow parting of his eye-lids, and an evident attempt to take a sly peep.

"Hush! hush!" she softly said, "Mr. Grubbs is about to awaken. Poor man! how distressing he looks."

"Raally distressing," ejaculated Mrs. Jones.

"Are you awake, Mr. Grubbs?" asked Mrs. Smith, placing her hand on the brow of the old bachelor.

There was a slight tremor beneath the coverlids, but no response.

"He must be dreaming," continued the lady.

"Or maybe he's gone out of his head, and got the flighties," intimated Mrs. Jones.

"You had better wake him up," suggested Mrs. Brown, "That bed is really distressing, and must be made up. Wake him, and we will lift him into a chair, while we renew the sheets, and put things to rights."

"Mister Grubbs," said Mrs. Smith, as she slightly shook his shoulder. There was no response. Again she shook, again she called him, and again she received no answer.

"He is sound asleep," she said, "and we had better not disturb him. Let us noiselessly arrange the furniture in order, and by that time he may awake."

"Not a hand stir," urged Mrs. Brown, "until the bed is made!"

"Not a hand stir," repeated Mrs. Jones.

"Let me at him; I will wake him up," continued Mrs. Brown. "There is no use of being delicate about it, when the man is dying for the want of a little womanly comfort. Mr. Grubbs!" she fairly screamed, as she gave him a heavy shake.

The old bachelor still lay "possuming," though every moment he was becoming more and more angry.

"Hang the man!" exclaimed Mrs. Brown; "if he did not breathe I would believe him dead. If he can be aroused, however, he shall be."

She was about giving him another shake, when the trio of neighborly ladies were frightened almost out of their wits by the old bachelor suddenly raising himself in his bed.

"If you insist on seeing me in my shirt, say so, and I'll get up," he coolly remarked; "but if you have the natural modesty of women, and wish to be regarded as ladies, go home and attend to your own business and let me attend to mine. Get out of the house instantly, or by the powers I'll stand before you as naked as I was the minute I was born!"

The effect may be imagined. The ladies hastened from the house, while Cuff lay down on the floor, and rolled over and over, as he gave a tremendous "yah, ha!"

As may be supposed, the affair created quite a sensation among the ladies of the neighborhood, all of whom declare that old Grubbs may rot in his bed before they again tender their merciful services to him. He laughs heartily at it, however, and declares that the incident made him a well man, as he was able to walk out the next day.

POD II.

INVISIBLE CALLS UPON THE FORTUNE-TELLERS.

How fascinating is Mystery! Even in this enlightened age and country, thousands upon thousands seek by every means to learn the hidden things of the future. The result is that Astrology, Card-cutting, and other modes of pretended Fortune Telling, have experienced a revival, and, to-day, thousands bow in reverence, within the Temple of Humbug, erected by the Masters of these self-styled Arts. Even I, yes, I, Invisible, have knocked at the door, obtained admission, bowed at the altars, (but with twinkling eyes!) and sought, (with a very doubting heart,) the revelations of Astrology! Anxious to penetrate the mysterious depths of the humbug, I sought the Book of Fate in several quarters, and — got my money's worth!

In company with officer Rose, I called on a Clairvoyant, who advertised herself in the City papers, as being able to see into the future, with an unerring eye. We ascended a narrow flight of stairs to the second story, where we came to a door all be-pasted with the circulars, advertisements, etc., of the Clairvoyant. We knocked, and a young looking woman opened the door, invited us to take seats, and then suddenly disappeared behind a curtain stretched across the room. We found ourselves in company with an elderly woman, who was evidently "in waiting," and who not only manifested a disposition to avoid conversation, but contrived to keep her face hidden from our view.

A whispering behind the curtain gave us the impression that the clairvoyant was "opening up the future" to a customer, and as we could hear nothing distinctly, we occupied the time in examining the room. The apartment was about thirty feet square, a dirty curtain extended across one end, dividing the *sanctum sanctorum*, from the place allotted to those in waiting. The room was well furnished, but in considerable disorder.

A rustling behind the curtain, and a chinking of money, warned us that the clairvoyant was through with one customer. The curtain was raised, and out came an apparently young woman closely veiled. She could not resist taking a good look at us as she passed out of the door, and as she did so, I recognized a pair of black eyes, which I knew belonged to an acquaintance. Her veil could not disguise them.

The clairvoyant again made her appearance, and invited the elderly woman to a seat behind the curtain. The fat old lady arose with difficulty from her chair, and tottered to the sacred recess of the oracle, a perfect specimen of deluded *wo*manity. The curtain dropped.

"Listen," said the Lieutenant, "we can hear them."

"Laws-a-mercy!" exclaimed the old lady, "I wonder if you kin tell true?"

"The science never fails," replied a voice we had heard before. "Will you choose clairvoyance or the cards?"

"It does not matter a mite to me. I just wanted to ax you a few questions, an' I want you tell me the truth, an' I don't care how it is done. Laws-a-mercy! d'you think you kin tell true?"

Without replying to the question, the fortune-teller took the cards, and after shuffling them, asked the old lady to "cut," at the same time inquiring of her the subjects upon which she wished information.

"I want to know," replied the old lady, with a sigh, "what's a goin' to become of my darter?"

"She's had a misfortune?" asked the shrewd clairvoyant.

"I know that," sighed the old lady, "but what's a goin' to become of her?"

The fortune-teller ran over the cards, and then told the old woman just what her daughter was going to do. Of course, a "black-haired gentleman," and "riches," and "honors" were in store for the girl and her mother. After some further conversation in relation to other members of the family, the old lady paid a half-dollar, and went off satisfied.

It was my turn next. I insisted on being accompanied behind the curtain by the Lieutenant, but to this the lady objected, on the ground that the presence of more than one person disturbed her mind. My inquisitiveness at last overcame my modesty, and I consented to go alone behind the curtain, with the good-looking and mysterious woman. In the darkened corner I found two cane-bottomed chairs, a table covered with a dirty cloth, and a lap dog. I seated myself in the nearest chair, at the same time informing the clairvoyant that my fortune had never been told, and I wished her to give it in full, for I was certainly ready to believe it. She sat down by my side, and took my right hand in hers. She then shook her body as if some mysterious influence was overcoming her, closed her eyes, and rested her head upon her left hand for a moment. Then shaking her body again, she drew her fore-finger across her eyes, as if wiping tears away, gave a heavy sigh, shook her body again, and then made a motion as if to assure me she was magnetized!

No sooner was she in the mysterious sleep than she commenced talking. She told me I was born near a great water, (Deercreek!) that I had been poor, but better days were in store for me; that I was born under Mars and Venus, the former lucky, and the latter unlucky; in June, the planets would change, and then I would have most excellent luck for seven years. She thought she saw a "dark spot" in my past life. She could not tell exactly what it was, but she could perceive that I had been fortunate sometimes, and unfortunate at other times.

"Did you ever deal in lottery tickets?" she asked.

"No," was the honest reply.

"Well, try it after next June," she replied, "you are sure to be successful in drawing prizes. Try speculation in real estate, too, for under Mars you will certainly succeed."

Keeping her eyes closed, she proceeded to describe my disposition, and I give her credit for coming quite near the truth. She next approached a very tender subject, by asking me if I was married? I hesitated; but at last, concluded to deceive her, and responded, "No!" One word threw me back into the miseries of single blessedness. That answer was all she wished, and immediately the following conversation ensued: —

Clairvoyant.—Just as I thought. I could see no wife before me. But you wish to get married, do you not?

Invisible.—(One fib bringing on another.)—Yes.

Clairvoyant.—As I expected. I see standing before me a fair lady, with dark complexion and dark hair. She lives in a red brick house. She loves you, and you desire to marry her, do you not?

Invisible.—Yes (Fib No. 3.)

Clairvoyant.—She dresses very finely and is fond of show, but she will make you a good wife.

Invisible.—Do you think I will marry her?

Clairvoyant.—Beyond all doubt. You are almost a husband to her now, are you not?

Invisible.—What do you mean?

(I respectfully decline giving the answer, particularly as it caused a smothered laugh from our friend the Lieutenant, who, it appears, heard all.)

Invisible.—How long do you think it will be before I can call myself a married man?

Clairvoyant.—I will never deceive. I might tell you the exact time, but that you may not be disappointed I will say within fourteen months.

Invisible.—Will I marry the dark-haired woman?

Clairvoyant.—Yes, and she will bear you seven children. But you will not have her always. She will die, and then you will get another wife.

Invisible.—Indeed!

Clairvoyant.—Yes, you will travel a great ways and get another wife, who will bear you nine children.

I thought she was coloring the picture rather too highly, and changed the subject by asking her some questions as to the past She thought I had "seen trouble," had probably speculated too much in real estate, (never owned a foot outside of the graveyard) but, after a certain period my fortune would change. After giving me sundry other items of importance, she roused herself from her magnetic sleep, going through the same contortions of the body, manipulations, etc., she had at the beginning. She then told me I would receive a letter within a week, which fact she forgot to relate while in a magnetic sleep. I gave her a dollar, her regular charge for gents, popped from behind the curtain, and with my police friend bade her good day, and took my departure. She gave me a very earnest invitation to call again, manifesting great desire to tell my future by cards, a method she said she preferred to clairvoyance, and assured me I would find my future the same by both methods.

We next visited an old negro, who lived in an alley just above, and who pretended to possess not only the gift of prophecy, but great power in the healing art. We found some twelve or fifteen white women in his parlor, awaiting the good pleasure of Sir Oracle. The only men present were three young mulattoes, whose appearance and conduct led me to believe them confederates of the old darkey. We learned from one of them that this was "medicine day," and as we could not have our fortunes told, we departed. The females present were mostly elderly women, and I judged nearly all poor. Some of them were evidently sick, and had called for advice and medicine. In the doctor's room were various mysterious devices, calculated to impress upon the visitor the belief that the house was inhabited by no ordinary personage. It was tolerably well furnished, but the atmosphere was so freighted with disagreeable smells that it was positively sickening. I was glad to reach the open air again. At the gate we met the old doctor himself, with a bottle in his hand, and a would-be dignified look on his face. I think he is the ugliest "brack man" I ever looked upon.

"Hallo, doctor," said the Lieutenant, "I have brought a young friend of mine here to consult you, but it seems he can not see you to-day."

"What does the youn' man want?" asked the doctor dignifiedly.

"To consult you," I answered.

"What for? med'cin' or de future?" he asked.

"The future," was my answer.

"Den you isn't gwyin to cum in dis day," was the reply.

"Why not?"

"Kase, 'tain't de right day for dat."

"When will be the right day for it, then?"

"Dis would be if it war only clar," replied the doctor, slamming to the gate and entering his domicil. We concluded to let him pass.

We next visited a German lady, "over the Rhine," and one, too, who has some reputation in the city as a veracious foreteller of human events. Two negro and one white woman were in waiting. The white woman, I found, had come as company with another, who was then having an interview with the fortune-teller. Ten minutes spent in conversation with the master of the house, was all the time I was delayed. I was given preference over the "ladies ob color." I ascended to a room in the second story, where I found the fortune-teller. The apartment contained a table, two or three chairs and a bed. Everything was as clean and neat "as a pin." The fortune-teller was seated at the table, with a pack of cards in her hand. Her appearance was clean and neat, but she was dressed in shocking bad taste. A faded black skirt and a calico waist, were the visible garments. Barring a crooked eye, her countenance was handsome, while her form was of that plump nature for which German females are noted. She apologized for her appearance, stating she had not been in good health for some days.

"Vat you want to know about?" was her question, as I took my seat.

"I am in search of a wife," was my answer.

"Vat, your vife run away?"

"No, no — I want to know where I can get a wife."

She made me cut a pack of cards three times, and then throwing out three on the table, said she saw a *light haired* woman, (the clairvoyant said dark haired,) with whom I was in love. She, (the light haired woman, not the fortune-teller,) loved me, and wished me to wed her, but I was jealous of her, and disliked to marry on that account. She assured me the light haired woman was virtuous and true, and if I became her husband I would be a happy man. Jealousy, she knew, was the cause of my distress, but I was jealous without cause. The cards told her that married life would suit me best after I had tried it awhile.

"You goin' avay, hey?" she asked.

"Yes," I replied.

"You goes far, mit a long distance?"

"May be to Constantinople."

That reply was satisfactory. She then made me choose nine cards from the pack, and spreading them before her, she continued my fortune. The cards, she said, declared, that I, feeling disappointed in the light haired woman, intended to go to Europe to get a very handsome wife, whom I would bring back to this country to tantalize the light haired woman. I would find many friends in Europe, and stay there until Spring.

The cards told her I was rich! I had traveled much in my young days, and had been very fortunate in accumulating riches. I had plenty of money, and all I wanted to make me happy was a wife!

She asked me if I did not think much of a dark haired woman. I replied, I could not tell. She then said there was a dark haired woman in this city who loved me; and after looking over the cards again, she observed I did not know the woman. She was quite sure, however, the woman loved me, and thought if I would call again she could tell me where I might find that woman.

A good deal more she told me, about as correct as the above, which amused me very much. She charged me only fifty cents, which though only half what the clairvoyant asked, was as much as the "fortune" was worth.

Our next visit was to an aged woman residing on John street, not far from Richmond. She lived in an old one-story house, and occupied two rooms. Our "call" was made about three o'clock in the afternoon, and we found the "enchantress" at home. Beside herself there was another female present, whom she called Mary. Mary, who appeared to have reached venerable maidenhood, was tall and slim, with red blotches on her face, and anything but agreeable in person. She had a broom in her hand, and scarcely noticed our entrance.

Madame was sitting at a table, and as we approached, saluting us with "Good Day," asked us to take seats. She seemed to be about sixty or seventy years of age, and to weigh some two hundred pounds. Her face was much shrivcled, and her eyes were dim; but she was quite talkative, and appeared to prosecute her profession with great zest. She had on a dark, dirty dress, an antiquated silk mantilla, and a greasy-looking "hood" bonnet.

The appearance of the room was disgusting, being dirty in the extreme. The bed was not made up, the chairs were covered with dust, and the walls looked as if they had not been cleaned for a century. Old rags, bottles, and different household articles were piled up in corners, cooking utensils, medicines, table ware and clothing were packed indiscriminately on the shelves, while here and there upon the walls hung branches of herbs wrapped in remnants of worn-out clothing. In fact, everything betokened a want of tidiness, industry and intelligence. True, the old woman informed us that the apparent confusion of the furniture was caused from the fact that Mary was "cleaning house;" but I am inclined to think that Mary would never, were she to undertake the job, get through with it.

"Do you tell fortunes?" asked I of Madam, after the Lieutenant and myself were seated.

"Well yes, sometimes," was the reply — "Do you want yourn told?"

"Yes."

"And yourn, too?" asked she of the Lieutenant.

"Well, no, I guess not," replied the officer, "as I am not anxious to know the future."

"Just as you like, sir," was the reply of Madam.

"Mary, give me the cards, and shut the door, as there's no knowin' who might come in."

Mary obeyed, and retired to the back room, and apparently busied herself in domestic concerns.

"How will ye have yer fortune told — by the planets or cards?" asked the old woman.

"By the planets," was my ready reply, that being, to say the least, the more romantic method.

"Well, I'm afeared I can't tell by the planets to-day. You see I've been sick, and I've sorter got the head-ache, and I don't feel a bit like reading the planets."

"I would much prefer that mode."

"But if I tell ye by the planets, I'd have to charge ye a dollar, when I charge only half a dollar by the cards."

"That makes no difference," was my reply, feeling somewhat liberal, on the strength, perhaps, of the Twelfth street Astrologist assuring me I was so immensely rich.

"I hardly feel able to read the planets to day, so ye'll have to take the cards," was her answer. As she shuffled the pack, she asked me, "Well, what is it ye seek — love or luck?"

"Luck."

"And not a bit of love?"

"None — I've had enough of that."

"Well, that's strange for a young man; but I suppose ye

knows best. Afore I commence, I must tell ye that ye must make the change for me."

"I guess I can do that."

"Ye see there is so much counterfeit money goin' about, that its mighty easy for one to pass it on them as aint a judge. I can't tell one from tother, and they've got a good deal on me; so I'm detarmined not to lose any more, but jist make them what gets their fortune told give me the change."

"Ye has had bad luck, that's plainly to be seen."

"That's all right," I replied, "I will give you the change."

She bade me cut the pack, which I did, and then running her eyes slowly over the cards, she told me what each one indicated. Her words, as near as I can recollect, were as follows:

"Ye has had bad luck, that's plainly to be seen. At present yer luck's good, and there's better days comin' to ye. You've got an enemy — he's been an enemy to ye some years. He's a dark complected man, and has worked hard agin ye. Don't ye know of any dark complected man as is yer enemy?"

"I do not."

"Well, there is one, certain, and he's tried to injure ye,

but without success. He comes behind yer luck all through here. And here's a woman—a fair and lovely woman—and I should say she is yer wife. Aint you got a wife?"

"No," answered the Lieutenant for me, seeing I hesitated.

"No! I believe ye are telling me a lie, for here's yer house, and yer either got a wife, or yer boarding with a woman; there's no mistake about that. Well, yer to have luck about yer house—everything will prosper amazingly. This woman that yer living with, be she yer wife or not, she's yer friend, and is devoted to ye. But here's another woman, with dark complexion. She's yer enemy. She's been tryin' to make trouble about yer house, an' she is a goin' to keep tryin'. But as she's behind yer luck, she can do ye no harm. Here's a letter for ye; it contains a large amount of money and good news. Ye'll get it in a few days, for it's coming now. Don't ye expect a letter?"

"Yes—but none with money in."

"Well, this has got good news and a heap of money in it. It's writ and on its way now. Soon after ye get it, ye'll sign a contract or paper of some kind, which will be a fortune to ye. Ye'll sign the paper with a light-complexioned man—now, havent ye dealings with a light-complexioned man?"

"I believe I have."

"Well he's a friend to ye. Ye'll git a fortun' I think by him. Yer enemy appears here agin', but still he's behind yer luck. Yer to take a journey afore long. This card says yer to go on wheels, and this one that yer to cross water. The journey will be a long one, and ye'll be a little disappointed at first, but ye'll have luck on the journey. Ye'll git what ye go for, and come back pleased. The dark complexioned woman appears during that journey, but she can do ye no harm, for she's behind yer luck. There's good luck all through the cards, and ye'll certainly have it. Now lets try it again," and so saying she commenced shuffling the cards.

While she was mixing the cards, the Lieutenant gave me a nudge with the toe of his boot. Looking at him, he directed me to a certain part of the room, where two mammoth rats seemed to be enjoying a social chit-chat. A third and a fourth one came through the hearth, and went capering about the floor apparently in search of food. The Lieutenant stamped on the floor with his foot to frighten them, but they merely gave a roguish look, and then resumed their frolicking. They were afterwards joined by others, and all kept us company until we left the house. They evidently had no fear of the Fortune-Teller.

Again I cut the pack, when Madam declared I had cut my own thoughts. Glancing slowly over the cards, she told pretty much the same story as she did before. My enemies she declared were behind my luck all the time, and it was impossible for them to harm me.

INVISIBLE AT A PIC-NIC.

I WAS invited to attend a Pic-Nic. The day for the excursion was a lovely one, the sky being clear, the air exhilarating, and nature, refreshed by a late rain, clothed in her fairest garb. We were going on a steamer to North Bend, and were to leave the wharf *precisely* at 7 o'clock. At that hour I proceeded to the boat, and was not a little surprised to find no one but the crew aboard. Thinking I had made a mistake in the time, I sat down to patiently await "the turn of events." A long, long hour rolled by before any of the party appeared, and they then came leisurely along, and in small crowds. There came old men, with locks of gray, and young ones, who had endeavored to extend their hight, by rearing enormous pieces of linen beneath their ears. Each had upon his arm a heavy laden basket, covered with a neat white napkin. The ladies, whose countenances displayed dispositions

"From grave to gay, from lively to severe,"

clung closely to their protectors or their gallants, as they walked carefully over the miserable pavement of the levee. Our boat had but one place for the party, and that was the boiler deck, so arranged as to make a kind of sheltered promenade. To the boiler deck, then, all came, and for a while we had a scene of beautiful confusion, caused by the hurrying to and fro to stow away baskets and bonnets, the greetings of acquaintances, the smacking of female lips upon female lips, (a horrible sacrilege!) and the exclamations each gave vent to. Let the reader imagine him or herself at Invisible's side, and pay attention to what is going on. Listen:

"Bless me! I was so afraid I would be left, that I hardly closed my eyes all night. It is —— "

"John, where did you place the basket? You are so careless, that if I don't watch you, we will be without any —— "

"Just look at Miss Clark, with what care she has dressed herself. I apprehend this is her first appearance at a picnic, for a white dress soon presents a horrible appearance in the —— "

"How terrible Miss Baker looks in that calico dress and shabby kiss-me-quick. Really, I should think Mr. Thompson would be ashamed of her appear —— "

"Billy! Billy! come here, darling. If you wander from me you will certainly be drowned."

"Oh! gracious, I have left my woodland shoes at home. Mr. Johnson, will you please go after them?—it will not take long." (Johnson flies up the levee.)

"Why, Mrs. Jenkins, how do you do? I am so glad ——"

"Oh! Oh! catch my bonnet; it's flying overboard, and —— "

"Do you think the boat perfectly safe, Mr. Jones?—I'm so timid when —— "

"I declare, I forgot those preserves. I told Nancy to set them near the basket, and she —— "

"What a sweet bouquet you have, Blanche, it is really inspi—— "

"Where's the music? Ain't we to have no danc—— "

"I'm so fatigued—the walk was so long that —— "

"How long are we to wait? It is certainly past the hour."

A blow from the steam whistle causes a general shriek among the ladies, and a laugh from the gents, but has the good effect of hurrying up a few laggards who are coming down the wharf. The Captain informs one of the committee that he is ready, but one of the committee says he must wait for the music. The music arrives in a half hour, and then it is ascertained that the Wiggins branch of the party have not yet arrived. Another half hour brings the Wigginses, and then we are ready to shove off. The Captain rings the bell for the twentieth time, the planks are pulled in, the hawser let loose, and at half-past 9 o'clock the boat leaves the wharf

Now it is more pleasant. The speed of the boat gives us a fine breeze, which proves an agreeable offset to the scorching rays of the sun upon the deck overhead, and the heat of the boilers beneath our feet. To be sure, we might have started at the hour named in the cards, and had our ride upon the river before old Sol became so furious. But we are glad to get off at last, and feel confident of having a pleasant time after a while.

While passing by the city, we return the greeting of those raftsmen, who stop their work and whirl their hats, and of those ladies in the houses upon the river banks, who wave their handkerchiefs while we are in sight. We are inclined to pity them, as they are laboring in the hot sun, or cooped up between walls of brick and mortar. The contrast between their position and ours makes us feel contented.

The musicians now tune their instruments, the floor-managers place with pride their gay rosettes upon their breasts, and preparations are made to commence the dance. The signal is given, and then we have a rush, all striving to be the "head couple" in a quadrille. Those who obtain that honorable (?) position appear glad, and those who don't, very much displeased. But now we discover another inconvenience! — the boat is either too small for the party, or the party too large for the boat. All wish to dance — none will give way — and the consequence is, the deck is crowded, the cotillions considerably "mixed," and there is no room to move without running against somebody.

"Never mind," says one of the committee, who appears to be a real philosopher, "we will have plenty of room when we get into the woods." With this consolation we commence the dance, and by squeezing, pushing and crowding, manage to get through the figures. To be sure, corns suffer not a little, while the exercise, with the crowded condition of the deck, draws the perspiration in streams even from the leanest. Those who have been blessed with a good proportion of flesh suffer excruciatingly, and would wish themselves at home, if they were not *enjoying* a pic-nic excursion.

The dance continues with slight intermissions until about half-past 12 o'clock, when we arrive in sight of North Bend. The boat rounds to, lands, and now all our troubles are at an end. How happy we are! The ladies have scarcely patience to await the erection of a gangway, that they may pass safely off, while the gentlemen talk of leaping from the guards to the shore. None venture, however, to perform the daring feat, wisely concluding it better to wait and perspire, than run the risk of a broken neck. The gangway is at last erected, strong and secure, and off we go.

There! that lady with the orange-colored dress has had it dreadfully torn by a nail, which so frightened the one with the blue scarf, that she would have fallen overboard had not the gentleman with the brass buttons on his coat caught her. What a distressing occurrence! Will our miseries never end? Heavens! Miss Thompson has become so intimidated in walking ashore, she has dropped her fan into the river, and in trying to catch it, young Mr. Wiggins follows after! How the ladies shriek when they see him spluttering about in two feet water! The mate of the steamer, with a cunning look in his eye, offers to throw him a rope, but Mrs. Wiggins, a heroic lady, protests it needless, because she knows he is a good swimmer! He scrambles out of the water uninjured, the sudden bath doing him more good than harm. After this warning, those who were yet on board were more careful, and in the course of half an hour, the party were all safe on shore. We scrambled up the banks, to a delightful grove, where, throwing ourselves upon the long grass, we soon forgot the troubles of the past in the pleasures of the present.

"Oh! what a pleasant place is this North Bend! To us, confined day and night, within the limits of a busy city, toiling over the desk and the work-bench, it is a Paradise. Here, in this ancient grove, we breathe a pure air, which quickly invigorates our system to a surprising degree. The superb scenery around charms us, while the enchanting music of the forest songsters thrills our very hearts. How magnificent the foliage of the trees, here shooting high into the air, and there spreading their giant arms in every direction.

How these enormous oaks bow to the breeze which fans our foreheads, careless of the burning sun-rays which here and there pierce through their branches. And there is *La Belle Riviere* right at our feet, a pretty stream indeed, as it rolls gently at the base of these high hills. The lofty cliff above us looks grand from here, with its dark gray rocks partly covered with green moss. If I can ever be persuaded to move from this spot, I will ascend to the top of that cliff, and view the surrounding country. But here to my left, rugged nature has received an embellishment. Look at that hillock, with its deep green grass and pretty shrubbery. It is inclosed all around, near its base, with a plain open board fence, without even a gate to admit those who would seek entrance there. The massive trees outside the inclosure shade the whole hill, and the slow waving of the long grass, gives it a melancholy look. That spot was chosen by one who died while occupying the Presidential chair, as his last resting-place. It overlooks the country for miles in every direction, including the site of the old log cabin which was once his residence, and the valley which, by his own hands, was, from a wilderness, made to blossom like a rose. How uniform upon all sides is the elevation of that hillock, so regular, that one would think it thrown up by the hands of careful men. Right upon its summit is a low brick vault. That vault is the Tomb of Harrison. No monument marks the grave or indicates the gratitude of a people to the slumbering soldier, who battled so nobly during the war of 1812. He

"Sleeps his last sleep"

in that lonely, yet lovely spot, selected by himself years

before his death. As you approach it, tread softly, for I know you revere the memory of Harrison."

Thus spake old Mr. Wiggins, while many of the wearied company gathered around him, upon a grassy knoll, but a few paces from the boat. He was proceeding, at our request, to give some incidents in Harrison's life, when we were startled by a deafening shriek not far from us. It came from Miss Johnson, who, white as a sheet, and trembling like a leaf, cried "snake! snake!" Instantly twenty clubs, supported by twenty hands, sailed through the air to Miss Johnson's rescue. Approaching her with the rapidity of lightning, the deliverers commenced beating — *a crooked piece of wood,* which, lying in the grass, appeared to Miss J. to be a real live snake, and nothing else. In fact, even after she had recovered from the shock by means of several heavy drafts from a smelling-bottle, she could not be convinced that her fears had been groundless, until young Mr. Wiggins broke the deceitful stick in two, and put a piece in his mouth. After this occurrence, however, the ladies insisted on moving out of the high grass, for fear of snakes. The gentlemen consented, and lugged their heavy baskets up the hill. But there was very little shade there, and the ladies, after hard persuasion, decided to submit to the long grass and run the risk of snakes rather than be exposed to the scorching sun; so down they marched again.

While the gentlemen were erecting swings, the ladies prepared dinner. Each emptied her basket upon tablecloths spread upon the grass, and then arranged every article in its place. As soon as they were ready, all commenced screaming "dinner! dinner!!" and laughed and clapped their hands, as the wearied and exhausted men came running from all directions to partake of the welcome refreshments. A merry dinner was that. There was not one but was hungry, and some ravenously so. They talked, chatted, and laughed, as squatting upon the grass they ate without knives, forks, or spoons. Every thing, too, seemed to taste so much better in the woods, though cooked at home, and then, as Miss Jenkins insisted, there was something so romantic in it.

It was three o'clock before the company rose from the table, or rather tablecloths, and then the amusements of the day commenced. While some enjoyed a dance upon the green, others were swinging, or playing with grace-hoops or balls. Conventionalities were thrown aside, and all enjoyed themselves as they thought best. For instance, Mr. Brown put on Miss Jones' bonnet, and Miss Jones, out of revenge, wore Mr. Brown's hat. Then there was a general exchange —ladies strode around with coats and hats on, and gents strutted about with mantillas on their shoulders and bonnets on their heads. Miss Dandy and Miss Scruggs dared Mr. Rush to a set-to, and he, accepting the challenge, the ladies got him by the hair and made him cry "Enough!" Mrs. Johnson and Mr. Potts ran a foot-race, the former winning, by the latter falling over a stump and skinning his nose. Young Mr. Wiggins made a wreath of clover, which he placed on the head of Miss Jenkins, as he eloquently (as he thought,) delivered a portion of the "May Queen." Some of the elderly ladies jumped the rope, for the first time, as one of them declared, for thirty years.

These were some of the pleasures the party enjoyed in the wild, wild woods, but as there is no sweet without its bitter, they also met with many casualties, some of which it will be well enough to mention.

The corpulent, Mr. Thumps, slipped while attempting to climb a tree, and came near breaking a leg. As it was, he limped ridiculously. Miss Pattie fainted on discovering a caterpillar crawling down her neck. As she fell into the arms of Mr. Snooks, no great damage was done. Mrs. Brown was accidentally struck in the face with a ball, which caused a circlet of black around one of her blue eyes, that by no means enhanced her beauty. Mrs. Jenkins and Mrs. Jones had a very narrow escape, having been chased by a furious bull out of a pasture, whither they had strayed in search of wild flowers. While descending a hill, the modest Miss Clark, who had been careful to dress all in white, slipped and rolled a distance of some forty feet. As may be imagined her dress was spotless no longer. In endeavoring to save Miss Clark, Mr. Thompson burst his pants in a shocking manner, and was obliged to retire to the boat, until the damage was repaired. While playing blind-man's buff, Miss White ran against a tree with so much force as to set her nose to bleeding. As Mr. Black was endeavoring to take a comfortable snooze in a retired part of the grove, a large bug crawled into one of his ears. It gave him a severe pain and he came dashing into the party like a madman. Fortunately Dr. Pinch was present, and by the use of his instruments, he soon pulled out the intruder. A naughty bee stung Miss Pluck upon the arm and caused her to screech dreadfully.

Yet, amid all these mishaps, there was general joy and hilarity. The birds were hushed by the sweet tones of some of the ladies, as they occasionally hummed over a favorite air, while the woods resounded with joyful acclamations and heartfelt laughter. What a treat it is, indeed, to the resident of the city, to spend a social day with friends in the woodlands of the country!

At 5 o'clock, the captain of the boat notified us to prepare for our return trip. Fatigued, and almost exhausted as we were, all disliked to leave that lovely spot. But go we must, for steamboats, when chartered by the day, wait for no man. What a time the ladies had, in finding their capes, their fans, and their bonnets! — scattered here, and there, and everywhere. The boat's bell rung, for the third time, and a screeching noise came from her whistle, which could not be misunderstood. Aboard we must go — and aboard we went in a hurry. Fortunately, no one fell overboard this time, and we soon bade adieu to the pretty scenery of North Bend.

The trip up the river was very much the same as the trip down, only it was not *quite* so suffocating. Many were "fagged out," and had no desire to dance; consequently, the deck was not so much crowded. The boat arrived at her wharf in the city about dusk, and each of the party wended his or her way home, all, of course, "highly delighted with the pleasures of the day."

INVISIBLE AMONG THE CLOUDS:

HIS PRIVATE JOURNAL OF HIS FIRST AND ONLY ÆRIAL VOYAGE.

City Lot, Monday, October 1, 3 o'clock, p. m. — Feel aspiring. Ruminate upon the follies of earth, and dwell upon the imaginary pleasures of the heavens. Below, the air is unwholesome; above it is pure and exhilarating: on earth, filth and wretchedness greet one upon every hand; in the skies all is clear and beautiful, from the tiny glittering stars of the night, to the gauzy clouds which float so sweetly through space, exposing every varying hue to the light of the God of Day. Cast my eyes at the monster passenger balloon, America, in process of inflation, and think I would like to go up.

Invisible before he went up.

3½ p. m.—Approach the agent to inquire relative to the fare.

"Good afternoon, sir," is my salute.

"Ah? Monsieur," is his reply; "bootiful day! — bootiful! — bootiful!"

"Mons. Godard intends taking several passengers with him this afternoon?"

"Godard? Passenger? Oh! yes-sare; seven passenger. Bootiful ride. Rise up ze easy as—as—as dey take sick man from ze bed—sail magnificent as great big ship wizout ze wave—grand, Monsieur! bootiful indeed?"

"Are all the seats taken?" I asked, animated by the agent's brief but extravagant description of an aerial voyage.

"Ze can have von, Monsieur," was his reply, holding up a finger. "Like ze American omnibus, ze has room for von more, all ze time—ha, ha, ha!"

"What's the fare?"

"Fifty dollare. Cheap, Monsieur, so beautiful is ze ride."

"Fifty dollars! That's a big pile my dear fellow—much more than I can afford. I would like however to take the ride, very much, and I tell you what I am willing to do. If you will dead-head one-half the amount, and—"

"Ze *dead*-head!" exclaims the agent, in amazement, shrugging his shoulders as he continued, "Ah, Monsieur is mistaken—ze balloon no kill—ze balloon no make dead-head. Ze go up so bootiful—ze sail so—so—bootiful, and ze come down gentle as ze baby on ze muzzer—muzzer—vot you call it? oh, yes! ze muzzer's lap!"

"You don't understand me. I intended to tell you that I can not afford to pay fifty dollars; but if you will take me at half-price, I will go. I will give you twenty-five dollars."

"Twenty-five dollare! Ah! Monsieur, too mooch little."

"It is all I can afford to give."

"Well, Monsieur, you mooch shentleman. I take ze

twenty-five dollare. No shentleman give me more, you take ze seat. You understand ?"

"Yes, sir."

"But, Monsieur, you say nosing to every shentlemans about ze twenty-five dollare."

"Not a word before the balloon starts."

"Ver good, Monsieur," and we shake hands, both evidently gratified at the result of the interview.

FOUR O'CLOCK, P. M. — Examine the balloon, and find all secure. Stiff wind, but a clear sky. Hope no fool, with more money to spare than I, will out-bid me for the seat.

HALF PAST 4 O'CLOCK, P. M. — Wind grows stronger; black frowning clouds overcast the sky, and altogether things above look rather dismal. Wish I had my money back.

FIVE O'CLOCK, P. M.—Monsieur informs me I can consider my seat secure. Try to feel elated, but after sundry unsuccessful efforts, postpone the attempt until we go up. The enclosure is crowded with ladies and gentlemen, the former everywhere expressing great anxiety to see the "daring individuals who are going up *in* the balloon." Begin to think I have received twenty-five dollars worth of importance, and *ought* to be delighted. Tell a few friends confidentially that I am to ascend, and they confidentially tell everybody else. Find I am a lion!

QUARTER PAST FIVE O'CLOCK, P. M.—Borrow an overcoat, and with my fellow-passengers, slip into the old steam engine-house, in a corner of the balloon enclosure, to avoid being bored, and to await orders. We cheer each other up, and joyously (?) anticipate delights in store. Try to feel happy and look smiling. Think of the Prophet who went

16

"up yonder" without casting off his "mortal coil," and wonder if he felt then as I do now.

Half past five o'clock, p. m.—Receive orders, and the passengers consisting of Col. Latham, Mr. Wm. Hoel, Mr. J. C. Bellman and myself, march out single file—all armed with overcoats — press through the crowd, and step into the car amid the plaudits of thousands. After seating ourselves, cast a glance at the rigging and think it is rather delicate. Friends crowd around to shake hands, wish us good luck and see if we look frightened. Monsieur is afraid they will injure the balloon, and after trying in vain to keep them back, curses like a trooper, in French. Amused at his gesticulations, and really begin to feel merry.

Twenty-five minutes of six o'clock, p. m.—"Let go!" shouts Monsieur, and the command being obeyed, we glide gently upward. In the crowd I recognise a score of familiar faces, waving us a hearty adieu. Animated by the scene, I involuntarily rise to my feet, and leaning over the side of the car, return the salutations. I am seized with the most thrilling sensations of pleasure and delight, and speechless I feast my eyes upon the scene below. The great city lessens to our view, until its houses appear like toys, while its streets seem animated with beings no larger than ants. Cheers reach our ears from every direction, and enthusiastically we wave our hats in response to the noises of our fellow-citizens below.

Quarter to six. p. m.—"Great Heavens! gentlemen, look there!" exclaims Mr. H—, our eyes are instantly withdrawn from the fast-receding city and cast in the direction pointed out. Oh! what beauty. There lies *La Belle Riviere*, its placid bosom glistening like silver in the setting sun. It winds its way east and west as far as the eye can reach, the tall hills which border its banks failing to hide it from our view. And what a charming earth! The forests are gone, the cities are gone, and the earth has the appearance of one vast garden, with its tiny groves, clusters of miniature houses, sparkling rivulets, and its well-planned walks. It has changed its form, too. We no longer see the earth of convex, but of concave form, and it lies below us an immense basin with its centre directly beneath us and rising uniformly upon every side. Oh! this is, indeed, delightful! —well worth seeing, even at the risk of breaking one's neck.

Six o'clock, p. m.—Flying on the wings of the wind! How pleasant to be thus floating between heaven and earth, no evidence of propelling power about you, yet conscious you are traveling at almost lightning speed! We seem to float as gaily along as the light clouds of a Summer day. It is glorious—delightful beyond expression! Passengers shake hands, and congratulate each other in their joy.

Quarter past six o'clock, p. m.—Monsieur Godard, who has been busily engaged in the rigging of his aerial ship, descends to the car, and shaking us all by the hand, exclaims: "Bootiful! bootiful!" We all unite in the expression of delight, whereupon Monsieur draws a bottle of wine from his hamper, and invites us to drink the health of all below us. One declines, for the reason that he is a pledged member of a temperance association. Another replies that the argument does not hold good in our locality. He has some knowledge of law, and is sure the jurisdiction of no temperance society was ever extended to our present altitude. The temperance man acknowledges the reasoning good, and as the atmosphere is rather chilly, concludes to take a sip of wine. Company getting rather lively.

HALF PAST SIX, P. M.—On! on! we fly. A bright golden cloud *below* us in the west, excites our admiration. Gradually its brightness pales, and suddenly its beauty changes to a frowning black. Dismal clouds seem to be approaching us from every side, indicating a storm and danger. Delightful as is the airy ride, begin to wish myself again on *terra firma.*

QUARTER TO SEVEN O'CLOCK, P. M.— We are now among the clouds. We seem to be floating between an upper and a lower tier. Above, all is calm, but below, vast masses of vapor roll over and over, as if driven by the fury of demons. We lean over the sides of the car and listen. Old Boreas has his harps in tune, and we can hear his terrible music as he flies o'er hills and through the valleys. The clouds heave and roll below us, and listening still, we hear the storm approach. Following the first gush of wind, comes the rain, and we hear it falling upon mother earth. The sound is not unlike that made by a railroad train when in full motion. We hope to escape the fury of that storm, and to land in safety.

TEN MINUTES BEFORE SEVEN O'CLOCK, P. M.—"No good! no good!" cries the commander of our ship, as he sees the upper and lower tier of clouds coming together. He drags all his ballast from beneath the seats, and prepares to heave it overboard. The upper layer of clouds still descends, and now we are enveloped in mist. Overboard goes the ballast, and up we fly with lightning speed. Monsieur evidently wants to get above the clouds. On that depends our safety.

SEVEN O'CLOCK, P. M.—Still we ascend. The clouds seem to shed a halo of mellow light into the car, enabling us to distinctly read the figures upon the barometer. The air is very chilly and damp, and all experience a strange rumbling noise in the ears. The water pours in torrents from the neck of the balloon into the car, making our position decidedly uncomfortable. Still I wish to go higher. I desire to scale the bank of clouds above us, and again, in the unobstructed ocean of air, gaze upon the bright stars, and witness the rising of the silver moon. Up! up! into the mysterious space, where meteors dance, and worlds vie with each other in brilliancy.

TEN MINUTES PAST SEVEN O'CLOCK, P. M.—Our ballast is all gone, and still we are in the clouds. Every moment the balloon becomes heavier, and now we must sink. Our commander, with his hand upon the valve-rope, shakes his head and says, "No good." The passengers, however, do not seem to apprehend danger. They joke quite pleasantly at their uncomfortable condition.

FIFTEEN MINUTES PAST SEVEN O'CLOCK, P. M. — "Down! down!" cries the captain, as seizing first one and then the other by the collar, he forced us to the bottom of the car. Out went the anchor, and then followed a sensation of rapid descent.

"Remember," says Mr. Bellman, "not a man leaves the car until it is safely secured."

"Not a man," is the response from his three fellow-passengers who lie closely huddled together in the bottom of the car.

"No good! no good!" fairly shrieked the aeronaut, as throwing one leg over, and resting himself on the side of the car, he grasps the anchor-rope with one hand, the valve-rope with the other, and casts his eyes into the darkness below.

Into the storm sinks our aerial ship, and now with the speed of lightning we seem to fly! Our anchor touches and drags upon the ground as we skim over the fields. Crash! it tears away a fence. The balloon seems to make a spring, and we feel the car gliding over tree-tops. The prongs of the anchor strike a tree, and taking a firm hold, the balloon is checked in its furious career. Like a monster baffled, the frail vessel struggles fearfully to be freed. The winds howl furiously, the rain descends in torrents, as it swings rapidly to and fro over the tall forest trees. Monsieur Godard still keeps his position on the side of the car, holding the valve open to allow the gas to escape, while the passengers lie in the bottom of the car in silent watchfulness.

TWENTY MINUTES PAST SEVEN, P. M.—The anchor breaks! The balloon gives a fearful leap, and falls almost to the ground. Now it rises again, and we feel ourselves being dragged through a cornfield. Now we are in a forest, and as we dash along, the weight of the car crushes the upper branches of trees. Again we are in the open fields, and our balloon, its power of ascent much weakened by the loss of gas, can not lift us from, but drags us over the ground. We encounter another blast of the storm, and up we go again, but only to fall heavily to the ground. Are we safe? No, the monster has not yet expended his power. Again we are lifted and borne rapidly through a field. Suddenly the car strikes a tree, and Mons. Godard is hurled to the earth. Thus lightened of its load, the balloon makes another and most fearful leap of it, this time in its descent bringing the car with terrible force against a tree. It was partially upset, and this time Col. Latham and Mr. Hoel were thrown from the car, at a great distance from the earth. The balloon rises again, and death seems certain to Mr. Bellman and myself.

EIGHT O'CLOCK, P. M.—Found myself about half an hour ago lying flat on my back on the ground, the trunk of a felled tree partially covering my body. I can not move. I remember an awful crash, which seemed to stun me, and my next recollection was the position described. The rain beating in my face revived me. Looking up, I descried a figure in the dark.

"Is that you, Mr. Bellman?" I asked.

"Ah! Invisible," he instantly responded, "are you there? I was fearful you were killed. Are you hurt?"

"I can not tell — I am pinned to the ground by this tree. Where are the balance of the party?"

"Heaven only knows, as I have not seen or heard one of them, since they were thrown out of the car. But you must get out of that position."

He instantly commenced removing the earth from under me, with his hands. I was soon able to move, and with his assistance regained my feet. I was rejoiced to find no bones broken, though I could scarcely stand alone. It appears, that in rising, the net-work of the balloon caught in the prongs of a dead tree. So strong was the cordage, and powerful the gale, that the tree was uprooted, and fell with a crash upon the car. Mr. Bellman escaped, but I was thrown out of the car, and directly beneath the trunk of the tree. A stout limb, which penetrated the car, and struck the earth not far from my head, was all that prevented my being crushed.

I was scarcely relieved from my uncomfortable position, before Monsieur came running up, frantically clapping his hands, and weeping. He supposed we had all been killed; but when he discovered his error, his joy was as nervously shown as his former grief. Next, Col. Latham came staggering through the dark, earnestly inquiring if we were safe. He reported himself only slightly injured; but said Mr. Hoel was badly hurt. He and Mr. Bellman returned for Mr. Hoel, and soon found him, and conducted him to the spot where I was receiving the congratulations of the little Frenchman.

The rain still fell in torrents, and a chilling wind brought it dashingly against us. We had no knowledge of our whereabouts, except that we were in a cornfield. Arranging that their shouts should be responded to, Col. Latham and Mr. Bellman started in search of a house. After wandering through the fields in darkness for some time, they espied a welcome light, which brought them to the farm-house of Mr. Smith, near Waynesville, Ohio. The farmer gave them a hearty reception, and on learning the state of affairs instantly dispatched a messenger for the nearest surgeon, and with his farm hands came to our relief. How welcome were their returning shouts! We are now seated around the cheerful hearth of Farmer Smith, who, with his kind lady, is doing all in his power to make us comfortable. I am done with balloon-sailing.

TUESDAY MORNING, 7 O'CLOCK, A. M.—Slept soundly last night, but wake up a dilapidated human being this morning. My arms are stiff, my legs are stiff, while my neck positively refuses to allow my head the slightest motion. I can not walk — can scarcely move. Dear me! but these airy flights do use a fellow up. And my clothes! all torn and soiled with mud! What a plight to return to the city in, after the gay departure of yesterday. Thank Heaven, however, I am able to return at all. I've had enough of ballooning.

Invisible after he came down.

The above ends the journal. Of the party of balloon-excursionists, Mr. Hoel was severely injured, having been thrown with his breast against a stump, when hurled from the car, and it was several weeks before he recovered; Mons. Godard and Mr. Bellman received but trifling injuries; Col. Latham was disabled by a sprained ankle; and it was many weeks before Invisible's "skewed" neck allowed his head to move with freedom.

PICKINGS FROM INVISIBLE'S CITY OBSERVATIONS.

A CLIQUE FRIGHTENED.

In the old Algerine Ward, no one commands a stronger influence at a municipal election than Knocking Bill, an individual who has not only exhibited his patriotism as a volunteer on the fields of Mexico, but did some sharp shooting and tall running, (when running was the order of the day), with the unfortunate Lopez fillibusters. At home, he confines his exertions principally to running "wid der masheen," and putting his friends into office. Ever surrounded with a party of kindred spirits, he may be termed the "Regulator" of his ward, and if things are not conducted to suit him, why—look out for a muss!

The Fighting Politician of the Algerine Ward.

It was in the Spring of 1852, that Knocking Bill fixed up the ward ticket of his party, some two weeks before the good people were called upon to select their candidates. He made no secret, either, of his work, and told all, "high and low," that must be the ticket, even if the nominating meeting were to break up in a row. Knocking Bill's edict was, of course, supreme, and his ticket was nominated without opposition.

The succeeding day, however, the "Regulator" heard that the "Water Street Clique" had publicly repudiated the nominations, and with

"Souls in arms and eager for the fray,"

were getting up a ticket of their own, which they were determined to "put through." This repudiation, too, was in the face of the fact that a "Water street man" was on Bill's ticket, and as may be supposed, aroused the indignation of the Regulator. He was not easily alarmed, yet he felt that this occasion was one which required caution to insure success; the more particularly as the ticket of the Water street clique was to be kept secret until the day of the election, which gave him no opportunity to worry the candidates into a declination. He soon determined on his course of action, and proceeded at once to ascertain the time and place of the next meeting of his dissatisfied political brethren. That information was soon acquired—the clique were to meet on a certain night in the parlor of a certain hotel.

The night for the meeting of the clique came, and found Bill and his "right bower" the first persons in the room. They had entered it noiselessly and unobserved. Their first business was to seek a convenient hiding-place where, unseen, they could see and hear the entire proceedings. The only place they could find was beneath a sofa, the legs of which, however, were so short Bill could not get beneath it. Nothing daunted, he ordered his companion to elevate the article of furniture until he spread himself upon the floor, and then lower it upon his ponderous frame, and press it down until his compressed body would permit the sofa to rest upon the carpet. This was done, and Bill's companion left the room. Nearly an hour did the Regulator lay under that sofa so squeezed he could scarcely breathe, before any one entered the room. At last the clique arrived, and securing the door, seated themselves around a table, uncorked their bottles, and proceeded to business. They completed their ticket, and in great good humor adopted their plans.

Bill was more than once the subject of their conversation, and though many hard things were said of him, he bore it all with patience. To be sure, at one time when the most puny of the clique, heated with liquor, declared he could "wallop" Bill in a fair fight, that individual came near giving him an opportunity to test the matter, but was fortunately enabled to control himself by giving a slight grit of his teeth.

About one o'clock in the morning, after the clique had disposed of its business, and a large quantity of liquors had been drank, the chairman, in high glee, remarked, "Now, boys, we'll adjourn. We've got everything fixed for success, and our ticket is sure to win. Ha! ha! won't Knocking Bill feel bad when he's beat, and, ha! ha! he won't know how we headed him. Ha! ha! ha! ha! but it's rich, boys. How he will rip and stave through the ward, and, ha! ha! ha! how we will laugh at him."

All joined most heartily in the laugh.

"I wish," continued the chairman, "ha! ha! ha! I wish Bill was here to laugh with us, for then——"

"Haw! haw! haw!" came in thunder-tones from beneath the sofa. The wine-heated politicians jumped to their feet, and stared each other in the face. "Haw! haw! haw!" came from beneath the sofa again, this time almost shaking the walls of the building. The chairman turned pale, and, seizing his hat, stepped softly toward the door, as he mumbled —

"By thunder, that is Knocking Bill's laugh. We're caught and done for. I'm off, sure as you're born, and will have no more to do with this ticket."

He left the room as soon as possible, and so did his companions. Knocking Bill kicked the sofa off his body, stretched his limbs, brushed off his clothes, disposed of the untouched drinks upon the table, and then gave one of his heartiest "haw! haw! haws!" His work was accomplished. The Water street clique dare not meet him in open battle; and now that they were aware of his presence at their meeting, they would be glad to "keep dark" until after the election. Such proved to be the result. Knocking Bill's ticket was elected without opposition from his party. He boasted much of that victory, and frequently declared that one of his hearty "haw! haw! haws!" was worth more than all the politicians in Water street.

A GLOOMY PICTURE OF LIFE.

Not far from the corner of John and Kemble streets, lives a young widow, the mother of some three or four children, whose history presents one of those instances in life which never fail to touch the heart. She is well educated and accomplished, and possesses those intellectual charms which adorn the highest positions of society. Her youth was happy; but in an unfortunate hour she married one who became a drunkard, destroyed her peace, and broke her heart. He is dead, and the wife is left penniless, to feed, clothe, guard and protect her children. Her condition may be readily imagined. She has accomplishments which, if she had been in a condition to use them, would have yielded her ample support. She is capable of teaching music, and those delicate branches of needle-work so much sought after in wealthy society; but she is poor, without friends, and all efforts to obtain a remunerative employment would have been in vain. Knowing this well, she resorted to the widow's last hope—sewing for "slop-shops." And, great heaven! what a life it is to lead! Constant toil from the earliest hour of dawn to the silent moments of midnight will not provide the bare necessities of life for a family like hers. It is unnecessary to recount this poor woman's struggles to keep comfortable her young and beloved children. Self was lost in a mother's devotion, and her constant application to the needle spoke volumes for a mother's love.

A few weeks ago, she suffered a heart-rending affliction. Her first-born, a handsome little boy, whose countenance always beamed with innocence and love, whose bright ringlets hung low down over his erect shoulders, and whose sweet disposition made him his mother's idol — that darling boy sickened and died. This event attracted some kind-hearted neighbors to the house, who did all they could to soothe the anguish of his parent's heart.

But what comfort could they administer? There lay the lifeless form of her CHARLIE, with that smile upon his sweet face which used to beam from it when he would throw his arms around his mother's neck and beg her not to cry, for he would soon be large enough to work as well as she. True, Heaven had transferred the cherub to a brighter world, but in so doing had newly afflicted an already bursting heart. Besides, the mother was poor, and could not even afford those tender demonstrations of love, which serve in a measure to relieve the anguish of the bereaved. She had no silken-cushioned coffin in which to lay his much-loved form, no flowers with which to deck his placid brow, no embroidered shroud to adorn his limbs. In a coffin donated by strangers, the little corpse was laid, and only three sympathizing female neighbors accompanied the mourning mother to his grave No tombstone yet marks the spot where he lies, for the mother, accomplished as she is, requires her entire energies to preserve her own life and that of her remaining children, who, in the midst of all her poverty and sorrow, have power to console her with their love.

ATTENDING FUNERALS—MRS. GADABOUT.

"Dear me," said Mrs. Gadabout, one Friday, tô Mrs. Thompson, upon whom she had just called, "I really thought I never could get an opportunity to call upon you. Two months have elapsed since my last visit. Do tell me how you have been?"

"I have enjoyed good health, I thank you," replied Mrs. Thompson, a good, sensible woman.

"Indeed! well, really I am glad to hear that. But poor Mrs. Jones! I presume you have heard of her death?"

"Yes, I have."

"Poor creature, she lingered *so* long. I did not know of her death until after it happened, or I certainly would have endeavored to attend her dying bedside. Although obliged to neglect my own business, I attended her funeral yesterday. Poor Mr. Jones took it so hard! Indeed, he was so overcome with grief, he neglected to order sufficient accommodations for the funeral. Would you believe it, wealthy as he is, he had only four carriages?"

"Indeed!"

"It is a fact, for I counted them myself. Why, I came near not going to the cemetery myself, and I would not have had the privilege, if Mrs. Jones' brother had not have taken an outside seat with the driver."

"Did he ride outside to accommodate you, and at his sister's funeral?" asked Mrs. Thompson in astonishment.

"O, bless your heart, it was no accommodation to me. I got into the carriage first, and then his wife and sisters filled it up, and he was too much of a gentleman to ask me to get out."

"But Mrs. Gadabout, did you do right?"

"To be sure I did. I have been to enough funerals to know that to obtain a seat in a carriage, all must look out for themselves!"

"But relatives should always have preference."

"Certainly, unless they are too stingy to order a sufficient number of carriages for friends. I have no respect for those parsimonious individuals who are sparing of money in the last sad tribute to the dead. I would have gone to Mrs. Jones' funeral if I had been obliged to crowd the husband out of the carriage."

"Why, Mrs. Gadabout!"

"I mean what I say. When persons pay so much respect to the dead, as to neglect their own families to attend a funeral, they should be accommodated. Now, on Monday I attended Mr. Bloss's funeral. There everything was superb—plenty of carriages, and two gentlemen in waiting at the door, to escort the ladies into the vehicles. On Tuesday, I attended the Rev. Mr. Smith's funeral, and there it was just the reverse. After the family were seated, there was such a rush for the remaining carriage, that I really blushed for the forwardness of our sex. I managed to get a seat, but nearly ruined the skirt of a new dress in the effort. On Wednesday I was at the funeral of the child of Mr. Simple, but I was shocked at the very slim attendance of the neighbors. I actually rode all the way to the Cemetery and back with no company but a gentleman, and I dont know how I would have passed the time if he had not been very agreeable. Yesterday I was at Mrs. Jones' funeral, and I am now on my way to attend the funeral of Mrs. Hobbs, whose husband is an intimate acquaintance of Mr. Gadabout's partner."

"Then you will not take off your things?"

"O, no, bless you, it is now near the hour, and I want to be there in time."

"You seem to delight in attending funerals, Mrs. Gadabout!"

"Indeed you are mistaken, Mrs. Thompson. I find it a very sad duty, but I can not bear the thought of a departed friend being conducted to her last resting place without due attendance. But I must be off."

"Can't you stay longer?"

"No, for I know a large number will be at the funeral to-day, and I want to secure an agreeable position. You understand, don't you?"

"I can not say I do. But, Mrs. Gadabout, I neglected to inquire after your family. How is your husband and child?"

"Bad enough, Mrs. Thompson. Little Emma is just getting over the measles. I left her with my next door neighbor—a very kind woman—while I ran over to the funeral. Mr. Gadabout is suffering dreadfully with the rheumatism. He has not raised his head for two weeks; but before I left home I fixed him comfortably, and he will need no more attention till my return from the cemetery. But it is now positively time for me to leave. Good-bye—call and see me when you can."

We need not give Mrs. Thompson's response, nor presume what her thoughts were. How many Mrs. Gadabouts there are!

THE RED FLAG.

See how it flutters, from the window of that princely mansion! What business has it there amid the evidences of opulence? It is the sign of Bankruptcy, the badge of Ruin; and can Ruin ever cast its mouldering hand, and Bankruptcy its withering grasp upon such a home of grandeur? It seems only yesterday eve, when that modern palace resounded with joy. Its wide, deep parlors were illuminated with the brightness of day, its costly decorations dazzled the eye, and the lord of the mansion strutted pompously o'er its downy carpets. Carriage after carriage arrived at the door—proud ladies and wealthy men sought entrance, and seemed honored by the privilege of assembling there, to do homage to unbounded riches. The softest music floated through the parlors, while the gay company enjoyed the merry dance; and though all were stiff with the silly etiquette of the day, the occasion was a happy one. And why should it not be? Such brilliancy was ne'er witnessed in this republican city of ours, for upon the table alone, in delicately wrought silver, lay a fortune. Happiness, we all feel, is in the enjoyment of wealth, and there wealth abounded; and there happiness must have been. Well might the lord of the mansion have been proud that night—proud of his wealth, proud of his unequaled festivals, proud of the homage done him.

Yet the red flag waves from the window of that mansion! Where is the lord of the palace? Run away! Where are those who clung around him so fondly, or worshiped at his golden temple so meekly, only a few evenings ago? They curse him! Where is that immense wealth which formed a grand circle for aristocracy? It has vanished. It never belonged to that house: it was cruelly extorted from pinching poverty, from hard labor, and from distressed humanity.

What disclosures that red flag has made; and what a change it has wrought! Carriages filled with proud ladies, and apparently wealthy gentlemen, still stop at the door; but they go not to pay homage to Mammon, but to endeavor to clutch the relics of a fictitious fortune. Now that the man who was Esq.'d as long as he lived in arrogance upon other people's money, has taken to flight, they are anxious to take his place as the center of the circle of fashion! Beware, good folks, of that red flag! It may one day wave boldly from your window, and you may be as deeply cursed as he whose princely furniture you now wish to possess.

The auctioneer, the owner of the red flag, commences his trusty work. He looks with surprise at the magnificent articles about him, and if his thoughts could be heard, they would, no doubt, say: "For twenty years have I been knocking off rich men's effects, but such grandeur I have never beheld as here. God help the poor people, whose hard earnings were made to contribute to this aristocratic show. What is the world coming to?" He hesitates to touch the first article for fear of soiling it, but he soon grows familiar with silver plate, downy carpets, inlaid furniture, and golden ornaments. Nay, he becomes animated, and with his "goin', goin', goin', gone!" excites the mirth of the visitors, and induces them to bid high. He cracks a joke over a one thousand dollar ottoman, speaks carelessly of splendidly-wrought silver knives and forks, and rattles the articles off at railroad speed. The crowd laughs, buys, and soon the sale is closed.

The red flag ceases to wave! It hangs stiffly on its rough pole, as if it durst not move. And then the long train of carriages drawn up to the curb, how like a funeral they look. Ah! it is a funeral. That red flag has buried the hopes of many poor men, who had confidently placed their little all in the hands of the once proud owner of that house. It is a death-signal to the expectations of many struggling widows, who had deposited with him the small earnings of Summer, to save them and their children from want during the dreary Winter. It is the funeral emblem to many whose bright anticipations have been blasted, and who have been deceived beyond recovery, wronged without a remedy. God help the poor!

Such were our thoughts while witnessing the sale of the household effects of an absconding banker. His assets will give to his depositors, who are numerous, many of them having their all in his possession, at least *five cents on the dollar!* Really, it seems as if law is made for the rich alone, and that the poor have no friends "at court."

VON SWEITZEL ON POLITICS.

"Mine neighbor, Vilhelm, vot you t'ink of bolitics, hey?" asked Peter Von Slug, of his neighbor Von Sweitzel, the Twelfth Ward blacksmith, one evening, as he seated himself beside him in a "Bierhaus."

"I t'inks mooch," said Sweitzel, giving his pipe a long whiff.

"Vell, vot you t'inks?"

"I comes to der conclusion dat bolitics is von great fool."

"Ah!" exclaimed Pete, after taking a draught from his mug, "how you makes him dat?"

"Vell, mine frien, I tells you," replied Sweitzel, after a few whiffs and a drink. "I comes to dish blace ten years last Spring, by der Dutch Almanack, mit mine blacksmit shop. I builds mine little house, I poots up mine bellers, I makes mine fire, I heats mine iron, I strikes mit mine hammer, I gets blenty of work in, and I makes moonish."

"Dat is goot," remarked Pete, at the same time demanding that the drained mugs be refilled.

"I say dat I make much friens," continued Wilhelm, relighting his pipe. "Der beeples all say, Von Sweitzel bes a goot man, he blow in der morning, he strike in der night, and he mind his bus'ness. So dey spraken to me many times, and it make me feel mooch goot here," slapping his breast.

"Yaw, yaw, dat ish gooter," remarked Pete, who was an attentive listener.

"Vell, it goes along dat vay t'ree year. T'ree? Let me see, von year I make t'ree hoondred toller, der next t'ree hoondred and fifty, der next four hoondred, der next four hoondred and swonzy, and der next five hoondred toller. Dat makes five year. Vell, I bes here five year, ven old Mike, der vatchman, who bes such a bad man, comes to me, and he say—'Pete, vat make you vork so hard?' 'To make moonish,' I dells him. 'I dells you how you makes him quicker as dat,' he say. I ask him how, an' den he dells me to go into bolitics, and get big office. I laugh at him ven he dells me dat Shake, der lawyer — vat makes such burty speeches about Faderland — bes agoin to run for Congress, and dat Shake der lawyer dells him to dell me, if I vould go among der beebles and dell dem to vote mit him all der vhile, he vould put me into von big office, vhere I makes twenty t'ousand toller a year."

"Twenty t'ousand! mine Got," exclaimed Pete, thunderstruck.

"Yaw, twenty t'ousand. Vell, by shinks, I shust stops der blowin', an' I stops der strikin', an' I goes to mine friens, an' I dells 'em all to vote for Shake der lawyer, and all der Yarmans vote for Shake, and Shake bes elected to der Congress."

Here Mynheer Von Sweitzel stopped, took a long draught

of beer, and fixing his eyes on the floor, puffed his pipe as if in deep thought.

"Vell, mine neighbor," said Pete, after waiting a due length of time for him to resume, "vat you do den, hey?"

"Vell, I ask Mike, der swellhead vatchman for der office, and he dells me I gets him der next year. I vaits till after der next krout-makin' time, and den I say again, 'Mike, vhen vill Shake give me dat twenty t'ousand toller office?' 'In two year, sure,' he say, 'if you vork for der barty.' Vell, I stop a blowin' mit mine bellers agin', an' I blow two years for de barty mit mine mout'."

"Two year mit your mout'?" asked Pete in astonishment.

"Yaw, two year. Den again I go to Mike, der swellhead vatchmans, an' dell him der twenty t'ousand toller about, an' he dells me in von more year I gets him sure; I dinks he fools me, yet I blow for der barty anudder year, an' den, vot you dinks?"

"Dinks? Vy, you gets him twenty t'ousand toller."

"Gets him?" Py shinks, Mike, der swellhead vatchmens dells me I pese von big fool, an' dat I might go to der bad place, an' eat sour-krout."

"He tell you dat?"

"Yaw. Sure as my name bes Von Sweitzel."

"After you do der blowing mit your mout' for der barty?"

"Yaw."

"Vat you do den, mine neighbor?"

"I makes a fire in mine blacksmit shop, I blows mine own bellers again, I heats mine own iron, an' I strikes mit mine own hammer. I say to mineself, 'Vilhelm Von Sweitzel, bolitics bes a humbug, and boliticians bes a bigger von.

Vilhelm Von Sweitzel, *do your own blowing, an' let der boliticians do deirs.*"

Neighbor Pete coincided in this expression of opinion, and, after wishing all sorts of bad luck to politicians, ordered the mugs to be re-filled, and changed the topic of conversation.

THE BABY IS DEAD!

A LONG black scarf, trimmed with broad, white ribbon, hangs upon the door knob. A death-like stillness pervades the entire mansion; all within moving with the softest tread, and speaking in whispers, as if fearful of disturbing the repose of some loved one. Those passing along the street observe the sombre scarf, and the instant change in the countenance betrays the thought, "the baby is dead!" Yes, the baby is dead, and not only those who have been familiar with its sparkling eyes, but the stranger, who receives the intelligence solely from the scarf on the door, feels that a home has been robbed of a precious idol. How deep was the love that had clustered around the innocent babe; and oh! how terrible is the blow its death inflicts.

The baby is dead! It no longer clings in innocent love to its mother's bosom, or stirs with fondest joy its father's heart. Its prattling has ceased forever, and its once laughing eyes are closed in an eternal sleep. But, even in death, it seems to have lost none of its sweetness. It lies so calmly in its silken-cushioned coffin, prepared with so much care; it has been arrayed in its costliest garments, its pure brow trimmed with a fragrant wreath, and flowers have been scattered o'er its lovely form. As it is thus arrayed, the babe seems only to be sleeping; but alas! it is that sleep which hath no waking.

The baby is dead! Around it are gathered many whose sympathies it has aroused, and whose love it has excited. The Minister leans over its cold form, and, touched with the sight, tears trickle down his cheeks while he exclaims, "Thus saith the Lord, 'Suffer little children to come unto me, and forbid them not; for of such is the Kingdom of Heaven.'"

The baby is dead! It is about to be shut forever from the sight of those who loved it as none others could. Oh! how the mother clings to the lifeless form; and as she imprints the last fervent kisses upon its cold cheeks, how her very heart-strings seem to break! And the father, though he has often manfully braved toils, cares, and dangers, now feels unmanned, and weeps like a child, as he bends over the corpse of his lost one. Sympathy, at other times consoling, is now of no avail, and the hearts of both suffer the deepest anguish.

The baby is dead! Tears have wet its grave, and crushed hopes lie buried with it. Though its mortal existence may have been brief, its death has desolated a joyous home. Sweet babe! Orators may announce a nation's loss in the death of patriots great and true, and poets sing in touching strains the memory of the dead, who have accomplished mighty deeds;—none but angels of heavenly birth will record thy life, so pure and beautiful, so early lost.

DRUNK

INVISIBLE never experienced "a drunk." His brain, fortunately or unfortunately, was never fuddled with the fumes of distilled extracts, and he has no idea of a drunken man's feelings. What charm there is in intoxication is a query he has put to many, but as yet has never received a satisfactory answer.

Some say, liquor drowns sad thoughts; and others, that it exhilarates, and makes one feel joyful. That sad thoughts are drowned in insensible drunkenness, no one can deny, but that intoxication produces joy, Invisible's observations flatly contradict. To be sure, when a man is just "boozy," or about "two-thirds tight," he appears to feel elevated, and in his anxiety to display his importance, utters volumes of nonsense, and shows himself a fool. He may laugh, shout, and act silly, but still there must be a consciousness in his own heart that he is degrading himself—falling below the level of a *man*.

Drunken men are met frequently in this community, and they are always objects for contemplation. Invisible saw one the other day, and could not avoid pausing and observing his actions. He was an old man, and, like most drunkards, poorly clad. He had fallen upon the pavement, but managed to regain his feet by clinging to an awning post. There he stood, in a half-erect position, the post tightly clutched in his hands, and his clothes bespattered with mud. His dull eyes were fixed upon his support, and, as his body moved to and fro, he seemed to be meditating, whether he was experiencing a reality, or merely dreaming. As if waking from a reverie, he let go of the post, and, with a curse, attempted to walk. He made only one step, when his trembling legs gave way, and he fell backward, as if some instrument of death had pierced his heart. A shout of laughter rose from the small crowd who surrounded him, and vulgar taunts were heard from more than one. The drunkard, however, did not attempt to rise again. He lay as if dead, and soon the blood came trickling from his hat, upon the cold pavement. A policeman came up, found the man had received serious injury in the fall, and roughly hustling him into an express wagon, had him taken to a police station. This is but one case in thousands, and now, where is the pleasure in getting drunk? Who will answer?

A CITY NUISANCE.

If there is anything the good wives of our city are troubled with, it is the innumerable hosts of pedlars who go from house to house to sell their wares. They are generally saucy, and oftentimes downright impudent. Imagine, if you please, an industrious, tidy little wife, with her hands in the dough, hurrying with all her might to have a nice dish of hot rolls for her husband's tea. She has been belated, perhaps, by the baby, which she has just succeeded in putting to sleep. There is a knock at the door.

"Gracious!" she exclaims, rubbing the dough from her hands, "who can that be!" Opening the door she espies a sickly-looking man, with a tin-shop on his back.

"Tin cups," he says, "ladles, pans, and—"

"Don't want any," replies the lady.

"Pie dishes, dippers, buckets and—"

"I tell you I don't want any. I have tin-ware enough."

"Rattle-boxes, pepper-boxes, match-boxes and—"

"No, no, no, no, nothing," exclaims the annoyed woman, shutting the door in the pedlar's face.

She resumes her work, but is hardly fairly at it, when there is another knock. Again she hurries to the door, and finds a big burly fellow there, with a dirty-looking bag on his shoulder. As soon as the door begins to give way, he exclaims —

"Rags, dree cent a bound."

"Haven't any," is the answer.

"Rags! dree cent a bound."

"I tell you I haven't any."

"Rags! dree cent a——" Slap goes to the door, and the pedlar pocketing the insult, moves off.

May-be the biscuits are made up and in the pan, when a third knock is heard.

"Another pedlar!" exclaims the wife. "He may knock until dooms-day, for I won't go to the door again."

The knock is repeated, when suspecting that it may come from a visitor, she peeps under the door. She sees two legs, and she knows they belong to the "tea man," so she resumes her work.

Still there is another knock, a soft one, just as if made by the kid-covered knuckles of a lady. The door is opened, when a little, delicate fellow, with a basket hanging to each side, squeals forth —

"Pins, needles, thread, *cheap!* Stockings, handkerchiefs, gloves, *cheap!* Laces, fringes, gimps, *cheap!* Scissors, kni—"

"Go along with you, and don't you come back here again," exclaims the tormented woman, provoked beyond endurance.

And thus it is in some parts of the city, hour after hour. Certainly pedestrian pedlars may here be set down as a nuisance.

RIDE IN AN OMNIBUS.

One day I stepped into an omnibus of the Union Line, intending to ride the entire length of the route, and hoping, with Mr. Micawber, that something would "turn up." I had but one "fellow-passenger," and she was a pretty young lady, dressed in the hight of fashion. She was from Newport, and I presume, from the number of times she examined and counted her gold, had come over to do her "shopping."

Driver cracks his whip, shouts, and starts. Proceed but a short distance before young lady espies a Lieutenant from the garrison, running quite nimbly after the "bus." She screams "stop," to the driver. I jerk the strap, and "bus" stops. Young officer gets in—is acquainted with the young lady—congratulations—conversation, mixed with silliness—the "bus" starts again.

At the foot of Broadway we receive the accession of a railroad runner. Knows the lady—has a swift tongue, and talks continually to the pretty miss. Young lady introduces him to officer—officer tries to talk, but can't get in a word edgewise—lady partial to railroad—officer bites his new-born imperial and looks daggers. Come to the conclusion that a slick tongue is better than a slick uniform.

At the foot of Main street two merchants get in. One is

from the East, and has come out to look after some slippery accounts. Shakes his head when companion tells him, thinks he will succeed in getting full amount. He expresses the opinion that a crisis has arrived in mercantile affairs, and complains of the awful condition of our streets.

At Walnut street take in a fat lady, from Covington, with her baby and black nurse. Officer helps her in, and pats baby on the cheeks. Fat woman is much fatigued—her replies to the inquiries of the Lieutenant are a mixture of sighs, puffs, and grunts. Baby cries, and fat woman tells black girl to bounce it. Says she is going to Fifth street to buy a bouquet for her grown-up daughter.

At Second street receive a hog-butcher, whose clothes are rather greasy, and who is puffing a cigar. He squeezes in between the Newport miss and the Lieutenant, to the great satisfaction of railroad, who politely changes seats with the miss. Butcher requested to throw away his cigar, but with a smile, rubs out the fire and puts the remains of his delicacy in his pocket. Lieutenant throws up his nose at the smell of venerable lard, and the fat lady wonders why such dirty people are allowed to ride in omnibuses.

At Pearl street receive a lady. She was helped in by three clerks, and had a pretty boquet in her hand. How everybody in the "bus" look at her as she comes in. Baby cries, nurse bounces, fat lady scolds, Lieutenant consoles, miss laughs, railroad smiles, merchants look demure, and butcher winks.

At Fourth street, receive three more ladies and two walking children. They all get in, but don't find seats. Driver tells everybody to move up — fat lady protests against a tighter squeeze—miss laughs, strange ladies ask the gentlemen to get on top—butcher responds, and I, thinking something had "turned up," left the omnibus in hot haste.

THE PROSECUTING ATTORNEY'S IRON CHEST.

In the office of the Prosecuting Attorney, of this county, stands an iron chest. It is of modern make, fire-proof, and will resist the encroachments of the most ingenious burglar's tools. There is nothing peculiar in the exterior of that safe, but unlock it, and allow its heavy door to swing open, and it presents a fearful sight. Murderous implements, many of them spotted with human blood, and ingenious contrivances for the commission of crimes, meet the eye. The most attractive is the remnant of the infernal machine, by which Allison and his beautiful wife were torn almost to pieces. The shattered iron, the burnt wadding, and the dark remnants of the box, call to mind all the circumstances of the horrid murder, and make one shudder.

Next to it is a long, much-worn carving-knife, covered with blood. Less than a year ago, a middle-aged mulatto woman, fired to frenzy by the ill-treatment of a brutal husband, seized that knife and plunged it into his side. He died; and a court of justice exculpated the woman from the charge of murder.

Next is a pistol, new and not much worn, which has inflicted a serious wound upon a human being. A young husband was happy in newly-wedded love, when rumors reached him that another had attempted to sully the character of his wife. Maddened at the thought, he procured that pistol, hunted out the alleged slanderer in a place of amusement, and convincing himself that what he heard was true, he drew the weapon and fired to kill. The wound he inflicted did not prove fatal, and the young husband was acquitted by a jury of his countrymen.

Next is a ferocious-looking bowie-knife. Its history is not known, but certainly the man who carried it possessed a malignant heart. That, as well as a neat little dagger by its side, is covered with blood.

Next is a dirk, for improperly using which, a man, once honored and respected, is now incarcerated in the State prison.

Next, way down in a corner of the iron chest, is a large knife, which, though covered with mould, has been the instrument of an exciting story. Years ago, a woman of great personal attractions, and strong mind, learned that her husband was bestowing his love upon another. Being convinced of its truth, she visited the favored one about dusk one Summer evening. The words which passed between them were few, for soon the jealous wife plunged a knife into the heart of the other. The one fell dead upon the floor, while the other fled to the residence of the Mayor, and delivered herself into custody. It was a bold premeditated murder. Yet the community sympathized with the injured wife, and few sorrowed for the dead. She, who had struck the fatal blow, was tried for murder—the jury knew she was guilty, but could not in their hearts condemn her to the awful penalty of the law. They declared her insane, and to the satisfaction of the whole community, nay, amid the applause of a crowded court-room, she was liberated from custody. Rust on, old knife! In being an instrument of a dreadful crime, thou didst bring sweet revenge to a wounded heart.

There is a lot of counterfeit money, which tells plainly how hard it is to resist temptation. A steady, sober, upright citizen of the Third Ward was made a policeman. The business bringing him in contact with all kinds of vice, he soon contracted pernicious habits, which eventually led to his disgrace, by dismissal from the city police. Henceforth he lived an idle life, and was at last caught with that batch of counterfeit money in his possession. He procured bail for his appearance, and then fled—a sure evidence of his guilt.

A bank note there tells a curious tale. One evening a well-dressed young man offered that note at the bar of the Theater for refreshments. The bar-keeper immediately pronounced it counterfeit, and called an officer to arrest the person who had offered it. As the policeman seized the young man, he thrust the note into his mouth, and endeavored to swallow it. He was choked until forced to spit it out, when he was conducted to the police station, and locked up. He had a preliminary examination, and was committed for final trial. At the trial it was proven, that the bank note he offered, and endeavored to swallow, *was genuine!* He was of course acquitted. His statement then was this: He was a country schoolmaster, and but little acquainted with the world. When he found he was accused of passing counterfeit money, believing the bar-keeper to be a judge, he thought that the production of the spurious bill would produce his conviction, and he followed the first impulse of his mind—to destroy the note. Shame for his disgraceful situation induced him to disguise his name, and keep silent as to his real position, though fully conscious of his innocence.

Beside the iron chest, is an old trunk, taken from a house in Newport, which contains evidence of one of the most stupendous schemes of villainy ever exposed. It contains piles upon piles of forged deeds, land warrants, and pension papers, many of the latter going back to the days of President Monroe. Bundles of correspondence show how these fictitious documents were sold for genuine; and no doubt hundreds have by this means been robbed of their honest earnings.

But enough of the Prosecuting Attorney's iron safe; its contents might found many an interesting tale.

A STONE OR TWO IN IT.

An individual well known in the community, and who has held several offices of honor and profit, was reduced to very stringent circumstances, like most public men of late, by the too free indulgence of intoxicating drinks. A warm friend of his who had advised him to a more moderate use of the "ardent," called on the proprietor of the house most frequented by him, and asked the landlord as a personal favor not to sell any more liquor to the individual referred to. He thought a rebuff at that house might bring him to his senses, or make him feel his real position. The proprietor of the coffee-house refused, however, for the reason that the individual was an old customer, and he did not wish to hurt his feelings. Unsuccessful there, the friend thought he would try one more appeal to the feelings of the almost ruined man.

He called on him one afternoon, and the two walked out together. After proceeding several squares, the one exhorting earnestly, and the other listening silently, the friend stopped, and pointing to a large and costly mansion, just being finished on the opposite side of the street, he said—

"Now look at that fine house. It is being built by a man who has received the most of your money for the last ten years. Your habit of drinking has made him wealthy and you poor. Now," he continued, believing he had touched the heart of his friend in the right place at last, "now, don't you see the folly of your ways?"

"Well," replied the drinker, after closely surveying the elegant stone-front mansion from bottom to top, "*Well, I guess I have a stone or two in it.*"

His friend was shocked at the naiveness of the reply, and could not muster courage to resume the subject. But how many ruined men are there, who can point to elegant mansions, and immense business-houses, and claim that their money has purchased a stone or two in it, for which they have not had value received.

A SPECULATION.

"Tim, me boy," said the landlord of the Emigrant's Home, "Tim, me boy, an' wont ye tell us uv yer specelations?"

The Tim addressed was a tall, stout Hibernian, who, with some dozen of his fellow-countrymen, was seated in the bar-room, if it can be so styled, of the "Emigrant's Home," a story-and-a-half tavern, located on Dublin street. The Emigrant's Home is like most of the Irish boarding-houses in the West, composed of not more than four rooms—a drinking and sitting-room, a cooking and eating-room, and two lodging-rooms. The landlord boards his patrons at cost, looking to the bar, and his weekly dances or "shin-digs" for profits.

"An' it's mesel' that'll do that same," was the reply.

"An' it's a gintleman I know ye are, Tim," responded the landlord, "an' ye shall have a drop uv the crathur to moisten your lips."

"A betther boy than mesel' niver left howly Tipperary for Ameriky," remarked Tim, with a gladdened face, as he helped himself to the proffered grog.

"An' yer right there, me boy; so tell us uv yer specelation, man," said the landlord.

"None uv yer blarney now, Misther landlord," replied Tim; "its mesel' that can spake for mesel'. I tould ye a betther boy than Tim niver left Old Tipperary for Ameriky, an' hav'n't I me aut'ority for spaken so? Didn't Father O'Roork tell me that, an' did Father O'Roork iver lie, except when he was at prayers?"

"It's the trut' yer spakin now, Tim; but tell us uv the specelation!" urged the landlord.

"That I will. Ye see, me darlings, whin I first landed in Ameriky, I thried hard to be a polaceman, but me legs were too short, an' me tongue too thick. Thin I thought to mesel' I'd try a bit uv a specelation, an' so I married Dinnis O'Garraty's widdee."

"Och! but was it that ye done?" exclaimed the landlord.

"It was mesel' that did it," continued Tim, "an' the widdee had the money too, I tell ye."

"An' a swate crathur was she too?"

"Divil a bit! Two weeks afther the weddin' she packed up, an'—an'—an'—run'd away wid Pat McDugan, as ugly a baste as iver broke a poor husband's heart."

"Murther! an' was that yer specelation?"

"Sure, an' wasn't it?" continued Tim, somewhat excited. "*Didn't I git me two weeks bed an' boord for nuthin, an' divil of a cint did it cost me to git away from the wicked widdee?*"

"Och! an' yer right, boy," said the landlord, after a moment's hesitation; "it was a specelation, shure! Now ye'll trate lad, wont ye?"

"An' its Tim will do that," responded the speculator; and drinks were ordered for all hands—on the strength of the speculation.

ANOTHER SPECULATION.

"PLEASE ma'm, can you tell me where I can get a place?" asked a pale, thinly clad girl, about thirteen years of age, of two richly dressed women, whom she met on Fourth street, one morning.

"A place? What can you do, girl?" inquired one of the women.

"Most anything, ma'm. I've always been used to hard work."

"Who have you been living with—can you produce certificates from your last mistress? I want a girl, and think from your looks you may suit me."

"Oh! I do wish you would take me, ma'm. I have never

worked out; but now my mother is sick, and I want to get work so I can support her."

"You support your mother, girl? Ha, ha! that is decidedly jovial. You must be content with supporting yourself. Why, how much do you expect to receive a week?"

"I don't know how much they give girls, ma'm, but I would like to support my mother if I can."

"Your ideas of wages are too extravagant, girl," responded the woman, with a pompous air, "but if you can do house-work, I am willing to take you, and give you good wages."

"How much are you willing to give me, ma'm?"

"Well, I will give you twenty-five cents a week, and let you eat at the second table."

"And find me in clothes?"

"Gracious, what an idea! In clothes? — no, indeed. You must clothe yourself out of your wages."

The girl was evidently sadly disappointed. The woman continued:

"If you are disposed to accept of my offer, call at No. —, Seventh street, at 9 o'clock to-morrow morning;" and then walking on with her companion, she said, "I am now paying my girl fifty cents a week, and if I can get this one at half that salary, it will be quite a speculation."

Speculation, indeed! If it is by such speculations, madam, you bedeck your person so gaily, and live in idleness and ease, Heaven have mercy upon you. Twenty-five cents a week, for the hard services of a poverty-stricken girl, anxious to relieve the sufferings of an afflicted mother! Shame! shame! upon the woman, so heartless as to make such a proposition.

A TREACHEROUS MEMORY.

MARTIN STUBBS, do you know him? He lives out in the Twelfth Ward, and is noted for his volubility of tongue and treacherous memory. One evening Martin was sitting in front of the Brighton House, reading a newspaper.

"That's nothing," said he, concluding a paragraph, to a crowd of half a dozen sitting near him.

"What?" was the inquiry.

"This feller in here," pointing to the paper, "walked one hundred miles in one hundred consecutive hours."

"I guess you never saw it beat," spoke up one.

"I haven't? You don't know me, young man. Did you ever see me walk? I'm used to it. When I was six months old, I'd pick up a cheer and run off with it; and when I was a shaver, I always preferred walking to riding. Just the very day I was nine year old, I walked fifty mile in five hour."

A laugh followed this declaration.

"It's a fact, by ginger! I'll tell you how it was. You see, we lived in the country; and one night a peddler stopped with us, and on the same night he slipped away with ten thousand dollars of the old man's cash, and—"

"Ten thousand dollars!" exclaimed a by-stander.

"Yes, sir, just even ten thousand. You see, in them days the people didn't care as much for money as they do now. Every feller owned a farm big enough for himself and children, and they worked along sort of easy, and having no use for money, they cared nothing for it. Why, once my old man went to market, and sold his load for five hundred dollars, and—"

"Five hundred dollars for one load?"

"Yes, sir, they had awful big wagons in them days. My old man's wagon was bigger than our house, and he never thought of hitching up a team of less than twenty head of the—"

"Twenty head? Why how did you drive them?"

"Easy enough, bless your soul. We'd starve the critters just before we wanted to use them, and then carry oats before their noses along the road. They were always careful to keep within smelling distance. I've driv eighty head that way, and—"

"Eighty head?"

"Yes, sir, and I was the only boy in the whole neighborhood that ever did it. You see, I was always counted smart, and—"

"But about that walking fifty miles in five hours?"

"O, yes, I forgot that. Thank you for putting me in mind. Well, as I said, two peddlers—"

"Two?"

"Yes, two. They stopped at the old man's, and during the night stole twenty thousand dollars, and—"

"Twenty thousand?"

"Yes, certainly; that's what I said before. And twenty thousand was twenty thousand in them days, I tell you. My old man was the only person in the whole country who had a cent, and he was mighty careful of it, so much so, indeed, that he never went away from home."

"Never?"

"No, sir."

"Not even to market?"

"Him? Why, you couldn't get him out of the house except it was to feed old Tom, the only horse in the whole section of country."

"The only one?"

"Yes, sir. People couldn't afford either horses or wagons in those days. Talk of hard times now! You ought to have lived just about that time. I never had—"

"But tell us about walking fifty miles in five hours."

"Fifty miles in five hours?"

"Yes."

"That never was done by human."

"Didn't you do it once?"

"Me? Never. I always was stupid at walking—couldn't crawl about until I was four years old, and have never been limber in the legs."

"Why, Stubbs!"

"Fact, upon my honor."

"Why, what a liar."

"Liar! I can pocket an insult from a man who can't appreciate truth when he hears it," indignantly replied Stubbs, as he threw down the newspaper and walked away. The crowd who had kept serious faces during Stubbs' recital, now gave vent to their suppressed laughter, much to the indignation of Stubbs.

POD III.

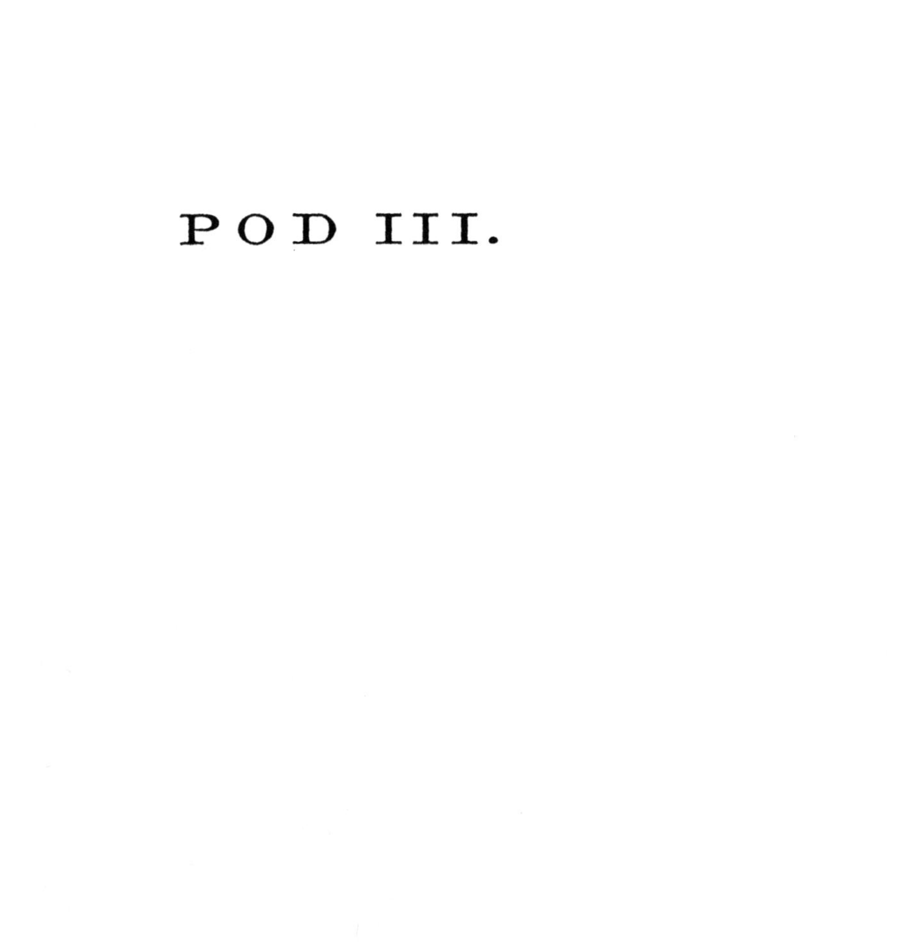

POLICE SKETCHES.

QUARREL OVER A DISH OF KROUT.

Everything was ready for the trial. Esquire Rowekamp had thrown his dignified personage back in his easy chair, his young clerk had seated himself by his side, like another Sancho by his master, and the constable had posted himself, like a trusty sentinel, at the gate of the inner bar, to preserve the court from improper intrusion. In the outer bar, on either side of a long green-baize-covered table, were arrayed a half-dozen lawyers, two with pen in hand and hair erect, ready for the work; and though they ranked from a judge down to a brainless pettifogger, the great money-making qualification of each, was the fact, that they commanded the ready use of two languages—English and German. Within the same bar, upon one side of the room, were arrayed, Jake Breakstein, the complainant, and his witnesses, and upon the other side, face to face with their opponents, sat Frau Haverstraw, the accused, and those upon whose testimony she relied. Beyond this, in the space between the outer railing and the front door, was a crowd of spectators—some attracted by friendship for one or the other of the parties, and others by mere curiosity. Their general rough appearance, stained and patched garments, uncombed hair and greasy faces, told plainly that they belonged to the "unwashed" class; while their tiny cloth caps, their short-tailed jackets, their very coarse linen, and their iron-bottomed shoes, indicated beyond doubt their Teutonic origin.

Looking at the scene, the stranger might infer he was in "Faderland," and that the "Burgomaster" of the district was about to hear an important case; but the citizen of Porkopolis would know he was in a Magistrate's court "over the Rhine," and that a German trial was about to take place, after the American fashion. Such scenes are frequently witnessed in all our large cities, now-a-days, particularly in those where the foreign population is large, and the languages of other climes are nurtured by the community.

"Mrs. Haverstraw," said the court, "you are accused in this warrant, with having assaulted, with intent to injure, Jacob Breakstein. Are you ready for trial?"

"Vat?" asked Mrs. H., a stoutly-built woman, with arms like sections of stove-pipe, and a face that would pass for an almanac representation of a full moon, and who had understood only her name, in the solemn announcement and query of the Magistrate.

"Sit down mit you," instantly interposed her lawyer, who, after telling her in German that he would do her talking, said, "May it blease der court, *ve* are now ready to be dried."

"Remember, sir," announced the attorney upon the other side, "that the trial once commenced, we will allow of no delay. We consider ourselves in personal danger from your client, and shall demand the full protection of the law."

"Ve vill put you in shail before you gits t'rough mit us," was the prompt and cutting response of the defense.

"Call your witnesses, gentlemen," remarked the Magistrate, "and leave the merits of the case to the Court. Is the prosecuting witness here? Call him, Mr. Constable."

"Jacob Breakstein! Jacob Breakstein!" shouted the officer.

"Here bes Shake," responded the owner of the name, who was sitting within four feet of the constable. He was ordered to the witness-stand, where the oath was administered in English, in quite a solemn manner, and the nature of it explained in German.

"Now, Jacob," said the Court, "proceed and tell us all about this business, and remember, you are sworn to tell the truth, the whole truth, and nothing but the truth. How, and in what manner, did Mrs. Haverstraw assault you?"

"Vell, 'Squire, I tells you all about it," responded Jake, a short, thick-set man, whose form resembled a beer-keg, resting upon short legs, with a cabbage-head on the top. "I live on de Bremen strasse, mit mine frow, an' drive a bier vagon mit der horse."

"Vat dat do mit der assault?" interrupted the attorney for the defense.

"May it please the Court, we demand the protection of our client," bawled the attorney upon the other side. "We come here seeking justice, and will not be brow-beaten by any member of the bar. We—"

"Keep cool, gentlemen," interrupted the Court. "The witness evidently is not familiar with Court proceedings, and must be allowed a little latitude. Go on, Jacob."

"Vell," continued Jake, "I live on der Bremen strasse mit mine frow, an' I drive a peer vagon mit der horse. Mine neighbor Haverstraw live in der same room mit me, mit his frow. Vell, I comes home on Donnerstag, mit mine peer vagon: I puts mine horse in der stable, an' I goes to mine house, for mine breakfast-supper. Mine frow sets out der table, mit some peer and some krout, and some pretzel, and me and mine frow sets down, and eats der peer, and drinks der krout and der pretzel."

"Trink der krout und der pretzel?" asked the attorney for the defense. "Vy you say dat—vy you no tell the trut'?"

"Yaw," replied Jake, not in the least disturbed, "I trinks der pretzel mit mine teeth."

"Eat, you mean," interposed his lawyer. "A mere slip of the tongue, your Honor will notice."

"Yaw, yaw—by mine tongue—dat's him," responded Jake. "Vell, vhile me und mine frow trink der krout und der pretzel, mine neighbor's frow, der Haverstraw, vot sets over there pehind Shon der blackschmidt—"

"Yaw, yaw," interrupted the defendant, as she was pointed out, "frow Haverstraw—yaw, frow Haverstraw."

"Yaw, dat vomans, 'Squire; she come und she set down mit me und mine frow; vell, she take her finger, so, (making the motion) she take some krout in her finger, so, und she put it in her mout', so," he said, with vehement gesture and indignant action, which brought forth a roar of laughter from the audience.

"Silence! Order in Court!" shouted the Constable, in a terrific manner.

"Vell," continued Jake, "I say to mine neighbor Haverstraw's frow, 'vot for you do dat?' Mine neighbor Haverstraw's frow look me in der face mit von eye, so, (making a grimace) und she say, 'Shake, you bes von big Dutch fool.' I say to her 'Vat?' und she say to me, 'Shake, you bes von big Dutch fool.' I say, 'Vhy you tinks so, frow Haverstraw?' und she say, 'Shake, you tinks I no like krout.' I say, 'Ha! frow Haverstraw, you no stand under mit me; I tink you don't like your own krout, but, py shinks! you like mine krout too mooch to blease Shake.'"

"Stand back, Madam! stand back! No intimidation of witnesses here!" shouted Jake's attorney. His demand was addressed to frow Haverstraw, who, hearing the witness mentioning her name frequently, and being unable to comprehend what he was saying, came forward to get a better understanding of what was going on. The lawyer took advantage of her movement, to endeavor to create an impression of foul play, a little pettifogging trick, often resorted to, in the lower courts of justice. Frow Haverstraw was ordered to resume her seat.

"Vell," proceeded the witness, "after I tell her dat, she take her hand, shust so, (making the motion) she put it in mine krout dish, shust so, und she take out all der krout, mitin her hand, und py shinks, she t'row it all on mine cope!"

A burst of laughter from the spectators caused another demand for silence from the constable, and a burst of indignation from the witness's attorney, who could not "see anything to laugh at."

"Vell," continued Jake, as soon as order was restored, "I scrape der krout from mine cope, und put him in der dish again to eat him once more, when mine neighbor Haverstraw's frow take anudder time some more again an' put him in her mout'. Says I, 'vot for you eat mine krout?' und she say to me, 'Shake, you be von big Dutch fool.' Den I gets madder as not'in', and I takes der krout in mine hand shust so, I catch frow Haverstraw by der head mit von hand, an' I—"

"Stop! stop!" exclaimed his lawyer, "you need not tell that."

"Yaw," innocently remarked Jake. "I catch her by der head mit von hand, an' I—"

"Stop! stop!" shouted the lawyer.

"No, no, I nix stop, but py shinks I puts all der krout vot had been on mine head—"

"Won't you stop?"

"No, I nix stop, but I put all dat krout from mine head into frow Haverstraw's mout'."

Even the Court could not preserve its equanimity after this rich development of the termination of the quarrel over a plate of sour-krout, while the spectators roared with laughter. Jake underwent an examination and cross-examination very calmly, and resumed his seat without taking one word from his testimony in chief.

"What other testimony have you to offer?" asked the Magistrate of the prosecuting lawyer.

"I am prepared to prove the peaceable character of my client."

"That is unnecessary," remarked the Court. "Have you anything else to offer?"

"No, sir."

"Then we dismiss the case. Though the throwing of the krout by Mrs. Haverstraw at the head of Mr. Breakstein may be construed into an assault, we think sufficient punishment was inflicted at the time by Mr. Bre .kstein taking the krout from his head, and, as he testifies himself. cramming it into the mouth of the lady. Mrs. Haverstraw, you can go home, and Mr. Breakstein, you can pay the costs."

"Dunder and blixen!" exclaimed Jake, casting a woful look at his attorney.

"Yaw, yaw, dat is goot," shouted Mrs. Haverstraw, who now, for the first time, understood the decision of the Court.

As is usual in all legal contests, one party left the court-room chop-fallen, and the other in the hight of good humor; the friends of each showing their feelings, and the disinterested spectators applauding the decision of the Court. Jake will hardly venture into Court again, particularly if his case is tainted with sour-krout.

MY HUSBAND'S MINIATURE.

Amid the lowest degradation, bright jewels of the heart can often be found. It seems almost impossible for the human heart to become so debased, that it is lost to all feelings of kindness and love; and, however low God's creatures may become, they have something around which their hearts will cling with pure affection. An illustration of this occurred in the Police Court one morning.

For several months an intelligent, and once a good-looking Irish woman, had been before the Court for drunkenness. Each time she appeared to have sunk lower and lower in the scale of degradation, until at last her associates were the most debased of the negroes of the city. She did not appear to have any shame for her position, receiving her sentence to jail, as a vagrant, with perfect indifference, and always refusing to escape punishment by promising to leave the city. On the occasion alluded to, when brought before the Court, she said:

"I've got my locket, now, Mr. Pruden, and if you will let me go this time, I'll leave the city to-day."

"Your locket," asked the Court, "what has that to do with your leaving the city?"

"It's got my husband's miniature in it, sir, and I could not leave the city without it. Here it is, sir, a little broke, but the face is uninjured."

She handed the locket up to the Court. It was a costly gold one, and had the face of a good-looking man in it.

"Has it been out of your possession?" asked the Court.

"Yes, sir," she replied, a tear stealing to her eye; "one night, when maddened and almost insensible from liquor, I was induced to pledge it for whisky. I regretted it the next day, but, poor woman that I was, I could not get it back. The parting with it made me wretched, and I drank more and sank deeper in sin, until your Honor sent me to prison. I then determined, when I came out to go to work like an honest woman, and save my money until I had accumulated enough to redeem the only thing dear to my heart. I got it last night, sir, and it so rejoiced me that I could not help taking a drop or two. That is the way I was in liquor last night."

"And you are now ready to leave the city?"

"Yes, sir. I have my husband's miniature, and I am

ready to leave the city to seek new associations, and, I trust, live a different life."

"Where do you think of going?"

"To New Richmond, sir."

"How can you get there?"

"Walk, sir. I have my husband's miniature, and I can endure fatigue."

Under these circumstances the Court discharged the woman, praying that the possession of that miniature so dear to her heart, might induce her to reform.

AN ETHIOPIAN PLEADING AT THE BAR.

"A HARD crowd we have here this morning!" was the side-bar remark of the Prosecuting Attorney of the Police Court one day, as a crowd of about a dozen negroes, male and female, were paraded from the watch-house entrance to the prisoner's bench.

"Dey is dat," responded Nat Lytle, one of the party, as he gave a contemptuous glance at his prison comrades. "Dey am hard cases, Massa, an' I doesn't want to be tried wid dem. I ax a seberance, under de constitution an' de laws ob de lan'."

"I am afraid we can not grant you a severance, sir," remarked the Prosecuting Attorney. "Have you a lawyer to defend you?"

"A lawyer? What does I want wid a lawyer, Massa? Hasn't I been hear nuff to get acquainted wid de law?"

"True enough," responded the official attorney, with a smile, as he proceeded to examine the documents in the case. The examination resulted in the calling of three witnesses—two watchmen, and one of the prisoners, who answered to the name of Mary Jane, and who had agreed to make a "clean breast," if, by so doing, she could procure her acquittal. The officers gave the entire party a bad character, and said they arrested them while engaged in a general muss.

The Natural Orator.

Mary Jane, however, insisted on the entire innocence of all the party, except Nat, whom she described as "a nasty, ugly, drinkin', cussin', good-for-noffin' nigger."

Nat asked the legal privilege of cross-examining this witness, which was of course granted.

"Mary Jane," said he, after clearing his throat with a cough, "look here at dis chile; Ise got de controllin' ob your language dis time. Look me right in de eye, colored woman, an' answer my questions. Whar did you come from?"

"From de watch-house, sure," replied the wench.

"Dat am a fac'. Now, woman, what fotch you to de watch-house?"

"Why de watchman—what you t'ink fotch me dar?"

"An' what did dey fotch you for?"

"For bein' in de company of such an ugly lookin' nigger as you is," responded the witness, to the chagrin of Nat, who finding the woman too smart for him, drew himself up, and with a dignified wave of the hand, said:

"Resume your seat, woman; resume your place on de bench. De truff am, dere is no truff in your bosom. Your heart am as brack as your face."

Nat could not produce a single witness, and all that remained to close the case, was for him to present his argument to the Court. This he proceeded to do. With one hand on the railing before him, he descanted as follows:

"May it please de Court. De merits of dis case can be summed up in mighty few words. De law reconnise all de time, de principle, dat ebery tub stan' on he own bottom. Whar does I stan'? Who am de individual what comes here, into dis Court, wid de foul words ob acceptation agin dis chile, upon her polluted lip? She am Mary Jane. An' who am Mary Jane? A brack woman who hab no truff in he eye, an' whose big feet hab treaded de paff ob ruin, lo! dese many years. Shall I, a man of honor, be condemn, jus' to please dat woman? No! de Court hab more ob de white man in he heart, dan do such a t'ing as dat. True, I hab no witnesses, but den my word am as good as dat brack woman's oaf. Now, if de Court will lend he ears, I will gib de whole truf ob de matter."

The Court full of laughter, nodded its willingness to listen.

"Mary Jane say I knock her down," continued Nat,

"Dat am false, false as de teef some beople had in der heads. Dis am de fact. I war a standin' out to de door, on!—no, I is too fast."

"Well you is, honey," interrupted Mary Jane.

"I war standin' in de jinin house, meditatin' upon de folly ob a nigger bein' rich, when I hear a scream. Ah! did I know dat scream? Was it not from de froat ob Sarah sittin' right dar, an' who is my wife by de laws ob de lan! Did I do but to rush to de rescue? Sartin I did. I flies ober de groun'; I reach de door, an' what did mine eyes see den? On de floor lay Sarah, de woman ob my heart; an' ober her stood de ole woman, a lammin' her like de debbil. Where was Mary Jane? A standin' in de corner shoutin' 'put in de licks old woman.' What did I do but foller de dictate ob my own conscience, an' rush in an' grab de old woman by de har, an' pull her off ob my abused Sarah."

Here, the laughter in Court became really uproarious, and Nat was obliged to stop, while the Marshal demanded order. Quiet restored, he continued—

"Look at dat (pointing at Sarah,) face—see dem eyes—behold how de flesh am bruised. Who done dat? Why de ole woman wid Mary Jane egging her on. Did I, could I, make dem woun's? Neber. I stan's here innocent ob de charge; yet dat wicked brack woman gets up here an' swars it all on me. I specs to 'pear on de Judgment Day, an' I now say, if it war my dyin' words, dat I neber lay hands on de woman. Yet Mary Jane swars it all on me, an' I spose I must suffer, like de innocent lamb brought to de slaughter.

But who is dis Mary Jane? She does nuffin but drink whisky, an' fight, an' kick up musses all de time. Las' night she cum down dar wid six bitts; she buys de whisky, she sets de table, an' she git us all to drink. Who can belieb her? Dar's not one dat knows her, dat would belieb her. She swars to an untruf to-day, jis to git herself out ob trouble. Does you hear dat? I is a man ob peace; I tries to lib in harmony wid all de world, but dat woman (pointing to Mary Jane) wont let me. Dat's de truf, an' dat's all I's got to say on dis occasion. I axes de Court to discharge dis prisoner from de custody ob de law."'

This speech, so seriously delivered, did not touch the heart of the Court. The whole party, including Nat. were condemned as vagrants, and sentenced to imprisonment for twenty days on a diet of bread and water alone.

ALL ABOUT A PAIL OF "WATHER."

Mrs. O'Dorothy is a "gintale" little widow, who, having a half-dozen "childer" depending upon her for support, has opened a little grocery in Friendship Alley. She occupies but one room, and her stock is therefore easily enumerated. She has soap (an article much needed in that locality) for the ladies, candies for the juveniles, and whisky for the men. That the "childer" love her candies, let her numerous penny sales testify; that the men love the whisky poured by her tender hands, and which dances from the decanter to the glass in the light of her large, piercing black eyes, let her extensive traffic in the article bear witness; that the neighboring women are jealous of her charms and whisky, can be established beyond all doubt.

21

Mrs. O'Dorothy is a poor widow, and lives in a frame tenement; Mrs. O'Connell, who has a husband, and resides next door, occupies a brick house. Mrs. O'Connell, like most women with good husbands, despises widows, looking upon them as snares erected by old Satan himself to entrap married men into evil habits. Mr. O'Connell loves whisky, especially whisky sold by bewitching young widows, and long since became a customer of Mrs. O'Dorothy—merely, however, out of sympathy for her forlorn condition. Mrs. O'Connell, though possessing a good-looking countenance, has red hair, and consequently soon learned to hate the next door neighbor, to whom her husband seemed so much attached.

One cold Winter's day Mrs. O'Dorothy found her hydrant closed with ice. She could as well live without water as without whisky, so she hied away to her neighbor's hydrant, with the full determination to help herself. She found Mrs. O'Connell's hydrant in running order, and without speaking a word to anybody, filled her pail. She was about returning, when Mrs. O'Connell, with a pitcher in her hand, appeared before her.

"Good mornin' to yez, Mrs. O'Connell," sweetly said the widow.

"An' it's not good mornin' to yez, ma'm," was the reply. "Yez has no business to be stalin my wather."

"I beg yer parthen, Mrs. O'Connell, but it's not staling I'm afther. Sure an' yer own dear husband tould me to help mesel'."

"Yez lies!" shouted Mrs. O'Connell, the flush of anger covering her face. "Me husband is a gintleman, an' will have nothing to do with the likes uv yez."

"Och! an' is it jealous ye are, Mrs. O'Connell? Pace be wid yez, thin; for me poor heart is broke intirely, since me good Mike wint to Purgatory. Not a man do I want to touch since that, at all, at all."

"It's nice spakin yez al'ays have upon yer tongue, Mrs. O'Dorothy," replied the jealous woman; "but yer mighty low to be stalin wather."

"Stalin wather! Mrs. O'Connell, yez tells a falsehood, if yez tells me that."

"It's a liar I am, thin, Mrs. O'Dorothy? That I niver took from man or baste. Take that for yer impedence!" and suiting the action to the word, Mrs. O'Connell brought her pitcher flat upon the widow's head.

Where is the Irish woman who is not used to blows? Mrs. O'Dorothy surely was, and she had not only learned how to receive them, but how to pay them back. She dropped her bucket, and made at her antagonist.

Their fingers went into each other's hair, then into each other's eyes, and then into each other's mouths. Though the smaller, the widow proved the better fighter, and had just got the jealous wife into a "pelting" situation, when a third person took part in the affair. Mrs. Doolan, another neighbor, saw the fight through her window, and was a disinterested spectator until the widow seemed to be getting the better of it. She then raised the window and yelled, "Watch! murther! watch! Sure an' Mrs. O'Dorothy is a killin' of Mrs. O'Connell. Watch! murther! watch!"

Her screams aroused the neighborhood, and brought Watchman Flack to the spot, who, in duty bound, took both the ladies into custody. They appeared before Judge Pruden, and the above facts having been brought forth, the widow was dismissed, and Mrs. O'Connell fined five dollars and costs. So much for one pail of "wather."

A TATTLER.

Of all things in the world, save us from a tattler—one of those ever-moving busy-bodies, who are always ready to construe the most inoffensive remarks into wicked assertions, and to make evil out of an entirely harmless act. With eyes ready to peep into the most sacred privacies, noses continually stuck into premises not their own, ears open to hear every word spoken within hearing distance, feet prepared to fly, and tongues that can run off news faster than a double-cylinder press, they delight only in doing evil to others, even when they can accomplish no good to themselves. They are a pest to their neighborhood, and their breath is as poisonous as the bite of a snake. We hate them, and would a thousand times prefer the company of a skillful pick-pocket to one of these useless, mean and contemptible species of the human race. A tattler! Who can like, or even respect one? Her presence is significant of bad news, dissensions among friends, and difficulties among neighbors; she carries misery wherever she goes, and sorrow, needless sorrow, follows her train. She is a walking contagion, infecting all that come within her influence.

We saw one of these venomous females at Esquire Rowekamp's office, one day. Her name was Amanda Blossom, and she was there as the prosecuting witness in a case wherein she charged Mr. Godfrey Vontam with assaulting her, with intent to kill. She was a tall, slim woman, with grayish, sunken eyes, sharp nose, low and narrow forehead, long chin, thin lips, and a very wide mouth. She was dressed rather stylishly, though the slovenly manner in which she wore her garments, gave her a disagreeable appearance. We thought her a busy-body at first sight, and concluded to witness the trial and its results.

The defendant, or rather prisoner, in the case, was a Mr. Godfrey Vontam, the keeper of a grocery near the railroad depot in the Sixteenth Ward. He was a small, but stout-built fellow, apparently with about mind enough to buy and sell groceries on a small scale, and to make a little more than a living by devotedly attending to his own business, and not troubling himself with what his neighbors or the world might be doing. Though, as we learned from him after the trial, he had lived in the city ten years, he wore a suit of clothes, which had the appearance of having been made "a long time ago," in some quiet corner of his Faderland. True, they were but little the worse for wear, but might he not have kept them safely locked up, free from dust and dirt, for many a day, only using them on such special occasions as the one we write about?

The hour for the trial of the case arrived, and Esquire Rowekamp, with that easy grace which characterizes all his movements, arranged the parties in a proper position; namely, opposite each other. He then read the warrant to Mr. Vontam. Mr. Vontam attempted to explain, but was interrupted by the Magistrate, who knows as well as the most learned judges, just at what points the law allows a prisoner to speak.

Mrs. Blossom was then called to the witness-stand, duly sworn, and requested to relate the particulars of the assault committed upon her by Mr. Vontam. After clearing her throat with several coughs, and giving the little German on the other side of the table several *very* hard looks, she proceeded—

"'Squire Rowekamp, I am the most peaceable woman in the world,—I never bother in my neighbors' affairs, or act deceitful toward anybody; but what I have to say, I say it right out. Nobody ever heard me back-bite (looking hard at Mr. Vontam) or scandalize my neighbors. I defy any of them to prove—"

"But, Madam, your character is not in question," interrupted the 'Squire; "we wish to know about the assault."

"Well, sir, I am going to tell you; but you must let me have my own way. I can't cut a long story short like some people, and I wont, either. Just let me go ahead, and you will save time."

"Well, then, be as brief as possible, Madam," rejoined the 'Squire, "and come to the facts of the case as soon as you can."

"Yes, sir. Well, this man (Vontam) keeps a grocery in my neighborhood. When he first moved there, he hadn't a cent to buy bread for his dinner. His poor little children were suffering for a morsel of something to eat, and his now mean stuck-up wife, hadn't a change of clothes to save herself. Besides, they were all dirty and filthy, and were—"

"Come, come, Madam, I can hear no more of this," again interrupted the 'Squire, "if Mr. Vontam assaulted you, tell us how he did it. I haven't time to sit here and listen to scandal."

"It is not scandal, sir," snappishly replied the witness. "I *seed* it with my own eyes. They needn't laugh, either, the poor, dirty stuck-ups—my memory is not treacherous. Do they remember when I loaned them linen to cover their nakedness, and bought blue ointment to clear their children's heads?"

"Never mind that, Mrs. Blossom—tell us of the assault."

"Well, sir, I will. You see, some time ago I was at Mrs. Thompson's, to spend the evening. Besides me, there was Mrs. Black, whose husband owns a large distillery in Kentucky; and Mrs. Jones, who has been unfortunate in her marriage, and got a divorce, and is now earning an honest living with the needle; and Miss Johnson, who, in her younger days, declared she would always remain a virgin, and has refused several offers to get married; and Mrs. Smith, whose health is so feeble through the ill-treatment of the man to whom she was bound out when a girl, that she is obliged to have three hired girls to do her work; and Mrs. Brown, who is as nice a woman as ever lived, though her husband treats her like a brute; and Mrs. Baker, who everyday has a crying spell, because the neighbors tell her how attentive Mr. Baker is to Jemima Spriggins, who talks to him as he goes to and comes from work; and Mrs. —"

"But what have these ladies to do with the assault?" inquired the 'Squire.

"Why, they know all about it."

"About the assault?"

"No, but about the scandal that was going through the

neighborhood. Did not Mrs. Baker tell me that she saw Mr. Vontam put sand in his sugar, and Mrs. Smith that she knew he gave short weight, and Miss Thompson, his next door neighbor, that she saw him, through the cracks of the fence, kiss Mrs. Klappingham, who goes there most too often to buy groceries?"

"What has that to do with the assault?" inquired the Magistrate, who began to manifest some impatience.

"Why, sir, a good deal. The veracity of those ladies can not be doubted, and when they told me these things, I thought it my duty to put the neighbors on their guard, for I do despise a cheat and a swindler. I made mention of the short weights and the sanded sugar to Mrs. Jenkins, and Mrs. Sprouts, and Mrs. Donkers, and other neighbors, and I instantly withdrew my custom from Vontam's grocery. Besides, I intimated to Mr. Klappingham, that he had better change his grocery, or he might hear of something that would arouse his jealousy. I always suspected an undue intimacy between his wife and Vontam, and Miss Thompson's timely observations through the fence-crack confirmed my belief.

"When did Mr. Vontam assault you?" asked the Squire, abruptly.

"Last Saturday, as I was going to remark, after he had heard ——"

"Where did it happen?"

"In his grocery, where I had gone to buy some articles, being in a hurry, and Mr. Scott's grocery being further off."

"Did he strike you?"

"No, but he shook his fist in my face, and called me the most outlandish names."

"What did he call you?"

"Epithets that should never come to the ears of a lady!"

"You must tell it all, madam, or you will fail to make out a case."

"He said that I was a busybody, a mischiefmaker, and, sir, a *liar!*"

"What else did he say?"

"He said I went about the neighborhood injuring his business and character, which is false. I never whimpered a word about his character. I only told that which I heard with my own ears, and saw with my own eyes."

"What did you say to him, then?"

"I was so thunderstruck, that I said nothing. To think that I should be accused of carrying news among my neighbors, so affected me, that I became nervous—I could hardly stand."

"Well, what did Mr. Vontam do?"

"He told me—to his shame, be it said—that if I did not go out of his grocery, he would *kick* me out."

"Did he do it?"

"No, sir. I threatened to take the law on him, and he dare not do it; but Mrs. Von—"

"Never mind his wife: have you told all Mr. Vontam did."

"Yes, sir; and, for heaven's sake, aint that enough?"

"Not enough to make out a case, and I therefore dismiss it, at your cost."

We cannot describe the horror depicted on Mrs. Blossom's countenance, on hearing the decision of the Court. She gave him about four yards of her tongue, and then flew out of the office in a desperate flurry. We don't know, but we'll venture the assertion, that Squire Rowekamp caught "scissors" in her neighborhood, not many minutes afterward. She certainly did not eat, drink, or sleep, until she gave him a "blizzard" in every ear that would listen to the rattling of her tongue.

A COMMODORE BEFORE A HUMAN JUDGE.

CANAL-BOATMEN live a reckless life. Though always afloat, they are ever within stepping distance of the shore, and though used to skimming the water, generally use it internally pretty well mixed. Compelled to slow locomotion in the canal, they are naturally "fast" when on dry land, and once clear of the perplexing changes of the tow-path, and the stubbornness of low bridges, they seek to spend their time gaily, amid the perfumes of the extract of corn, and the merry strains of some canal-boat fiddler. To get "tight," and have a "stag dance" on shore, is the delight of a canal-boatman, be he captain, horse-engineer, steersman, or guardian of the line. That canal-boat captains sometimes get drunk, can not be denied, for one of them, even the "Commodore of the Whitewater ditch," was before the Police Court one morning upon that charge.

"I found the Commodore on Front street, last night," testified a watchman, after the canal-boat captain had been properly arraigned. "He was quite drunk, sir, so much so, indeed, that he was unable to navigate."

"What is his business?" asked his honor, the Judge.

"He is the Commodore of the Whitewater canal, and commands a boat."

"Is he in the habit of getting drunk?"

"Can't say, sir. Never saw him intoxicated until last evening."

"What have you to say to these accusations?" asked the Court of the prisoner, a thick-set, coarse-fac'd fellow, with shoulders broad enough, seemingly, to bear the weight of Barnum's baby elephant.

The Commodore of the Whitewater Canal.

"I war drunk," replied the Commodore, as he stepped forward. "I war drunk. That story's as straight as a tow-line on a stretch."

"Well, don't you know that is bad business?" asked the Judge reprovingly.

"It ar," responded the Commodore, sighing, as he removed his quid from the starboard to the larboard side of his mouth.

"Are you in the habit of getting drunk, sir?" inquired his honor, in a serious tone.

"I am not," replied the prisoner, at the same time assuming a belligerent posture, as if to resent the insinuation.

"But you drink habitually."

"That I takes my dram are sartin, but whar's the Com

modore who don't? Arnt I as good a right to tea it as Stockton, an' all t'other great fellows? But get drunk? That are aint in my bill of ladin'."

"Where do you reside?"

"In Ingeeanar, when I'm among my folks; on the Rantin' Belle when I'm at home."

"And you are not in the habit of getting drunk in Indiana?"

"Nary time. They've got the Maine licker-law out thar, and a feller can't git a drap, unless he smuggles, an' you know I'd never do that. I tell you what it is, 'Squire, I haint been drunk afore since I was twelve year old, an' if ye'll jest let me off this one time, I'll give ye all the money I've got, an' on my honor as a Commodore, never git drunk agin."

"How much money have you?"

"Half a dollar, countin' the coppers."

"Is that all?"

"I've got more on the boat, but she's left port."

"What will you do, then, if your boat has left?"

"Take the tow-path an' overhaul her."

"Will you do that, if we discharge you?"

"Sartin."

"And will you never get drunk again?"

"Sure as I'm a Commodore."

"Then take your hat and leave."

The Commodore was overjoyed at the result. He walked briskly to the door; then stopped, took a long look at the Judge, slapped his hat upon one side of his head, rammed his hands into his pantaloons' pockets, and then, as he made his exit, exclaimed:

"May my boat sink on the next trip, if that thar aint a human Judge."

He moved off in the direction of the tow-path.

THE TROUBLES OF A NEW HOOD.

"WHAT do you want, Madam?" inquired the Judge of the Police Court one morning, of a squatty, red-faced, pug-nosed, big-mouthed Irish woman, who had a handkerchief slightly smeared with blood around her head, and who had elbowed her way into his presence.

"I'm a witness, yer worship," she replied with a courtesy.

"A witness against whom?"

"Johanna O'Nale, sur, who sits forninst the watchman there, yer worship; and a swately bad woman she is, too."

"Johanna O'Neil," asked the Court, "are you ready for trial?"

"Fait, an' I be, yer honor," replied Johanna, quite a young woman, with a pleasant face and sparkling black eyes, who had on a dirty calico dress, with a bran new brown hood, lined with bright blue silk, covering her "frowsy" head.

"What is your name, Madam?" inquired the Court of the anxious witness.

"Mrs. Raymond, yer wurship.

"Your Christian name?"

"Before I was married, do ye mane, yer wurship?" inquired the witness, not understanding the question.

"No, your first name."

"Is that it, yer wurship? Well, it's Ann, yer honor, but me good mon calls me Anna, yer wurship."

The witness being sworn, she was told to proceed with the complaint she had to make against the accused. She said—

"Well, yer wurship, I'll tell yez like an honest woman, that I am. Last night, sur, I was sittin' in me house wid me childer, whin there cum a saft tap at me doohr. I opened it gintalely, yer wurship, whin this woman, Johanna O'Nale, put her ugly head widin the doohr, an' wid her fisht, she sthruck me wid this tay cup, yer wurship."

"She did?" asked the Court, "and without your saying a word to her?"

"Not a word, yer wurship."

"The Saints forgive yez," exclaimed Johanna.

"Och! but I'm spakin the trut'," replied the witness.

"Satan will get yez!" continued Johanna.

"But not till he burns the wickedness out uv yez," promptly returned Mrs. Raymond.

Generally in cases of this character, testimony without qualification is as reliable as with it, and his Honor, who is well aware of the fact, always allows the accused to make a statement as an offset to the testimony, and putting all the statements together, endeavors to arrive at the truth.

With this object in view, he asked Johanna O'Neil to state how the difficulty occurred between her and Mrs. Raymond.

"I'll tell yez," responded Johanna with apparent candor. "This woman, yer wurship, keeps a groggery. Well she sent word to me that she was sick, an' she asked me to plase come an' do up her work for her. Says I, uv course I will, as I am tender-hearted, an' feel in me heart for the sick.

Well, yer wurship, I had some money wid me, an' what did I do, but like an honest woman, go down town an' buy wid it this new hood upon me head. Whin I come back, I had fifty cents wid me in me pocket. Sez Mrs. Raymond to me, sez she, 'Johanna, wont yez wet the hood wid a trate?' Sez I to her, 'to be sure I will, me dear.' Well, yer wurship, I spint me half dollar for whisky in the house, an' I got droonk, and thin her baste ov a husband took me by the two arms an' put me out of the house, he did."

"Tell the trut', Johanna, tell the trut', me darlin'," exclaimed Mrs. Raymond.

"I am afther tellin' uv the trut', yer wurship," continued the accused. "The woman keeps a doggery, an' she entices poor lone women like mesel' there to spend their har-rd-earnt money for her nasty mane whisky. She's now got me locket, sur, worth fifteen dollars, which I pledged to her for whisky. an' she wants to chate me out uv it, yer wurship."

"Do you keep a groggery?" asked the Court of Mrs. Raymond.

"No, yer wurship," she replied indignantly, "I kape a grocery."

"And yez sells whisky Sundays an' week-days, too," exclaimed Johanna.

"Out wid yez!" impatiently shouted the landlady witness.

The Court very properly came to the conclusion that Johanna had been more sinned against than sinning, and discharged her from custody, much to the rage of the prosecuting witness.

A POOR THIEF.

THERE is as much classification among thieves as any other portion of the community. There is the gentleman thief, the genteel thief, the cute thief, and the dirty thief. The last class are those poor fellows who steal because they do not know how to do anything else. As they have no ingenuity, they no sooner commit a crime than they are caught, and consequently by far the greater portion of their lives is spent in prison.

Pittsburgh Bill is a fair representative of this class. He is a stout, thick-set fellow, fond of whisky, of a jovial disposition, and a steady, first-rate workman—when laboring for the benefit of the State or County; but out of jail, a lazy, worthless fellow. As a vagrant, or a thief, he has been almost a burden at the Rookery for some months, and the police are so used to arresting him, that they never see him in the street but they pick him up. Bill was brought before the Police Court one morning, and would probably have been quietly sent back to jail, had he not implored the Judge for freedom. After he was arraigned, on the charge of vagrancy, Bill said:

" Mr. Spooner, I just got out of jail yesterday afternoon, and I don't want to go back again. If you will only let me off, I will leave town right away; and if any of the officers catch me in town to-night, they can arrest me, and you can send me up, and I'll have no excuse. I'm sorry I ever came back to this place, for they've kept me in jail all the time. But I want to go home now—*I want to see my mother*

—I want to be free again. Do let me go, and I'll leave this town, and never return."

'Do you think we can place any reliance on his promises?" asked the Court of a policeman.

"Well, I don't know about that," replied the officer, who is something of a wag, "but I paid a quarter of a dollar to get him hauled up here, and I would like to get that before he is set loose."

"Let me off, Judge Spooner, if you please," continued the prisoner, fearful of the watchman's testimony; "if you do, I will leave town to-day, as sure as there is a God in Heaven."

"Hush! hush! don't make any such promises as that," said his Honor, and turning to the officer, he asked, "was he drunk?"

"Well," said the officer, "he was a little limber when I tossed him into the cart, but before he had been there long, he jolted up, gave the driver a bolt under the ear, and bounced out of the wagon."

"Indeed!" ejaculated his Honor.

"Well, I'll tell you how that was," said Bill. "I met some of the Pittsburgh boys, soon after I got out, and they made me tight. Indeed, I want to leave the city this time —*I want to see my mother*—won't you let me go?"

"On your solemn promise to leave the city to-day, I will," was the answer. Pittsburgh Bill waited to hear no more, but grasping his hat, he left the Court-room, apparently a happy man.

ORIGIN OF THE GOOSE QUESTION.

Miss Sharp is what the world terms a "little old maid." She lives, and has lived for many years, in a small, antiquated house, in the northern part of the city, which was once a retired spot, but is now in the midst of that thriving quarter known as "over the Rhine." She lives without any companion, save a snow-white goose, which she has often termed, her "darling pet." Its quacking is music to her ears—its presence happiness to her heart.

The 'Squire who decided the Goose Question.

Now, a few days since, Miss Sharp's next door neighbor, Mr. Heinrich Von Switchelheim, a sturdy old Dutchman, who loves nothing but money, beer, and krout, and who has never yet been able to see further than his pipe, except when driving a bargain—this near neighbor happened to stumble over Miss Sharp's goose. The poor pet, unused to such rough treatment, instantly set up a quacking, which almost frightened poor Mynheer Von Switchelheim out of his regular gait, and instantly brought Miss Sharp to the door.

The cries of her pet had aroused her most sensitive feelings, and when she saw the poor thing limping toward her, and her stout neighbor standing near by, with his hands in his pockets and his pipe in his mouth, she soon divined the cause of her beloved goose's misery. Catching her darling in her arms and folding it to her breast, she immediately demanded of Mr. Von Switchelheim why he had presumed to injure her only comfort? Mr. Von Switchelheim is a man of slow motion; and, knowing he had done no intentional injury, hesitated to reply. This affronted Miss Sharp to such an extent, that she suffered her angry feelings to get the better of her judgment, and grasping a small stone she hurled it at the stupid fellow. David took not better aim at Goliah, than did she at Heinrich, for the stone struck Mr. Von S. between the eyes. This aroused him, and made him feel "like fight," as he expressed it; but his belligerent feelings came too late. Miss Sharp had disappeared into her house, and locked herself up.

Mr. Von Switchelheim stood awhile, and reflected. He was determined on having satisfaction, but was too honest to destroy property, and too bold to fight a woman in his calmer moments. He would sue her, and teach her better manners. He procured a warrant from Esquire Rowekamp, and the next day stood face to face with the accused. Having all confidence in the integrity of the Magistrate, and in their own ability, neither party employed counsel. Mr. Von S. dressed in his best, and with his largest pipe in his hand, was the only witness. After he had detailed the circumstances, Miss Sharp, who, with her goose upon her lap, had not removed her eyes from him, while he had been upon the witness stand, cross-examined him as follows: —

Miss Sharp—Did you, sir, kick my pet?

Mr. Von Switchelheim—I walks mit der goose mit der boots, und her go, "quack! quack! quack!"

Miss S.—I demand of you to say whether you willfully kicked the poor creature?

Mr. V.—Oh! yaw, I kicks him mit a stum—stum—stum—vat you calls him?

Miss S.—You will please observe Mr. Rowekamp—ah! excuse me—'Squire Rowekamp—that he kicked the poor darling. Poor thing; [kissing the goose]—Mr. Von Switchelheim, have I ever done any thing to you, to cause this unjust attack upon my only companion?

Mr. V.—Yaw.

Miss S.—What is it, sir?

Mr. V.—Slap him un der cope mit der brick-stein.

Miss S.—When, sir?

Mr. V.—Ven der goose go quack! quack! quack!

Miss S.—But previous to that time?

Mr. V.—Yaw, yaw—I sees der fire all der times pefore mit der brick-steines in mine eyes.

Miss S.—You don't understand. Did I ever strike you before?

Mr. V.—Yaw, shust before mine eyes, on der headt.

Miss S.—Can't you comprehend plain English, Mr. Von Switchelheim? Did I ever injure you at any other time?

Mr. V.—Yaw, yaw, I forstay. Der time was shust pehind der sundown.

Miss S.—Mr. Von Switchelheim, you destroy my patience. You are a dunce.

Mr. V.—Yaw, dat ish all right.

Miss S.—I think so, and I am confident the Judge—ah! excuse me, (to the magistrate,) I mean the *'Squire*—will agree with me on that question.

Mr. V.—No, by dunder!—der goose say no question, but go quack! quack! quack! for not'ings. Der goose tell you mit a lie.

Miss S.—My goose never lied, Mr. Von Switchelheim, and I will let you know, sir, that you shall not add insult to injury here. I appeal to the 'Squire if I and my goose must be thus insulted, even in a Court of justice. Mr. Von Switchelheim, you are a nasty, mean, contemptible pup—

"Silence, silence, Miss!" cried the 'Squire, thumping rather loudly upon the table with his knuckles; "personalities have proceeded far enough between you and the defendant. As there is no other testimony, I will now take the case in hand myself."

The Magistrate then reviewed the evidence, although several times interrupted by Miss Sharp, who either "begged leave to correct him," or to "assure him that he misunderstood the testimony." He concluded with saying that an assault had been clearly made out, but as the defendant was a lady, and had committed the assault under a false impression, he would fine her only one dollar, and relinquish his costs in the case. Miss Sharp complained very bitterly at this mild sentence, but finally agreed to it, if Mr. Von Switchelheim would enter into a written agreement never to harm her goose again. Under the impression that he was to get the dollar, Mr. V. readily agreed to the bargain, and Miss S. left, apparently well satisfied. Mynheer waited some time for the dollar, but not getting it, he put his pipe in his mouth, his hands in his pockets, and meditatively walked out of the office for home. He no doubt thought there was something in the law entirely above his comprehension. This was the origin of the "goose question."

A RICH TRIAL.

ONE day, at the tail end of the prisoners before the Mayor, was a real darkey, who flourished the tremendous name of Junius Brutus. He was an Ethiopian in looks, manner and action. He was charged with assaulting a "little nigger" some ten years of age, named Moses Johnson, the evening previous.

Junius Brutus, after having made room for his feet, took a seat by the side of an attorney he had engaged, and the lawyer on the other side having "squatted himself" opposite, the trial proceeded.

Mose was called as the first witness, and testified that on the night aforesaid, the aforementioned Brutus did unlawfully strike him in the mouth.

LAWYER.—Tell what he previously threatened to do to you.

MOSE—Well, he tell my mudder, dat ——

BRUTUS—Shut your mouf, niggar!

MOSE—He say dat ——

BRUTUS—Wo-wo-wont you shut him mouf, niggar?

BRUTUS' LAWYER—Be quiet, sir—I am to conduct your case.

BRUTUS—Well den, (rolling his eyes terribly), make de niggar stop he gab.

MOSE'S LAWYER—May it please the Court, we protest against this rude interference with our witness.

MAYOR—What is the matter.

MOSE'S LAWYER—Why, sir, the prisoner has rudely interfered with the witness and appears disposed to mount him in open Court.

MAYOR—Brutus, you must keep quiet.

BRUTUS' LAWYER—Please the Court, the matter was on the impulse of the moment. It shall not occur again.

MOSE—Well, dat Brutus say de furst time he kotch me he lam me out ob my boots.

BRUTUS—Look out colored individual.

MOSE—Niggar, you knows I tell de truff, and nuffin but de truff, sure as ye're born.

MOSE'S LAWYER—Does the Court notice the conduct of the accused? (The Mayor nodded assent.) That is sufficient. Moses take your seat.

The next witness called was a white man named Tom Pepper. He said he saw "the nagers blarneying, but divil a bit a stroke was passed."

Then came Tom Fire, who proved to be an important witness, "Well you see boss," he said, "I was stan'in' down on 'Commodation, when who would come 'long but dat ugly niggar, Ingin Bill. 'How is you, Tom?' says he to me, just so. 'Ise well,' says I, just so. Den says he, 'cum 'long Tom, you brack niggar, and wood up,' just so. Says I, 'don't care if I does, distinguished colored man,' just so. Den we gwyes 'long to blin' Pete's, where we takes a slug all 'round. Just at dat moment, in comes dis little niggar, Mose Johnson, yelping like a dog wid his tail cut off, and roaring like Injuns. 'Who-what's de matter niggar,' says I, just so. 'Dat darkie, Brutus, hit me,' says he, just so. Den I turns round to Brutus, an' says I, 'you'd better not hit dat little darkie 'gin, while Ise about,' just so.—'Go to de debbel, niggar, says he,' just so.—Den he runs his han' into his pocket, as if he was gwyn to pull out a shootin' iron, an' says I, 'give up de weapon, colored man, and go on to de hill, or down into de butcher's hollar, an' I'll lam you out ob yer boots,' just so.—Den Ingin Bill say, 'go 'long niggar, what's use habbin a fuss,' and off I goes, just so.—An' dat's all I know ob de struggle."

Mose's Lawyer—Ain't Brutus considered a dangerous man?

Tom—Nuffin shorter.

Mose's Lawyer—He shoots don't he?

Tom—Sure as yer born.

Brutus' Lawyer—Yet you wanted to fight him.

Tom—On de squar, sartin.

Brutus' Lawyer—Didn't you pull out a knife at him?

Tom—I takes de knife from dis pocket and puts it in dat.

Brutus' Lawyer—Didn't you try to cut him?

Tom—Neber.

Brutus—Bewar' niggar, you under oaf.

Tom—I knows de responsibilerty ob an oaf, well as you, Junius Brutus; an' you needn't roll your eyes at me dat way.

Brutus—(grinning)—See dem teef!

Brutus' Lawyer—Be still, I tell you, or I will not conduct your case any farther.

BRUTUS—Den make de niggar stop his freats at my indi-widual pusson.

MOSE'S LAWYER—We ask the Court to protect the witness.

MAYOR—Do you know anything more about the case, Tom?

TOM—If my recollection serbs me right, I doesn't.

Tom was ordered to sit down, and Miss Feliciana Rover was called. She said that all she knew about it was, that she didn't see Junius Brutus pull out a pistol.

MOSE'S LAWYER—Aint Brutus your beau?

FELICIANA—No; an' if he is, taint none ob your business.

MOSE'S LAWYER—Don't he call an' see you occasionally?

FELICIANA—Better lookin' niggars 'an him wait on dis chile.

MOSE'S LAWYER—I insist on a direct answer; does not Brutus *pay* his addresses to you?

FELICIANA—Brutus neber tried to get my lub, and dat's more 'an you can say.

MOSE'S LAWYER—Take your seat, impudent Miss.

Miss Josephine Bright was next got upon the stand, but not without some difficulty. Hiding her face with her shawl, she refused to answer any questions, until Mose's lawyer asked her if she was married. She then gave him a dignified look, and flirting herself into her seat, said, "Guess I is most."

Injin Bill next appeared. He threw some light on the matter, asserting unequivocally, that "de niggar Mose run against de niggar Brutus' hand, and de blow was an accidentul sarcumstance, as far as de measure ob his eyes could penetrate into de facts ob de case, as dey war spread before de vision ob his bodily faculties." Such at least were "de mental impressions ob his mind."

Brutus was fined five dollars and costs, and to the surprise of the complainant, "forked over" the cash. He then asked the Mayor, "Am Brutus free?" Receiving an affirmative reply, he "socked" a plug of tobacco into his mouth, gave his opponents a terrible scowl, and walked out of the office as stately as a Numidian prince.

THE REIGN OF PETTICOATS.

"Timothy Brown, stand up," said his honor, the Mayor, while trying the watchhouse cases one morning, to a slim, nervous-looking creature, in the prisoner's dock.

Timothy stood up, but instead of casting his eyes toward the Mayor, he kept them fixed upon a short and somewhat corpulent lady, with a *highly* figured shawl thrown over her rather broad shoulders, and a bonnet on her head covered with flowers, who sat on the opposite side of the court-room. At the time Mr. Brown's name was called, she was engaged in packing sundry little articles in a highly ornamented reticule. As he raised his body, however, she raised her head, and their eyes met. A kick from a horse could not have shocked Timothy more severely, for he certainly would have fallen, had not his hands nervously grasped the railing of the dock.

"Mr. Brown," said the Mayor, "you are charged with abusing your wife."

"Yes — that's the charge," replied the lady mentioned, rising and making a courtesy, "for may it please your honor, I am his better-half."

"Has he been abusing you, madam?"

"I—I—I—never—did," stammered Brown, "as she—"

"Mr. Brown," cried Mrs. B., stamping her foot upon the floor, which stamp apparently chilled the heart of her husband. "Mr. Brown, will you hold your peace while I am speaking? Remember, sir, that we are not now alone in our domicil, where peace once reigned supreme, but which, alas! is now the abode of misery. I stand now under the protection of the law; and Justice, with her blinded eyes and unerring sword shall decide the differences between us."

"Mary, for Heaven's sake don't——"

"Mr. Brown, hold your peace; you are a prisoner—prisoners are not allowed to speak."

"You," said the Mayor to the woman, "charge your husband with abusing you,—did he strike you?"

"No, sir—that he *dare* not do. Strike *me!* Let him ever attempt that, if he wishes the broom-handle broken over his head."

"In what manner, then, did he abuse you? I must know this before I can further proceed with the case."

"Please your honor," tremulously said Brown, "I can tell you all——"

"*Mister* Brown, *will* you be silent?" interrupted Mrs. B., with another stamp of her foot, which effectually stopped the tongue of her husband. Then turning to the Mayor, she said—"That man, sir, was once the idol of my heart. I believe he loved me at that time, but Heaven knows, sir, I have discovered my mistake. He is a tailor by trade, sir—a journeyman tailor—as good a tailor as ever stitched a pair of pants—but it profits me nothing now. What is a husband, your Honor, without affection—devoted affection—that blissful affection which is the admiration of our sex—the acme of our heart's enjoyment?"

"Mary! Mary! I do love you," cried Mr. Brown.

"You once did, Timothy—you once did, but you do not now. My heart is shrouded in darkness, Timothy—black, dismal darkness."

"Will you please to tell me, madam, in what manner your husband assaulted you?" inquired the Mayor, now growing impatient.

"Oh, pardon me, sir," replied Mrs. B., but my troubles so distract my mind, that I know not what I say. Timothy, you will one day repent all this." Here Mrs. B. rested her forehead upon her hand for a minute, as if in deep study, and then addressed the Mayor as follows—

"I will tell you all, though shame parch my lips. I have told you we were once happy, but a change in his habits has ruined our peace. For your better understanding, allow me to say, that woman naturally yearns to disseminate good among the children of Eve. Her heart, naturally more refined than man's, seeks to penetrate the recesses of darkness, and shed righteous light upon poor humanity. I am a woman, and have the feelings of a woman, and therefore seek to aid with my feeble powers, the various reforms which now agitate the world. I have attached myself to a sewing society for the relief of distressed emigrants, the members of which meet——"

"To talk about other peoples' business," slyly whispered Brown.

"At Mrs. Smith's, every Tuesday evening, and I am bound to attend it. I am also a member of the Ladies' Society for the Diffusion——"

"Of domestic discord," again whispered Brown.

"Of Internal Knowledge, which meets every Wednesday evening. Being a member of the Female Improvement Association, I necessarily attend its sittings every Thursday evening, to——"

"Learn nonsense and mischief," softly whispered Brown.

"See that the important interests of the Association are not neglected. My Friday evenings are spent at Squire Hill's, making——"

"Mischief among neighbors," said Brown.

"Clothing for the suffering Heathen. Every Saturday evening, the Married Women's Debating Society meets, and being Monitress, it demands my attention above——"

"Your domestic duties," sarcastically whispered Timothy.

"Everything else. Sunday is the day of rest for us all."

"Except me," said Brown, bravely.

"For relaxation, I attend, every Monday evening, the Rev. Mr. Longbreath's popular lectures on popular ideas."

"Does your husband attend you to all these places, madam?" inquired the Mayor.

"Bless you! no; and thereby lies my complaint. Formerly he objected not to my doing good; but lately he seems disposed to forbid me all these privileges. Last evening, when I put on my bonnet, preparatory to accompanying my particular friend, Mr. Adams, to the lecture, he threw down the baby, (Mr. Brown began to tremble again,) and declared openly he would neither nurse the brat or clear up the supper dishes. My feelings were so shocked that I nearly fainted; for in six years of married life, Mr. Brown never before refused to perform his share of our domestic duties."

"What did he do after that?" coolly asked the Mayor.

"Nothing, sir, but obstinately refuse to do his duty. After persuading him in vain, I called in the officers of the law and had him arrested. I intend to show him that law and justice will sustain me."

"You are mistaken, madam. He has not offended the law, however much he may have offended you. I discharge him."

"Discharge him! Heavens! is there no remedy for our sex? and will even the law insult us when we ask for redress? Oh! woful, woful indeed, is the condition of society!"

She looked the Mayor in the eyes for a few moments, as if expecting a response, but getting none, turned to her husband. She gave him a glance which almost melted him in his seat; and then harshly stamping her little foot, she said to him:

"Timothy, begone! I'll seek redress among those who deal out justice."

Mr. Brown obeyed, but with a trembling step. His wife followed him, amid the laughter of all who had witnessed the rich scene.

HAPPY.

"HA! ha! he! he! don't, I tells you—keep your han's off—ha! ha! ha! hi! hi! ho! ho! o-o-o-oh! but you does tickle me," shouted a robust, plump-faced negro woman, with a full and melodious voice, one morning as she was ushered into the presence of the Police Court.

"Order!" shouted the Marshal, as every head in the dense mass outside the bar was stretched forth to obtain a fair view of the prisoner.

"It makes me laugh to t'ink ob him."

"Order?" was the woman's response, not in the least abashed at her position. "Ha! ha! ha! ha! does you 'spect a body to keep order when dey is tickled? Ha! ha! ha! he! he! he! he! ho! ho! ho! gor-a-mighty but I feels funny."

"Come, no more of this," remarked the Court, authoritatively. "Be quiet, or we will have to punish you for contempt of Court."

"Wha-a-at?" asked the woman, as she gave a cunning glance at the Court. "What's dat you'll do, Judge?"

"Punish you for contempt."

"Contempt! What' dat?—ha! ha! he! he! ha! ha! ha!—gorry a-mighty, but what am dat—ha! ha! ha!—but what am dat, say?"

"Take that woman below!" gravely ordered the judge.

"No you doesn't—no you doesn't—keep your han's off—ah! gorry, but how you does tickle," shouted the woman, at the same time sending forth a deafening roar of laughter. She wriggled, and jumped about so, as she laughed, that the officers found it impossible to hold her; and it was at last thought best to let her have her laugh out. She roared and shouted incessantly, for some five minutes, when she gradually began to calm down, and at last ceased her boisterous merriment.

"You appear to be happy," remarked the Court, addressing her after she had become quiet.

"Yes, sir-ee," she replied, as she rose to her feet. "You see, Ise a great gal to laugh, an' when I gits in dat way, gor-a-mighty Ise so tickled, dat when dey touch me, I couldn't stop a-laughin, if it killed me."

"What put you in such a happy mood, this morning?" enquired his Honor.

"Ha! ha! ha! an does you ax me dat! Ha! ha! ha! an' does you want to know dat? I tells you boss; but, ha! ha! gorry, he! he! gorry, ho! ho! but I must laugh."

"Go on!"

"Well, dis am de fac'. You knows dat nigger what war up here jus' afore now? Lor' what a nigger! ha! ha! ha! but it makes me laugh to t'ink ob him," and away she went into another fit of cachination. Ending her laugh, she heaved a long sigh, assumed a gravity of countenance, and then continued:

"You didn't do right wid dat nigger, boss; an' I tell you why. I hab an' ole grudge agin him, an' las' night I pass him up. He wor comin' along de street, an' I ups an' ats him. I sneak along up close to him back, I cotch him by de wool, an' I beat him—gorry how I beat him. Ha! ha! you ought jes' to have seed de—ha! ha!—brack man roll him—ha! ha! ha!—eyes, an' bite him lips, an'—ha! ha! ha! ha! he! he! ho! ho! ho! o-o-h—gorry, but he did squall," she said, with an uproarious laugh.

"I whaled de nigger," she continued, as soon as she could. "I whaled de nigger good, an' he didn't gib me nary a scratch. De watchman come along jus' den, an' toat us boff off to de lock-up. I whip de nigger—de nigger didn't do noffin, an' yet you fotch him up here, an'—ha! ha!—you socks him—ha! ha! ha!—for five dollar—ha! ha! ha!—an' de nigger comes down—ha! ha! he! he!—to de watch-house—ha! ha! he! he! he!—an' he looks so brack—ha! ha! ha!—at me, dat, oh! gorry a-mighty, I jus' t'inks I die—ha! ha! ha! ha! ho! ho! ho! o-o-oh!"

The prisoner was still laughing, and boisterously, too, when the Court made up its mind, that she had told a true story. The fine of the person to whom she had alluded, was transferred to her, and he ordered to be set at liberty. This appeared to delight her still more, and skipping and laughing, she made her way to the watch-house, without escort, where, after being locked up, she "just laid down and roared."

DISAPPOINTED LOVE.

A MAIDEN of some forty years standing, entered complaint before Esquire Rowekamp, one Saturday, against a young man of eighteen summers, for an assault with intent to maim. The substance of the lady's evidence was that the young man had been waiting upon her for "some several weeks," and when, after she thought he had been coming quite long enough to arrive at "the point," she intimated that his ultimate wishes ought to be made known, he became aggravated, and besides other ungentlemanly acts, endeavored to bite her ear!

The attorney for the accused, who, like many others of his profession, never allows gallantry to interfere with the rights of his client, brushed up his hair and assumed a position which plainly told that he intended to put the witness through a scorching examination.

"Miss," said he, with an impudent, brazen look, so becoming lawyers of the lower degree, "Miss, look at me. *I* have a few interrogatories to put to you."

"Well, sir," replied the witness, unawed by his terrible appearance.

"You said this young man waited on you?"

"I did, sir."

"Did he ever say, or even intimate the wish to marry you?"

"That is my business," remarked the witness, with a haughty air.

"Yes, and it is mine, too. You must answer. Please the Court, we wish that question answered."

"The lady can do as she pleases," replied the 'Squire.

"As the Court pleases," remarked the lawyer, not a whit discomfited. "Now, Miss, you said my client committed many ungentlemanly acts toward you. State particularly what he did."

"Must I answer that question?" asked the lady of the magistrate.

"Yes," was the reply.

"Well, sir, he put his arm around my waist."

"Was that all?"

"No, sir; he pressed me."

"Tightly?"

"Pretty tight."

"Sufficient to hurt you?"

"I can not say, sir, that he actually hurt me, but it was an immodest act, to say the least."

"And so it was, but did you never press him?"

"That is none of your business, sir."

"Hasn't he often pressed you?"

"I shall not answer such impertinent questions, sir?"

"Very well," replied the attorney, "then we will leave that point. Are you sure he attempted to bite your ear?"

"Yes, sir."

"Did he not merely attempt to kiss it?"

"Kiss my ear? The lips are to be kissed, not the ears, sir!"

"I am aware of that fact, Miss, but what I want to get at is this: whether you have not been in the habit of kissing each other, and if you did not tell him on this occasion that no one but an engaged beau could ever kiss you again; and that in endeavoring to kiss you, he accidentally got your ear in his mouth?"

"Sir, your impertinence is intolerable," replied the lady, the color rising to her cheeks.

"I insist, Miss, on the question being answered."

"Well, sir, you wont get a reply from me."

"Does the Court hear that?" asked the attorney, in triumph.

The magistrate insisted that the question was a proper one. The lady hesitated, but her passion being aroused by repeated appeals, she approached her late beau, gave him a terrible slap in the face, told him she would not "have him for his weight in gold," and then hurriedly left the office. Though jealous of the dignity of his court, the magistrate thought it best to let her go; and with the remark that he supposed the complaint was made from disappointed love, discharged the accused, and entered the costs against the disappointed old maid.

WHAT ARE YOU LAUGHING AT ME FOR?

Herman Killer is a Dutchman—but he can't help that. He wears a pair of antique breeches, a half-dozen woolen shirts, and a little green-cloth cap, with an immense leather rim—but he can't help that. Like a genuine Dutchman, Herman scorns the frivolities of fashion, the forms of gentility, and scoffs of the world; and devotes himself to the praiseworthy objects of accumulating money, and increasing the stock of little Deutchers. His home is his castle, and his work-shop his play-ground. He cares for nobody, and is indifferent as to any one's care for him.

It happened that at noon, one Saturday, after Herman had demolished his meridian dish of krout, and kissed his wife and all his babies, previous to again departing for the soap-house, where he labors, he was just passing through his gate on Bank street, when a red-faced, red-haired, red-mouthed Irishman came riding by in a furniture car. Herman looked at the Irishman, and the Irishman looked at Herman. Herman thought of his wife and his nest of babies, and smiled. The Irishman, ever ready for a fight, and supposing the smile was in derision of his fiery top-knot, stopped his team and shouted:

"What bes yez laughing at me for, ye grazy specimen of a dirty spalpeen?"

Herman was too busily engaged in his own thoughts to hear, much less respond to the query of the Milesian. He closed his gate, carefully secured it with a rope, and then with a slow and steady step turned his face soap-house-ward. With his hands in his pockets he wended his way thoughtfully along.

The Hibernian was enraged at his indifference. Jumping from his car, he pursued, with that sprightliness for which his countrymen are celebrated, the phlegmatic Dutchman. With the cunning of a cat, he slipped up behind him, and suddenly gave him a kick, which lifted poor Herman from the ground.

"Mine shinks!" exclaimed the astonished soap-boiler, as he clapped his hands to his injured parts, "who hits me mit a brick-stein?"

"It's mesel' that's a belaborin' uv ye," responded the Hibernian, his face now rivaling his hair in intense redness.

"Vat you do dat for, ha?" asked Herman, still rubbing his tender parts.

"What did yez laugh at me for, thin, ye ugly booby yez?"

"I nix laugh," indignantly replied Herman. "I laugh mit mine frau only—mine shinks! but you hurts mine back bone side."

"It's a liar, yez calls me thin," shouted the Milesian, now determined on a fight, seeing that his antagonist exhibited no pluck. "Faith an' the best boy in the ring niver tould me that, an' kept his teet' in his mout'. I'll murther yez in cowld blood."

At that, he made "a stroke" at the Dutchman, who seeing himself in imminent danger, at that moment took to his heels, and escaped the lick. He was pursued to the soap-house, where the Irishman succeeded in collaring him, and was about pummeling him, when a pistol was pushed in his face by one of Herman's fellow-workmen. Not liking the looks of the "baste" he retreated, muttering vengeance, however, upon Herman, at the first opportunity.

The Dutchman, like a law-abiding citizen, immediately proceeded to the Police Court, and had a warrant issued for the Irishman. The trial came off, and resulted in the defendant being fined ten dollars and costs. Herman left the Court satisfied, but the Irishman came near getting into further trouble.

"What are yez laughing at me for?" he asked of a spectator, who, leaning far over the railing, was amusing himself at his red head. The spectator replied with a laugh, and instantly the Irishman's fist was raised, but fortunately his arm was caught by an officer. He was immediately escorted to the lock-up below.

GEORGE WASHINGTON IN JAIL.

In these days of spirit-rappings and supernatural intercourse between mortals and the beings of the heavenly "spheres," the world is being constantly favored with the present opinions of long-departed great men, upon topics which agitate the human mind. Indeed, the dark labyrinth of death—the once impenetrable gloom which shrouded the future existence of the soul—seems to have been illumed by a new light, enabling "progressive" inhabitants of the world to stand upon the brink of eternity, and communicate freely with the spirits of the dead. Has not Napoleon, through a mortal medium, predicted the taking of Sebastopol? Did not Jefferson foretell the great Gasconade Railroad catastrophe? Has not Franklin indorsed Free-Loveism? and has not Paine declared himself a Know-Nothing?

But the most astonishing of all is the fact, that George Washington has again really descended to earth, and once more walks among the people of the land! We saw him one morning—saw him, alack-a-day—sitting upon the prisoner's bench of the Police Court! He is a mulatto, with a profusion of hair upon his face, of stalwart form, brawny arms and tremendous feet.

"Who is the witness against George Washington?" asked the Court, to the great horror of the mixed crowd which daily fills the Court-room as spectators.

"Hear-ah she is, honey," responded an old negro woman, with face and apparel as black as charcoal.

"Take the stand then, madam."

"I does dat, sure-ah," she said, as she hobbled up to the stand.

"What is your name?" asked the Judge.

"My name, child," answered the witness, "doesn't you know dat? My name's Jane Washington."

"Is the prisoner your husband?"

"He my husband!" she exclaimed, with a most disdainful look. "Nebber! nebber! My husband is dead, but *he* was a *brack* man—none ob your half-way niggers. You knowd my husband, Judge."

"We have no recollection of his acquaintance.'

"He war small-poxed all over, and was here-ah, I know he was here-ah, afore he died."

"Then probably we did form his acquaintance before his decease. But tell us what charge you have to make against the prisoner?"

Mrs. Washington, who declared her age to be fifty-six, and who indignantly denied all relationship with George, told a very long story. George and herself were neighbors, and had been living in a neighborly manner. Last night, according to her account, she sent her little girl into George's to borrow a broom. Instead of loaning the article, he gave the girl a *sweeping* blow, and sent her home with a torrent of curses. The old woman protested against this unkindness, when George, still enraged, entered her apartment and "fotched her a lick."

"Did I hit you?" asked George Washington; exercising the law-defined right of a prisoner to cross-examine.

"Sartin you did—you knows you did, George," answered the witness.

"Whar?

"Dar—whar de skin's brack—doesn't you see it?" responded the witness, shoving aside her hood.

"Didn't you fotch me a lick on the cocoa-nut wid a stick ob wood? Answer dat if you dar."

"De Lor' help de nigger," exclaimed the witness, holding up her hands in astonishment. "Dar has not bin a stick ob wood in my house dis winter. I burns coal, an' ye knows I burns coal, George."

Failing to make anything of the witness, the prisoner next turned to the Court. He gave his version of the difficulty, which exculpated him from blame altogether. Notwithstanding the general reverence for the name he bears, the Court was fòrced to disbelieve him, and, finding him guilty of an assault, sentenced him to the dungeon for two days, and to pay the costs of the prosecution. George Washington in a dungeon! Shame, where is thy blush?

A HUMAN CROSS.

In this country, where the influx of foreigners from other countries is so vast, intermarriage is said to exert a very beneficial influence. It is urged that it has a tendency to dissipate all foreign nationality, and to unite all upon one broad American platform. Be that as it may, there are exceptions, as in the union of Herman Von Slickerman, as pure a Dutchman as ever smacked his lips over a beer-mug; and Bridget O'Doolan, as plump a woman as ever made the acquaintance of Sir John Barleycorn, in the bogs of old Ireland.

A Human Cross.

Though six months have elapsed since their hymeneal union, Biddy says she has not enjoyed an hour's "pace," with the "ugly hathen" known as her husband. Indeed their difficulties were so frequent, and at last became so serious, that they found themselves ushered one morning into the presence of the Police Judge. The testimony produced against them by the officers of the law, was not explicit; and his Honor, as is his custom, concluded to hear the statement of each, from which he hoped to arrive at a satisfactory conclusion, as to who was more at fault—the man or his wife. Ordering the unhappy couple to stand up, side by side, he inquired,

"Now, what is the difficulty between you?"

"Der difficult?" said Herman, looking first at his wife and then at the Judge, "der difficult? Py shinks it pes mooch. Dis voomans bes vorse den dem beebles vot dey calls der—der—der—der—ah! ha! vot you call dem beebles vot gets der election in Newport, eh?"

"The Wild-Cats," suggested an Attorney.

"Yaw, yaw, dat ish it all der vhile. Vell dish vomans, who, mine Got! bes mine frow by der 'Squire—dis vomans she bes vorser den all dem vild cat fellars, py shinks!"

"Arrah! now Herman an' would ye be spakin to his wurship in that way about yer own luvin wife?" pathetically inquired Biddy. "Will yer wurship plase to let me spake a word?" she urged with a courtesy.

"Certainly, I wish to hear both sides," replied the Judge.

"Thank yer wurship. Didn't I know ye were a gintleman, because ye thrate me like a lady? It's mesel' that's a dacent woman yer wurship, an' it's niver a word of wrong ye'd hear from me tongue, if the baste uv a husband didn't bate me all the time, yer wurship."

"Me peat you?" exclaimed the astonished and indignant Herman, "vot I peat you mit, hey?"

"Now aint that a swate question to be a axen uv yer own luvin wife right here before his wurship? Och! an' see how the paple are laughin at ye, ye ugly Dutch spalpeen ye."

"Boo—dey laugh mit you, you old Irish t'ing," responded Herman with a comical scowl.

"Ye know ye bate me, Herman, ye know ye did," continued the wife somewhat excited.

"You lies mit your mout'," exclaimed the husband, "I hit you nex time, but you trinks all mine moonish mit your viskey, an' you gits trunk, an' den vhen I comes home I finds not'in' for mine pelly but slap on der cope all der vhile. Ah! ha!" he shouted with an air of triumph.

"Murther! but yer a baste to be a talkin' that way to me, so ye are. An' was it for this I took yer dirthy name?"

"Yes," responded Herman, who did not seem to comprehend her language, "you do all dem t'ings. You puys not'in' but viskey mit mine moonish—you give me not'in' but dis, (pulling his hair), an' dis, (running his nails across his cheeks), an' dis, (striking his face with his fists), an' dis, (jerking his clothes as if he would tear them to pieces). By tam, you bes von great, pig, grazy wild-cat!"

Biddy could stand no more. She made one "lunge" at her lord and (ought to be) master, and had her hands fairly planted in his hair, when Herman mustered his superior strength, and gave her a blow which stunned her. The officers instantly interfered, and separated the unloving couple. His honor, convinced that no good could come out of Nazareth, sentenced both to ten days' imprisonment, to be fed on the simplest diet, and expressed the hope that the jailor would keep them as far apart as possible. This match certainly is a human *cross*.

A PUNSTER.

AMONG the prisoners before the Mayor one morning, was one Deuteronomy Brown, a person who looked as if he belonged to the lower order of the literary species. Watchman Jacobs was the only witness against him, and the following is a faithful report of the trial.

" Mr. Jacobs," asked the Mayor, " where did you find Mr. Brown ? "

" Leaning against a lamp-post, sir, unable to navigate."

" Ah ! indeed, you were drunk then, Mr. Brown ? "

" Rather toddled from drinking tods," calmly replied Mr. Brown.

" What is your business ? "

" From the evidence, I should judge I was a *post*-man. Had I held the post, I might be call a *post*-master ; but as the post held me, I can not aspire any higher than a *post*-clerk."

" When you let go the post, you fell," said the watchman.

" Aye," replied Mr. Brown, " and what a *fall* was there, my countrymen. Do you mean to insinuate that I am a *Falls* pilot ? "

" Not at all, I know not what you follow."

" I followed you last night, and have found it a poor business."

" Come, sir," said the Mayor, sharply, " no more of this nonsense. If you do not give an account of yourself, I shall commit you as a vagrant."

"Please your Honor," replied Mr. Brown, "my accounts would display very empty pockets. Is it my present occupation you wish to know?"

"Yes, yes, and be quick with your answer."

"I am a gamester."

"A gambler?"

"No, sir, not quite; but a dealer in *game*cocks. They *gambol* sometimes, but I never do."

"You are disposed to pun, this morning."

"That is because I hope to escape *pun*-ishment thereby."

"But you can not, you must go up under sentence of bread and water for ten days."

"You believe, then, that I belong to *up*-per-*ten*-dom, do you? Your *sentence* is badly composed and miserably pointed, yet I must acknowledge you have done it up *Brown*."

"You can retire below."

"Just as you please, but you just now ordered me to be sent *up*. I suppose, however, I must court the Court if I wish a favor. Please your —— "

Here Mr. Brown was suddenly seized by a deputy Marshal, and ordered below. After he was locked up, he offered a pair of cross-barred breeches to any one who would make a *breach* in the bars which confined his person. No one accepted the offer.

AN IRISHMAN'S FIRST SUP.

"THOMAS DOOLY, stand up," cried the Prosecuting Attorney of the Police Court, one morning, during the hearing of the watch-house cases. A tall, broad-shouldered individual, with a decidedly Hibernian appearance, responded to the call, bowing as he did so, first to the Attorney, and next to the Court, as if he was used to doing homage to his superiors.

"Mr. Dooly," continued the Attorney, "you are charged with having been drunk and disorderly last night. Stand forward, and hear the evidence against you. Watchman Carrol, take the stand."

This last expression was made without cause, for watchman Carrol was already upon the stand, and had his hand raised in signification that he was ready to take the oath. A faithful "star" always knows his victims, and Carrol being one of that kind, needed no pressing to compel him to mount the witness-stand. He was there, standing face to face with his prisoner. His story was short. He had found Thomas in Fifth street market-space, drunk, noisy, and riotous.

"You hear this, Thomas," said the Court; "what have you to say for yourself?"

"Faix an' it's thrue, yer Honor," replied Thomas, with a blush. "Ye see, yer Honor, I went to New York wid me brother; an' he died there, yer Honor, so he did. Well, yer Honor, I came back, an' I took a sup, an' I thought uv me brother, an' thin I cried, so I did."

"Well, I suppose we must fine you one dollar, Thomas, for getting drunk."

"Och! yer Honor, but wouldn't that be thrating me badly? I've no money sur."

"It appears you had money enough to get drunk with," returned the Court.

"Not a bit uv that, yer Honor," was Thomas' reply. "I was threated by a friend to a sup, an' I took to me only one sup, yer Honor. Sure, an' its mesel that niver took a sup before, in all me life."

"You never did?" asked the Court, somewhat astonished.

"Niver, yer Honor, in all me life," replied Mr. Dooly, his face coloring with the flush of modesty, as his knees gave way in a spasmodic effort to be humble.

"Why, where were you raised?" inquired the Court, still astonished.

"In ould Ireland, sure."

"And never drunk before, in all your life?"

"Be me soul, I niver was."

"Then you can go," remarked the Court, in a tone, and with a look which bespoke surprise.

"Thank ye, sur," said Thomas, as with another obeisance he made his way to the front door.

Mr. Dooly is the first son of Erin brought before our Police Court, on his "first sup," and his Honor therefore did right in bestowing upon him a distinguished mark of esteem, viz: a dismissal without punishment.

LOVE—PISTOLS WITHOUT COFFEE.

SAM BROAD, though colored, is a lover. A bright-eyed "yaller gal" has bewitched his heart and tickled his affections. He loves with the intensity of a noonday sun, and is as jealous of the honor of the fair being to whom his heart is devoted, as the Bogens are of the fame of their sausage-meat. He called to see his darling one night. As he sat beside her, upon a rude settee, his arms around her slender waist, her eyes shedding rays of love upon his, and blushes flushing her sun-proof cheeks as he whispered soft words of bliss into her ear, he was as happy as any nigger can be, beneath the stars of heaven. How sad it is for lovers to part! Sam Broad felt this that evening, when the girl of his heart was torn from his presence to wash the supper-dishes. He stole from her lovely lips one kiss, and then another and another, and would have taken a fourth, had she not, in her modesty, shrunk from the frequent repetition, and softly said:

"Don't make a fool ob yourself, niggar."

Sam left his fair one's home with a light and joyous heart. He felt as if he could defy the world, when the fair Arderbeller became his. His long heels no longer impeded his step—he walked on his toes, and seemed to skim o'er the pavement, supported by an aerial power. Sam felt big—proud—lofty—far above himself—a man fortunate beyond expression.

Under these circumstances, is it a wonder he was confident he could beat the world at a game of poker? Nay, so confident was he, that he stepped into the new "billiard" saloon on East Sixth street, and bantered the house to take a "hand" with him. Sylvanus Thompson, a sporting character of some repute, instantly took him up.

"Whar has you been propelling to, Sam?" asked Sylvanus, as he commenced shuffling the cards.

"Whar?" responded Sam, in astonishment, "why, down to Arderbeller's, in course. Whar else should you inspect dis darkie ob goin'?"

"Arderbeller? Guess I doesn't know dat gal."

"Why, yes, you does Syl. De yaller gal what libs down dar on 'Commodation street—de one wid de kurls what kum all down ober her neck."

"De one what sings in de Fird street quire?"

"De same."

"An' whose fader whitewashes wid all colors?"

"Ezackly."

"Oh, yes, I knows dat gal well," said Syl, complacently, as he made the first deal. "Pretty much ob a gal, Sam."

"Nuffin else," replied Sam, his eyes brightening.

"Ise got sum notion ob puttin' in dar myself."

"No use, niggar, no use," replied Sam triumphantly, Ise de chile dar, sure as you lib."

"De Lor' help your ignorance, darkie. Jus' let me tell you one t'ing. Dat gal wink to me last Sunday in church."

"Dat's a lie!" promptly responded the lover, rising to his feet and clenching his fists.

"None ob dat—none ob dat, niggar," replied Syl, rolling up the white of his eyes. "More'n one brack man's been sent head foremus to 'ternity for sayin' dat to dis chile."

"I tell you 'gin dat's de biggest kind ob a lie!" responded the now infuriated Sam. "Dar's only one man in dis worl' dat Arderbeller winks at, an' dat is dis chile himse'f. You try 'gin to stain de honor ob dat gal an' I shoot you froo and froo wid a bullet," shouted Sam, as he drew from his bosom a six-shooter, and pointed it at the breast of his antagonist.

Just at that moment Sam's arm was clutched with the firmness of a vice. He was about to make an exertion to release it, when the bright glitter of a star shot across his eyes. He instantly cooled down, and he and his companion were, after sundry explanations, marched off to the lock-up. In the morning they were fined five dollars each and costs, for disturbing the peace, though Sam endeavored to impress upon the Court the fact that he was only defending the honor of an injured girl. The last we saw of him, he was in a cell, endeavoring to persuade a policeman to convey the information of his sad plight — in prison and short of funds — to his "lubly Arderbeller."

A VICTIM OF LOVE.

"SIMON GIRTY, what brought you here?" asked the Mayor, one morning, of an inebriated-looking individual who occupied a seat upon the prisoner's bench.

"A watchman, please your Honor," replied Simon.

"What did he bring you for?"

"Ah! sir, that is more than I know," replied Simon, rising to his feet, and assuming a melancholy look. "Since I have become a victim of ——"

"Intemperance," interrupted the Mayor.

"No, sir, not of intemperance, if you please. True, I often drown my sorrows, my afflictions, in the cup, the bitter cup, sir, yet I am not a victim of intemperance, but of love; yes, sir, of love. And as I was remarking, since I have become a victim of love, it matters not to me what becomes of my personal self."

The Victim.

"Are you really in love, Simon?" inquired the Mayor, who knew the prisoner well.

"Oh! please, sir," replied Simon, apparently in great anguish, "don't pierce my heart with such an inquiry. I am indeed a victim, a heart-broken victim to the strongest of all the passions which rack the human heart."

"Can you not tell us your tale of sorrow?" asked the Marshal, his eyes twinkling with merriment, while his tone was grave; "we may have it within our power to relieve you. Here (pointing to the reporters), are a number of gentlemen of the press, and if you only excite their sympathies, they may do something for you."

"You who have tears to shed, prepare to shed them now," responded Simon, with great solemnity, "you see, gentlemen, I am a fallen man. The fire of energy no longer lights my eyes, the rosy hue of health blooms not upon my cheek, and my scattered locks are growing prematurely grey. Gentlemen, I am a victim of love, and would be much *obliged to one of you for a chaw of tobacco.*"

The listeners could not refrain from laughing at this odd termination of a serious sentence, but Simon remained as solemn as the grave. He was supplied with a "chaw," and then proceeded:

"Two years ago, I first met Mary Mayfield, and ah! heavens, my whole form trembles as my lips pronounce that name. She was matchless in beauty, a queen in action, and a divinity in form. Ah! gentlemen, need I tell you she robbed me of my heart; that my whole soul was fired by her resistless charms; that I forgot all things, saw nothing, felt nothing, save sweet Mary Mayfield?

"My love drove me to despair, and forced me at last to lay aside my native modesty. Would you believe it? I actually sought her presence, and prostrating myself at her feet, begged her to accept me as her own. Oh! that fearful moment! I felt as if my destiny lay upon the single word which would fall from her lips. There I was, prostrate before her queenly beauty; tears, manly tears, flowed like rivulets of liquid gems from my adoring eyes. She moved toward me like a breathing dream, as I fondly hoped and believed, to raise my humble form, and clasp it, thrilling with ecstatic bliss, to her high-heaving breast, the home, I thought, of love as true as mine. In a moment my joy was supreme, but the next, oh! horror of horrors, she gave me a kick with her pretty foot, and said, '*Get you gone, you fool, you lunatic, you madman, you dirty scrub!'"*

Simon was here overcome. He buried his face in his hands, as if in the deepest agony. Recovering in a few moments, he continued—

"I sprang from the floor, and in despair rushed to the street. My first impulse was to drown myself, and I fully intended to commit that dreadful deed. But a thought deterred me from acting thus rashly. From my days of childhood, I had a natural dread of the external application of water, and even in my frenzy, that dread induced me to pause. A moment's reflection convinced me that instead of making my body food for fishes, and withdrawing suddenly from this pleasant world, it would be far more congenial to my nature to drown myself by the internal administration of colored fluids. Gentlemen, I have drank, drank, and drank, but as yet I have not succeeded in drowning myself. I am now out of means, and I want help to aid me in accomplishing my determined purpose. A few more drams, and Simon will be in the spirit land. *Can't you loan a feller a picayune?*"

The Mayor was of opinion that water would be more beneficial to Simon's body than any stimulating liquid, and therefore sentenced him, before he had time to effect a loan, to twenty days' imprisonment, to be fed upon bread and water only.

"That's cruel, your Honor," responded Simon, "water is a stranger here, (placing his hand on his abdomen), and its intrusion there will certainly bring me to an untimely end. But 'tis well; if I die, I die a victim of love——"

"*Of whisky!*" exclaimed the Marshal, as he pushed the prisoner into the stairway leading to the cells in the watch-house below.

Simon, no doubt, is a victim, and a victim, too, to love—of whisky.

STUCK OR NOT STUCK? THAT'S THE QUESTION.

In the Police Court, one morning, a burly Irishman, named Michael Fitzpatrick, accused a little Dutchman, who acted as bar-keeper at the "Olive Branch," with assaulting and beating him. Michael came upon the witness-stand with an immense black neck-cloth around his head, and took the trouble to make various grimaces, that the Court might see he was suffering great pain. Patrick's statement, under oath, was, that he went into the "Olive Branch" in the evening, and bought a *half-gallon* of beer, and gave a bank bill in payment. After he drank the beer, he asked for the change, but the bar-keeper refused to give it to him. He sat down on a chair to wait awhile, and presently he asked the bar-keeper again for his change. This seemed to enrage the glass-washer, and he rushed out from behind the bar, and drawing a knife, stuck the said Michael right in the eye.

"Right in the eye?" asked the Court, with a shudder.

"Aye, yer Honor, right forninst my eye it was," responded the witness, contorting his countenance.

"That is frightful. Was the gash deep?"

"Och! but it was, yer Honor."

"Let me see it," continued the Court; "that is, if you

can exhibit the wound without inconvenience or great pain."

"That I will, yer Honor," replied Michael, lifting the cloth a little.

"I see nothing yet. Can't you raise the cloth higher?"

"Aye, yer Honor. Och! but it hu-urts!" said the witness, lifting the cloth clear off his eye.

"Why, where is the wound?" asked the Court, somewhat astonished.

"There, yer Honor," said Michael, laying his finger on his eyebrow.

"There! Why I see no wound there."

"Right here, yer Honor," replied the witness, stretching his eyebrow with his fingers. "*It is right betwane the hairs.*"

The Court still failed to see the frightful gash; but satisfied with the witness's honesty, ordered him to resume his seat.

The witnesses for the defense told another story. They stated, that Mike offered a bad bill for the beer, and that was the reason the bar-keeper refused to give him any change. After he had poured the half-gallon of frothy liquid down his gullet, he sat by the stove, and was soon in an unconscious stupor. While in that condition, he endeavored to rest his head on the hot stove, and being burnt, supposed he had been cut, and went after a police officer to arrest the bar-keeper.

The Court came to the conclusion, that Michael Fitzpatrick had not been "stuck," and therefore discharged the bar-keeper from custody. As Mike left the court-room, he shook his head, as if he thought the law was partial, when the contest lay between krout and paratees.

POOR OLD MAN.

It is a sad sight to see an old man, his hair frosted with age, a victim of intemperance; and especially so, when we know that in his younger days he was respected and beloved. John Livinton is such a man. Ten years ago he was a cheerful, prosperous mechanic, and with a devoted family around him, lived comfortably and happily. Whatever induced John Livinton to fly to the cup, has ever been a mystery to his friends; and what was more mysterious still, he drank deeply from the very start. Ten years ago he was a sober, and respectable citizen—and a few Saturdays since he was a prisoner in the Police Court. What a change those ten years of debauchery had wrought! Poor John Livinton, now a bloated, staggering wretch. As he sat upon the prisoner's bench, his silvery hair scattered over his still noble brow, one could but pity the condition of the poor old man.

A policeman testified, that he found the prisoner insensibly drunk, in an alley in the Thirteenth ward. Livinton was indifferent to the testimony, and only raised his head when the Judge, who had known him in his better days, inquired of him, whether he had any witnesses

"None, your Honor," was his reply.

"There is still no improvement in you, John," remarked the Court; "a fatality seems to attend you, and neither the persuasions of your friends, nor the rigors of the law, will save you from a drunkard's grave. You have been repeatedly before us of late. We at first treated you kindly, with the hope that our kindness might produce your reformation. That failed, and we were at last obliged to commit you to prison."

The prisoner gave a heavy sigh, but said nothing.

"Where have you been living, since your release from jail," asked the Court.

"I stopped one night in the Broadway House, somewhere up town," gruffly responded the prisoner.

"Where did you stop last?"

"Why I have been to the country, and I just came in to get my clothes."

"Whereabouts in the country have you been living?"

"Out on the Hamilton road, may-be about five miles."

"At what were you working?"

"Why gardening—that's what I work at."

"For whom did you work?"

"I don't know who owned the place—can't say whom I worked for."

"When did you return to the city?"

"Yesterday, I believe. I walked in and stopped at the Broadway House. Then I went down town after my clothes, and I met some acquaintances, got to drinking, and I don't know anything more."

"Did you have him hauled to the lock-up?" asked the Court of the officers.

"No sir, we carried him. He said he had an order to go to the Infirmary, but lost it," was the reply.

"Worse and worse. We will commit him to jail again, and this time as a vagrant, for twenty days."

"Oh, for God's sake, don't send me up," cried the old man, while tears streamed down his cheeks. "That place is too bad—the sentence is too hard, it will kill me; just let me off, this time—for God's sake, do, and in half an hour I will leave this city; all I ask is time to get my clothes; for God's sake, grant me that privilege, this once, and I will leave town."

"Will you refrain from drinking?"

"Oh! don't ask me that. I can't—you know I can't. The time was, your honor, when I could have paused in my downward career, but now it is too late. Oh! pity me. Let me go to the country, where I can drink and die. True, true, I am doomed to a drunkard's grave."

The agony of the poor old ruined man, touched the heart of his Honor. He orderd that John Livinton be released; and with all the hurry that trembling, feeble limbs would permit of, the aged drunkard tottered out of the court-room.

PROVING CHARACTER.

Attempts to prove character in the lower Courts, are often very amusing. Once a German, accused of abusing his mother-in-law, called upon a reporter of a German newspaper, to testify to his good character. The following ensued:

Judge—How long have you known the defendant?

Reporter—About five years.

Judge—What are his habits?

Reporter—Not very steady.

Judge—Does he drink?

Reporter—He is quite intemperate.

Judge—Does he work?

Reporter—But very little, if any.

This satisfied the Judge, and a penalty was inflicted upon the defendant.

On another occasion, an Irish woman, who had numerous "tinants," with whom she could not agree, and who was charged with beating one of them, called upon a watchman to testify to the general uprightness of her behavior. The following was the result:

Judge—Do you know this woman?

Watchman—I have been acquainted with her several years.

Judge—What is her character?

Watchman—She is drunk very often, and so quarrelsome, that she is a nuisance to the neighborhood.

Prisoner—Och! an' how can yez say that now?

Watchman—She has been drunk almost constantly for the last six weeks, and has given us a good deal of trouble. She wont behave herself any how.

The Court increased the fine to double of what was contemplated, previous to the testimony of this witness.

USES IT FOR MEDICINAL PURPOSES.

"ANTHONY FOUR!" called out the Attorney of the Police Court one morning.

"Present," responded a man some six feet in hight, whose straight and slim form was disfigured by a bruised face. His coat was buttoned to his chin, and in his hand he held a flimsily-bound novel. As he stood erect, his head towering high above those of his watch-house fellows, his arms akimbo, and his large bright eyes cast in meditative position toward the floor, he might have been taken—barring the dirt—for a colossal statue of some great statesman.

"What has this man been doing?" asked the Court of Watchman Marshall, who, knowing his duty, had stepped upon the witness-stand.

"We found him drunk, sir," responded the watchman. "He was quite unruly, and it was with great difficulty we got him to the watch house."

"Sir," said the prisoner, raising his head and addressing the Court, "I was not intoxicated. I went over to Newport, I know not how. There I took some medicine to recuperate my physical system, and I was obliged to mix it with spirits to make it the more palatable. Sir, no one deprecates the use of spirits as a beverage more than myself. I detest it, heartily detest it, sir, but in medicine I always considered it harmless, sir. I was not intoxicated, sir."

Here he paused a moment to recover his breath, and then proceeded—

"How is it, sir, that I, who am honest in thought and intention, should be treated in this manner? I assure you, sir, upon my honor, that it was medicine I took. There may have been spirits in it. Who gave it to me I know not—they were strangers; I never saw them before, and what *they* put in that mixture, I have not the remotest idea. Ah! sir, I have been imposed upon; I know it—I feel it—and for that reason, sir, I demand a vindication. I, sir, ask for my discharge!"

"Unfortunately, Mr. Four," said the Court, "we have had a previous acquaintance with you."

"Ah! that *is* true, and that *is* unfortunate," said the prisoner, a shade of disappointment covering his countenance. Reviving, however, he continued—"But, sir, in this case I am honest. Indeed, sir, I took nothing but medicine."

"What kind of medicine was it that affected you so strangely?"

"Indeed, sir, I do not know. It was an admixture—a preparation—something merely to stir up a sluggish system."

The Court seemed to have but little confidence in the statement of Mr. Four, sentencing him to three days' imprisonment, probably to give him an opportunity to sober off. He received the sentence with a burst of indignant eloquence, but when tapped upon the shoulder by the Marshal, and invited to walk down stairs, he put on his haughtiest look, and strutted down into the watch-house with all the dignity of a statesman.

AN OLD HOUSE WITH LOW TENANTS.

THERE is an old house located in Gas alley, noted in the Police annals of this city. It has witnessed more than one murder, and "they say" an honest man never lodged within its walls. It is an old house, a rickety house, a dirty house, a dilapidated house; just such a house as one would choose in which to devise stratagem and treason, and contrive means to accumulate spoils. It is not as might be supposed, in these degenerate days, a political head-quarters, or a place where politicians are wont to meet, to discuss over bottles and glasses the best means of getting possession of the spoils — it may be used for a nobler or a baser purpose.

Who owns this old house we do not know, but certain it is the landlord has no care for the reputation of its tenants. Their hearts may be as rotten as its timbers — if he gets the rent it is all he asks. It is now inhabited by a gang of fifteen or twenty hard cases, a sort of informal association of Free Lovers (of whisky,) who worship old King Alcohol, and claim the inherent right to live without working. They are mostly negroes, and many of them are familiar with the interior of our County Prison.

One night, Nat Bright, a slim, bony negro, whose countenance, not satisfied with the deepest color of his race had sought the addition of soot and coal dust, until it was pure black, visited this old house to rest his wearied body. There were no beds, so he took a chair, and a three-legged one at that, and resting his back against the wall, dropped off into a refreshing snooze. Nat was hardly fairly asleep, when

Bob Johnson, "the greatest nigger of them all," entered the room, accompanied by two white men and a bottle of whisky.

"Hurra!" shouted Bob. "Ise got the clar stuff, an' we's all gwyin to hab a spree. Wake up, boys."

Nat, however, was too sleepy to wake up, and Bob observing it, gave him a "clew" alongside the head.

"What's dat drap?" asked the startled negro.

"Drap? I hear nuffin drap," replied Bob.

"Drap on my head, I mean, nigga. Didn't you see nuffin?"

"Ya! ha! ya! ha!" roared Bob — "dat was dis chile's fis'. Ise got a bottle ob whisky, and two white men to help us drink it; so wake up, all you drowsy brack gemmen!"

For a wonder, Nat just then preferred sleep to whisky, and, instead of waking up, tried to drop off into a sleep again. Bob gave him a shake, asking:

"Isn't you gwyin to drink wid de white gemmen?"

"Go 'way," said Nat.

"Does you know who you's talking to?" asked Bob, indignantly.

"Go 'way, I tells you 'gin," continued the sleepy darky; "you is a nasty nigger, and you knows it.'

"What's dat?" shouted the indignant Bob; "you calls me a nigger, does you? an' you wont drink wid a white man? Take dat for your impertence"—and a blow laid Nat on the floor. He had recovered, and was on the point of returning the blow, when two guardians of the night entered. A stampede was made for the back window, but the watchmen secured the belligerents. The party were about moving watch-houseward when "Yaller Zack," a strapping fellow, unrolled himself from a quilt in the corner, and asked:

"Whar's you gwyin, niggers?"

"To de calaboose," sullenly replied Bob.

"Is ye? Den I goes along wid you, an' fotch dis quilt for you to sleep on."

"Dont trouble yourself, Zack," replied one of the watchmen, "you whaled your wife to-night, and we've been looking for you. We'll *take* you along."

"Gorry a-mighty!" shouted Zack, "wish I'd knowed dat fus time, an' de debbel wouldn't kotched me here-ah."

The trio were marched to the lock-up, and from thence the next morning to the Police Court, where a full exposition was made. Nat obtained his release by turning witness against his comrades—a fashionable mode now-a-days of escaping the punishment of the law. Bob indignantly refused to offer an explanation to the Court, while Zack only made matters worse by abusing his wife. They were both fined and sent to prison.

NATIONAL PLUCK.

In an oil-mill in the eastern part of this city, England could have been seen, at a late hour one night, in the person of a genuine Johnny Bull, shaving down oil-cakes. Near him sat Young America, stirring oil in a cask, and between the two was "Ould Ireland," in the shape of the fireman of the establishment, leisurely smoking a dudeen! Their conversation was at first upon the disputes between Britain and the United States; and, as might be expected, Johnny supported the course pursued by the government of his native land, while Young America, backed by "Ould Ireland," gave the British Ministry a severe overhauling.

From this they commenced discussing the relative merits of certain animals in the different countries, until they at last took up the subject of horses.

"You 'aven't no 'orses worth nothink, in this country," says Mr. Bull.

"Well, I calculate we haint got nothin' else," replied America. "Shavetail and Grey Eagle can just lam any English hoss you're a mind to bring out. Can't they, Patrick?"

"Sure, an' ye're right, my darlint," replied Pat.

"Shavetail's no 'orse at all," said the Englishman. "In Hengland, we've 'orses that can beat him as easy as ——"

"Your brag sailers beat the America, eh?" interrupted America.

"Be jabers, an' ye hit him that time, me boy," instantly put in Ireland.

"You don't know 'ow to run 'orses in this country," said the Englishman, spitefully.

"And I guess they don't know how to stop them in England," said America.

"Fait', an' they don't, my darlint," responded Ireland.

"They stop 'orses in Hengland same as vot they do 'ere," replied Bull.

"How's that?" asked the Yankee.

"By saying vo!" answered England.

"You're a liar," cried America.

"I vont take a hinsult from no man,' said England, giving America a fierce look, which reminded Ireland that the fire under the boiler needed stirring up, and off he went to attend to the duty.

"If you don't like the *hin*-sult," replied America, "take that," giving England a slap on the face.

"I don't want a fight 'ere," calmly replied Mr. Bull, "but I'll fight you fair for five-and-twenty dollar stakes."

America declined the offer of a prize fight, but expressed his willingness for a "rough-and-tumble" just at that moment. In fact he appeared so eager for it, that Johnny Bull left the mill, and hunting up a watchman, had America taken into custody.

A legal investigation resulted in both being fined—England for provoking an assault, and young America for committing one.

ILLUSTRATION OF A HISTORICAL FACT.

A VENERABLE Irishman, in giving testimony before the Police Court, one morning, stated that the prisoner pulled his hair out by the handfuls—acting worse toward him than Cromwell did to his ancestors in Ireland.

"Did Cromwell pull the hair out of the heads of the Irish, when he visited the Green Isle?" asked the attorney for the prisoner.

"Fait' an' he did, sir, an' in the manest way too, shure."

"In what way did he do it?" inquired the lawyer.

"If ye'll allow me, I'll show ye, shure."

"That's just what I want—proceed."

"But it'll hurt ye, sir."

"Never mind—go ahead, and when it hurts, I will tell you to stop."

"Fait' an' I'll do it, shure," and suiting the action to the word, he turned up his coat-sleeves and went to work. Taking a lead pencil about four inches long, he twisted the lawyer's bushy hair tightly around it. Then seizing both ends of the pencil with the fingers of his right hand, he braced himself for a pull, and gave a slight jerk.

"Oh!" cried the lawyer.

Patrick gave a little stronger pull.

"Ouch!" screamed the attorney.

The Irishman, holding the pencil tightly, gave a tremendous pull.

"Hold, for Heaven's sake!!" screeched the disciple of Blackstone, as the roots of the hair gave way, and the tears came streaming from his eyes.

It is almost needless to add, that the court-room resounded with the laughter of spectators, jury, and officers. Even the gravity of his Honor was destroyed. The attorney appeared satisfied with this practical demonstration of how "Cromwell persecuted the Irish."

WATCH-HOUSE LOAFERS.

We visited the watch-house at a late hour one night. In the room devoted to males, we found quite a number of persons spread out on the bare floor.

"Who are these?" we inquired of the keeper.

"They are *loafers*," was the reply, "who have no homes, and they come here for shelter. The floor of a warm room is all the accommodation we can give them."

Loafers! The word implies a lazy, good-for-nothing specimen of humanity, one who, though able, will not work, and whose aim is to get through the world with as little energy as possible. Webster says a loafer is "an idle man; a low fellow;" and the common acceptation of the word is, a lazy, debased being. If we are to believe the watch-house keeper, there was a crowd of them right before us, and while they were asleep on the hard floor, we thought we would examine them.

The first was a middle-aged man, his clothes all tattered and torn, his bloated face besmeared with dirt, and his body swelled by a life of intemperance. He slept soundly, for he no doubt was used to such a bed as that. He certainly was a loafer in the fullest meaning of the word.

The next was a mere stripling, a German, we thought, from his appearance. A check shirt, a pair of pants, a boatsman's belt, and a coarse pair of shoes, were all he had on. As he lay flat on his back, his long auburn curls partly covering his handsome face, we looked in vain for anything like the appearance of a loafer about him. His hands were hardened by labor, and the expression of his countenance was really pleasant. He assuredly was not a loafer. He must have been a stranger in a strange land, without means to pay for a night's lodgings, and in these ill-fated times unable to procure labor enough to prevent him from becoming a beggar. Poor youth! he was judged by the company he was forced to keep.

The next two were confirmed vagrants. We had seen them often before the Police Court and in jail. They never worked and seldom ate. Drink—the most burning, vicious deadly drink—was their joy, their sustenance. They had lost all manliness, and were dragging out their miserable existence to a drunkard's grave. How we would like to know their history—whether they ever enjoyed a mother's heart, or were the pride of a devoted father. Could such debased beings ever have been *men*, loved and respected as such? But these thoughts are out of place. The world takes people as they are, and it is now no matter what these loafers had been. The world now adjudges them as lost, and we must consider them so, too.

The next was a young man with but one leg. He was wide awake and sitting up. He said he came here for medical treatment, and having no money expected to get into the Hospital. The law prevents his admission, however, and he was forced to take lodgings in the watch-house. He did not know what would become of him on the morrow, but good naturedly remarked, he hoped to be able to "hobble" along some way. Crippled, sick and moneyless—what a fate!

Next lay a stout Hibernian, with shoulders broad enough to bear the weight of a barrel of flour. He was thinly clad, and from his appearance we would have taken him for a faithful son of toil; but the neck of a bottle of whisky, peeping out from a pocket, led us to fear he was in a fair way to become a loafer. Who would take the trouble to stop him in his downward career?

Near him, in a corner upon a quilt, with a chair-back for a pillow, lay "General Jackson," a very old negro, who had made the watch-house his home, for several months. In pity for his age, and perhaps in remuneration for his many interesting incidents of the "olden time," which he delights to relate, the watchmen supply him with an abundance of food.

What a pitiable object lay next to the "General." He was asleep, but he moaned most grievously. The fever-flush was upon his cheek, and it was evident the hospital, and not the watch-house, was the place for him. But he does not come within the terms of the law, and therefore can get no aid; he has no money, and sick as he is, dying may-be, the floor of the watch-house is his only bed. Well may he moan!

But enough of watch-house *loafers*. We are satisfied more than half of them are worthy men, whose only fault is their extreme poverty. What a world of good a true philanthropist could do among them!

WILL BE PUBLISHED IN JUNE,

BY

Q. K. Philander Doesticks, P.B.,

AND

Knight Russ Ockside, M.D.,

LIVERMORE & RUDD,
310 BROADWAY.

www.ingramcontent.com/pod-product-compliance
Lightning Source LLC
LaVergne TN
LVHW020221110826
845151LV00003B/779

* 9 7 8 1 4 2 5 5 3 2 5 8 1 *